Betty Crocker's

GOOD
AND
EASY

COOKBOOK

Macmillan • USA

MACMILLAN

A Simon & Schuster Macmillan Company
1633 Broadway
New York, NY 10019

Library of Congress Cataloging-in-Publication Data

Crocker, Betty
  (Good and easy cookbook)
  Betty Crocker's Good and easy cookbook.
     p.   cm.
  Includes index
  ISBN 0-02-861256-6 (alk. paper)
  1. Cookery, American.   2. Quick and easy cookery.   I. Title
TX715.C9216   1996
641.5'55—dc20   96-11022
                                             CIP

GENERAL MILLS, INC.

Betty Crocker Food and Publications Center

Director: Marcia Copeland
Editor: Lori Fox
Recipe Development: Altanette Autry, Nancy Cooper, Grace Wells
Food Stylists: Kate Courtney Condon, Katie McElroy, Cindy Lund

Nutrition Department
Nutritionists: Elyse A. Cohen, M.S., Nancy Holmes, R.D.

Photographic Services
Photographer: Carolyn Luxmoore

Cover by Iris Jeromnimon
Design by Rachael McBrearty

For consistent baking results, the Betty Crocker Kitchens recommends Gold Medal Flour.

You can create great-tasting food with these approved recipes from the Betty Crocker Kitchens. Cooking and baking have never been so easy or enjoyable!

Manufactured in the United States of America

10 9 8 7 6 5 4 3 2 1

First Edition

Cover: Grilled Shrimp Kabobs (page 390)
Back Cover: Ranchero Beef Pizza (page 244), Teriyaki Chicken Stir-Fry (page 124)

Contents

Introduction

When we asked, "What's your greatest cooking challenge?" Your response was loud and clear: "How to get dinner on the table every night!" The answer didn't surprise us. With everyone so busy these days, sometimes it seems as if making dinner is just another weeknight job.

Betty Crocker has the answer—the great-tasting recipes in *Betty Crocker's Good and Easy Cookbook.* You'll love the options here—meals that are quick to prepare at the end of a busy day; make-ahead dishes you can pull out of the freezer or refrigerator and cook whenever you like; and fix-and-forget oven meals that take very little preparation time and cook without your attention, leaving you free to do other things.

The recipes were designed to take advantage of the best new convenient ingredients and timesaving techniques. We've used crisp, fresh, pre-washed and -cut vegetables and greens, ready-made refrigerated pasta sauces, terrific new flavored canned tomatoes, pre-baked pizza crusts and the endless variety of frozen vegetable combinations. Add to that the exciting array of sauces, marinades, deli-foods, pre-cut meat and skinless, boneless chicken breasts available today. These all help to put together a meal in a new way—you could call it "speed scratch cooking"!

We also looked at the easiest cooking methods and created great skillet meals, satisfying casseroles, sizzling grill recipes, fresh soup and sandwich ideas, vegetarian main dishes, snazzy pastas, easy pizzas and express meals with five ingredients or less that are done in a flash. You'll also find ideas for the "sides," including salads, vegetables, breads and desserts.

Relax and enjoy these recipes—they will bring you back to the pleasure of a home-cooked meal no matter what day of the week it is, and you'll know that Betty Crocker has done the work for you!

Betty Crocker

Preceding page: Convenience products: (1) pre-sliced deli meats; (2) dip mixes; (3) salad dressing; (4) pre-packaged vegetables; (5) pasta; (6) salsa; (7) dressing; (8) canned soup; (9) soy sauce; (10) pasta sauce; (11) pesto; (12) prepared pizza crust; (13) chili; (14) fresh frozen pasta.

Drinks, Dips and
Mini Bites

Hot Spiced Cider

▼ 6 servings (1 cup each)

This cider takes the chill off any day! Keep extra cider in the saucepan over low heat and refill cups when you like.

Prep: 12 min

1 Serving: Calories 115 (Calories from Fat 0); Fat 0g (Saturated 0g); Cholesterol 0mg; Sodium 10mg; Carbohydrate 29g (Dietary Fiber 0g); Protein 0g.

  6 **cups apple cider**
1/2 **teaspoon whole cloves**
1/4 **teaspoon ground nutmeg**
  3 **sticks cinnamon**

1. Heat all ingredients to boiling in 3-quart saucepan over medium-high heat; reduce heat to low. Simmer uncovered 10 minutes.

2. Strain cider mixture to remove cloves and cinnamon, if desired. Serve hot.

Preceding Page
Fast Snack Garden Pizza (page 20) and Sparkling
Raspberry Tea (page 12)

Hot Spiced Cider ▶

Orange Slush

▼ 8 servings (about 1 cup each)

Prep: 5 min

1 Serving: Calories 260
(Calories from Fat 20);
Fat 2g (Saturated 1g);
Cholesterol 10mg;
Sodium 120mg;
Carbohydrate 51g
(Dietary Fiber 0g);
Protein 10g.

1/2 gallon vanilla frozen yogurt or ice cream
1 cup frozen (thawed) orange juice concentrate
1/2 cup milk

1. Place half of the yogurt, half of the juice concentrate and half of the milk in blender. Cover and blend on medium speed about 45 seconds, stopping blender occasionally to scrape sides, until thick and smooth.

2. Pour mixture into 8 glasses. Repeat with remaining yogurt, juice concentrate and milk. Pour remaining mixture into glasses.

Strawberry-Yogurt Cooler

▼ 4 servings (about 1 cup each)

Prep: 7 min

1 Serving: Calories 70
(Calories from Fat 10);
Fat 1g (Saturated 1g);
Cholesterol 5mg;
Sodium 80mg;
Carbohydrate 12g
(Dietary Fiber 0g);
Protein 3g.

2 cups whole strawberries
1 cup milk
2 containers (6 ounces each) strawberry yogurt

1. Reserve 4 strawberries. Place remaining strawberries, the milk and yogurt in blender. Cover and blend on high speed about 30 seconds or until smooth.

2. Pour into 4 glasses. Garnish each with strawberry.

Pineapple-Orange Colada

▼ 4 servings (3/4 cup each)

For an adult drink, add 1/4 cup rum before blending.

Prep: 5 min

1 Serving: Calories 245
(Calories from Fat 25);
Fat 3g (Saturated 2g);
Cholesterol 5mg;
Sodium 45mg;
Carbohydrate 55g
(Dietary Fiber 1g);
Protein 1g.

1 1/2 cups pineapple chunks or 1 can (20 ounces) pineapple chunks in juice, drained
1/2 cup frozen piña colada concentrate or pineapple juice
2 cups orange sherbet

Place all ingredients in blender. Cover and blend on high speed until smooth, scraping down sides if necessary.

Pineapple-Orange Colada ▶

Guava Spritzer

▼ 8 servings (1 cup each)

Prep: 2 min

1 Serving: Calories 170 (Calories from Fat 0); Fat 0g (Saturated 0g); Cholesterol 0mg; Sodium 50mg; Carbohydrate 43g (Dietary Fiber 0g); Protein 0g.

1 can (12 ounces) frozen guava or pineapple juice concentrate, thawed

6 cups lemon-lime soda pop, chilled

Mix juice concentrate and soda pop in 2-quart pitcher. Serve over ice.

Pineapple Limeade

▼ 8 servings (about 1 cup each)

Prep: 2 min

Refrigerate: 1 hour

1 Serving: Calories 105 (Calories from Fat 0); Fat 0g (Saturated 0g); Cholesterol 0mg; Sodium 15mg; Carbohydrate 26g (Dietary Fiber 0g); Protein 0g.

1/2 cup sugar

3 cups pineapple juice

1/2 cup lime juice

1 liter sparkling water, chilled

Lime slices, if desired

1. Mix sugar and juices in large plastic or glass pitcher. Refrigerate until chilled.

2. Just before serving, stir in sparkling water. Serve over ice. Garnish with lime slices.

Sparkling Raspberry Tea

▼ 6 servings (1 cup each)

(Photograph on page 7)

Prep: 3 min

1 Serving: Calories 40 (Calories from Fat 0); Fat 0g (Saturated 0g); Cholesterol 0mg; Sodium 20mg; Carbohydrate 9g (Dietary Fiber 2g); Protein 1g.

2 cups cold brewed tea

2 cups chilled raspberry or cranberry-raspberry juice

2 cups chilled sparkling water

Raspberries, lime slices or lemon slices, if desired

Fresh mint leaves, if desired

Mix tea, juice and sparking water. Serve over ice. Garnish with raspberries and mint.

Quick Tip: Use instant tea dissolved in cold water for the cold brewed tea for this refreshing drink.

Quick Guacamole

▼ About 2 cups

 2 large ripe avocados, mashed
1/3 cup thick-and-chunky salsa
 1 tablespoon lime juice
 Tortilla chips, if desired

Mix avocados, salsa and lime juice in glass or plastic bowl. Serve with tortilla chips.

Prep: 4 min

1 Tablespoon: Calories 20 (Calories from Fat 20); Fat 2g (Saturated 0g); Cholesterol 0mg; Sodium 20mg; Carbohydrate 1g (Dietary Fiber 0g); Protein 0g.

Hot Reuben Dip

▼ 2 1/2 cups

You don't have to limit this favorite flavor combination to sandwiches! Try this hearty dip version for a snack or as an appetizer—it'll become a favorite.

 1 package (8 ounces) cream cheese, softened
1 1/2 cups shredded Swiss cheese (6 ounces)
1/2 cup Thousand Island dressing
 4 ounces deli sliced corned beef, chopped
1/2 cup drained sauerkraut
 Pretzel crackers, if desired
 Cocktail rye bread slices, if desired

Prep: 10 min

1/4 Cup: Calories 220 (Calories from Fat 160); Fat 18g (Saturated 12g); Cholesterol 55mg; Sodium 820mg; Carbohydrate 2g (Dietary Fiber 0g); Protein 12g.

1. Heat oven to 400°.

2. Mix cream cheese, 1 cup of the Swiss cheese, the dressing and corned beef. Spread in pie plate, 9 x 1¼ inches, or quiche dish, 9 x 1½ inches. Top with sauerkraut and remaining ½ cup Swiss cheese.

3. Bake about 15 minutes or until bubbly around edge. Serve hot with pretzel crackers or cocktail rye bread.

Betty Crocker's Top 10

Recipe Shortcuts for Drinks, Dips and Mini-Bites

▶ **1.** Frozen drink mixes and bottled fruit drinks, such as piña colada, daiquiri, margarita, tropical fruit blends and berry-flavored

▶ **2.** Flavored teas and mineral waters, such as raspberry, peach, blackberry, lemon and lime

▶ **3.** Ready-to-go vegetable trays—try carrots, celery, broccoli, cauliflower and cherry tomatoes

▶ **4.** Dips from the deli or refrigerated case

▶ **5.** Cheese and crackers

▶ **6.** Chips and salsa

▶ **7.** Chicken wings from the deli or take-out restaurant

▶ **8.** Meat and cheese trays

▶ **9.** Frozen breaded cheese sticks or cheese-stuffed jalapeño peppers

▶ **10.** Cut-up fresh fruit from the deli or produce case, such as watermelon, cantaloupe, honeydew and pineapple

Corn and Olive Spread

▼ About 4 cups

Prep: 5 min

Refrigerate: 1 to 2 hr

1 Tablespoon:
Calories 35 (Calories from Fat 25); Fat 3g (Saturated 2g); Cholesterol 10mg; Sodium 100mg; Carbohydrate 1g (Dietary Fiber 0g); Protein 1g.

2 packages (8 ounces each) cream cheese, softened
1 package (1 ounce) ranch dressing mix
1 medium red bell pepper, chopped (1 cup)
1 can (4 1/4 ounces) chopped ripe olives, drained
1 can (11 ounces) whole kernel corn, drained
1 can (4 ounces) chopped green chilies, drained
Tortilla chips, if desired

1. Beat cream cheese and dressing mix in large bowl until smooth. Stir in remaining ingredients except tortilla chips.

2. Cover and refrigerate 1 to 2 hours to blend flavors. Serve with tortilla chips.

Corn and Olive Spread ▶

Beer-Cheese Dip

▼ About 2 cups

Prep: 10 min

1/4 Cup: Calories 220 (Calories from Fat 160); Fat 18g (Saturated 12g); Cholesterol 55mg; Sodium 820mg; Carbohydrate 2g (Dietary Fiber 0g); Protein 12g.

1 pound process cheese spread loaf, cut into pieces

1/2 cup regular or nonalcoholic beer

1/2 to 1 teaspoon red pepper sauce

Bite-size pieces vegetables, bread cubes or pretzels, if desired

1. Heat cheese and beer in 3-quart saucepan over medium heat, stirring constantly, until cheese is melted and mixture is smooth. Stir in pepper sauce.

2. Remove cheese mixture to earthenware fondue dish, electric cooking pot or chafing dish; keep warm over low heat. Serve with vegetables.

Let Go, Let Others Cook!

Do you do all the cooking? Then give yourself a break! Let someone else make one or two meals each week without any input from you. Although it may be hard, let them in the kitchen, even if it means that you end up with fried eggs and toast from one family member and peanut butter and jelly sandwiches from another. Sit back, relax and enjoy the extra time for yourself or your family instead of than worrying about a messy kitchen or perfect menus. Once family members get used to the idea of cooking, try letting them leaf through your favorite cookbooks—like this one. Trying new recipes is fun for everyone.

Beer-Cheese Dip ▶

Creamy Pesto Dip

▼ 1 1/4 cups

Skip the time-consuming preparation of cutting up vegetables by purchasing a package of baby-cut carrots and cut-up broccoli, cauliflower and celery. They're available in the produce section of the grocery store.

Prep: 3 min

1/4 Cup: Calories 170 (Calories from Fat 155); Fat 17g (Saturated 8g); Cholesterol 30mg; Sodium 65mg; Carbohydrate 2g (Dietary Fiber 0g); Protein 2g.

1   cup sour cream or plain yogurt
1/4 cup pesto
    Chopped tomato, if desired
    Assorted fresh vegetables, if desired

Mix sour cream and pesto until well blended. Sprinkle with chopped tomato. Serve with vegetables.

Savory Snack Mix

▼ About 7 cups

Prep: 5 min

Bake: 15 min

1/2 Cup: Calories 165 (Calories from Fat 110); Fat 12g (Saturated 2g); Cholesterol 0mg; Sodium 190mg; Carbohydrate 11g (Dietary Fiber 1g); Protein 4g.

3   cups toasted whole-grain oat cereal
3   cups corn chips (broken in half, if desired)
1   cup unsalted peanuts
1   cup thin pretzel sticks
1/3 cup margarine or butter, melted
1/2 teaspoon chili powder
1/4 teaspoon garlic powder

1. Heat oven to 300°.

2. Mix cereal, corn chips, peanuts and pretzels sticks in large bowl. Mix remaining ingredients; pour over cereal mixture. Toss until evenly coated. Spread in ungreased jelly roll pan, 15½ x 10½ x 1 inches.

3. Bake uncovered 15 minutes, stirring once. Cool completely. Store in airtight container.

Creamy Pesto Dip ▶

Golden Honey Snack Mix

▼ About 8 cups

Prep: 5 min

Bake: 10 min

1/2 Cup: Calories 185
(Calories from Fat 70);
Fat 8g (Saturated 1g);
Cholesterol 0mg;
Sodium 250mg;
Carbohydrate 24g
(Dietary Fiber 1g);
Protein 5g.

5 cups sweetened whole-grain oat cereal with honey and almonds

1 cup pretzel sticks

1/4 cup creamy peanut butter

2 tablespoons margarine or butter

1 cup raisins

1 cup honey-roasted peanuts

1. Heat oven to 350°.

2. Mix cereal and pretzel sticks in large bowl. Heat peanut butter and margarine to boiling in 1-quart saucepan, stirring occasionally; pour over cereal mixture. Toss until evenly coated. Spread in ungreased rectangular pan, 13 x 9 x 2 inches.

3. Bake uncovered 10 minutes, stirring occasionally. Remove from oven; stir in raisins and peanuts. Spread over waxed paper; cool completely. Store in airtight container.

Fast Snack Garden Pizza

▼ 6 servings

(Photograph on page 7)

Prep: 3 min

1 Serving: Calories 260
(Calories from Fat 115);
Fat 13g (Saturated 6g);
Cholesterol 20mg;
Sodium 570mg;
Carbohydrate 30g
(Dietary Fiber 2g);
Protein 8g.

1 container (8 ounces) dill or spinach dip

1 Italian bread shell or purchased pizza crust (12 to 14 inches in diameter)

1 cup chopped fresh vegetables

1/2 cup shredded Cheddar cheese (2 ounces)

Spread dill dip over bread shell to about ¹/₂ inch from edge. Sprinkle with vegetables and cheese.

Golden Honey Snack Mix ▶

Mahogany Chicken Wings

▼ 15 appetizers

Soy sauce, honey and molasses combine for a sweet-sour flavor and rich mahogany color in these chicken wings. Make enough—they'll disappear in minutes!

Prep: 5 min

Marinate: 1 hr

Bake: 50 min

1 Appetizer: Calories 130 (Calories from Fat 50); Fat 6g (Saturated 2g); Cholesterol 20mg; Sodium 500mg; Carbohydrate 12g (Dietary Fiber 0g); Protein 8g.

15 chicken wings (3 pounds)

1/2 cup soy sauce

1/2 cup honey

1/4 cup molasses

2 tablespoons chili sauce

1 teaspoon ground ginger

2 cloves garlic, finely chopped

1. Place chicken in shallow glass or plastic bowl. Mix remaining ingredients; pour over chicken. Cover and refrigerate 1 hour, turning occasionally.

2. Heat oven to 375°. Line broiler pan with aluminum foil. Remove chicken from marinade; reserve marinade. Place chicken in single layer on rack in foil-lined broiler pan; brush with marinade.

3. Bake 30 minutes; turn. Bake about 20 minutes longer, brushing occasionally with marinade, until deep brown and juice of chicken is no longer pink when centers of thickest pieces are cut. Discard any remaining marinade.

Good and Easy Substitutions

If you're looking for ways to make your meal preparation quicker, a change in your standard grocery list is in order. Check out the following chart for ways to make a "quick-change" to faster cooking.

Instead of	Use
Regular rice	Instant rice
Fresh potatoes	Refrigerated or frozen pre-mashed or hash brown potatoes, frozen French-fried type potatoes or instant potatoes
Whole fresh vegetables or produce	Pre-cut vegetables or produce and vegetables or produce from a supermarket salad bar
Fresh vegetables	Frozen or canned vegetables
Fresh garlic	Purchased chopped garlic sold in jars
Dried pasta	Fresh pasta
Whole cuts of meat	Pre-cut meats
Scratch cookies, brownies, bars and cakes	Boxed mixes, refrigerated cookie dough, bakery items or frozen baked items
Scratch sauces	Refrigerated, frozen, bottled and dry package mix sauces
Scratch soups	Canned soup or dry soup mixes
Regular barley	Quick cooking barley
Dry beans	Canned beans
Scratch salad dressings	Bottled salad dressings
Scratch spaghetti sauce	Jarred spaghetti sauce

Shrimp Quesadillas

▼ 8 servings

Here's a great recipe when you'd like to serve your guests something more than chips and salsa.

Prep: 8 min

Cook: 8 to 16 min

1 Serving: Calories 280 (Calories from Fat 125); Fat 14g (Saturated 7g); Cholesterol 50mg; Sodium 490mg; Carbohydrate 25g (Dietary Fiber 1g); Protein 14g.

8 flour tortillas (8 to 10 inches in diameter)

2 cups shredded Monterey Jack cheese with jalapeño peppers (8 ounces)

1 large tomato, chopped (1 cup)

1/2 cup real bacon pieces (from 3-ounce jar)

1 package (4 ounces) frozen cooked salad shrimp, rinsed and thawed

1. Heat 10-inch nonstick skillet over medium-high heat. Place 1 tortilla in skillet. Sprinkle with 1/4 cup of the cheese and one-fourth each of the tomato, bacon and shrimp. Sprinkle with additional 1/4 cup of the cheese. Top with another tortilla.

2. Cook 1 to 2 minutes or until bottom is golden brown; turn. Cook 1 to 2 minutes longer or until bottom is golden brown.

3. Repeat 3 more times with remaining ingredients. Cut each quesadilla into wedges.

Tip: To keep quesadillas warm, place on ungreased cookie sheet in warm oven.

Curried Chicken Turnovers

▼ 14 turnovers

If you would like to serve these tasty little turnovers with a dip, mix ²/₃ cup sour cream and ¹/₃ cup chutney.

Prep: 13 min

Bake: 23 min

1 Turnover: Calories 105 (Calories from Fat 45); Fat 5g (Saturated 3g); Cholesterol 15mg; Sodium 90mg; Carbohydrate 12g (Dietary Fiber 0g); Protein 3g.

1/3 cup raisins

1/3 cup sour cream

1/4 cup mango chutney

1 1/4 teaspoons curry powder

1 can (5 ounces) chunk chicken, drained

1 package (15 ounces) refrigerated pie crusts

1. Heat oven to 400°.

2. Mix all ingredients except pie crusts. Allow pie crusts to stand at room temperature for 15 minutes to soften. Unfold each pie crust as directed on package. Remove plastic sheets; press out fold lines. Cut seven 3¹/₂-inch circles from each pie crust.

3. Place about 1 tablespoon chicken mixture in center of each circle. Brush edge of each circle with water; fold circle in half over filling. Press edges with fork to seal. Place on ungreased cookie sheet. Bake 18 to 23 minutes or until light golden brown. Serve warm.

Curried Chicken Turnovers ▶

Super-Quick Nachos

▼ 5 servings

Some like it hot! For a spicy variation of this popular snack, substitute 6 jalapeño chilies, seeded and each cut into 6 strips, or ¼ cup canned chopped green chilies for the salsa.

Prep: 8 min

Bake: 4 min

6 Chips: Calories 155 (Calories from Fat 100); Fat 11g (Saturated 6g); Cholesterol 25mg; Sodium 350mg; Carbohydrate 8g (Dietary Fiber 1g); Protein 7g.

30	round tortilla chips
1/4	cup salsa
1 1/4	cups shredded Monterey Jack or Cheddar cheese (5 ounces)

1. Heat oven to 400°. Line cookie sheet with aluminum foil.

2. Place tortilla chips in single layer on cookie sheet. Top with salsa. Sprinkle with cheese. Bake about 4 minutes or until cheese is melted.

Pesto Tomato Toast

▼ 6 servings

Prep: 10 min

Bake: 8 min

1 Serving: Calories 175 (Calories from Fat 100); Fat 11g (Saturated 3g); Cholesterol 5mg; Sodium 250mg; Carbohydrate 14g (Dietary Fiber 1g); Protein 6g.

6	slices French bread, 1 inch thick
1/3	cup pesto
1	small tomato, seeded and chopped (1/2 cup)
1/2	cup shredded mozzarella cheese (2 ounces)

1. Heat oven to 375°.

2. Place bread on ungreased cookie sheet. Spread each slice with scant tablespoon of pesto. Top each with tomato; sprinkle with cheese. Bake about 8 minutes or until hot and cheese is melted.

Pesto Tomato Toast ▶

13 Timesaving Gadgets

Having the "right stuff" in the kitchen can really save time. Most of these items can be purchased for moderate prices in discount stores, large supermarkets or in the kitchenware section of department stores.

- **Apple wedger:** Quickly cores and slices apples and pears.

- **Garlic press:** Quickly crushes garlic. Look for the self-cleaning type—it presses all the garlic through the holes, instead of leaving pieces behind.

- **Ice cream scoop:** Quickly scoops ice cream, or use to fill muffin or cupcake pans or drop cookie dough. Choose a smaller scoop and use it for making meatballs.

- **Egg slicer:** Quickly slices hard-cooked eggs, mushrooms, small cooked potatoes or beets and kiwifruit.

- **Fat skimmer:** Separates fat from the pan juices of cooked meats and poultry.

- **Nonstick pan:** Cook without the added ingredient of margarine or oil; because food doesn't stick, clean-up is extra easy.

- **Vegetable peeler:** Quickly removes peels from fruits and vegetables.

- **Kitchen shears:** Quickly cuts up herbs, dried fruit, canned whole tomatoes, green onions, marshmallows and pizza.

- **Wire whisk:** Quickly blends and whips dressings and sauces so that they're smooth and creamy.

- **Food processor (regular and mini-sizes):** Quickly shreds, chops, slices, mixes, blends and purées.

- **Blender:** Quickly blends beverages, sauces, fruits and bread crumbs and chops nuts, onions and dried fruit.

- **Hand mixer with several attachments:** Attachments designed for specific jobs make an appliance quicker and more efficient. For example, some mixers have whisk attachments with the larger whisk suited for whipping cream, eggs and egg whites and the smaller whisk for creamy sauces and salad dressings. Mixing paddles work best for cookie, biscuit and pie crust dough.

- **Microwave oven:** Quickly reheats, defrosts, cooks, melts and softens.

Super Express
Cooking

Pesto Turkey and Pasta

▼ 4 servings

Prep: 5 min

Cook: 12 min

1 Serving: Calories 460
(Calories from Fat 205);
Fat 23g (Saturated 5g);
Cholesterol 55mg;
Sodium 160mg;
Carbohydrate 36g
(Dietary Fiber 2g);
Protein 29g.

   3 cups uncooked farfalle (bow-tie) pasta (6 ounces)
   2 cups cubed cooked turkey breast
1/2 cup pesto
1/2 cup coarsely chopped roasted red bell peppers
     Sliced ripe olives, if desired

1. Cook pasta as directed on package in 3-quart saucepan. Drain.

2. Mix hot cooked pasta, turkey, pesto and bell peppers in same saucepan. Heat over low heat, stirring constantly, until hot. Garnish with olives.

Sichuan Chicken and Pasta

▼ 4 servings

Prep: 5 min

Cook: 25 min

1 Serving: Calories 330
(Calories from Fat 70);
Fat 8g (Saturated 2g);
Cholesterol 65mg;
Sodium 980mg;
Carbohydrate 35g
(Dietary Fiber 5g);
Protein 34g.

   4 skinless boneless chicken breast halves (about 1 pound), cut into 3/4- to 1-inch pieces
   1 medium onion, cut into thin wedges
   2 cups water
1 1/2 cups uncooked fusilli pasta (3 ounces)
   1 package (1 pound 5 ounces) frozen Sichuan stir-fry mix with vegetables, Sichuan sauce and peanuts

1. Spray 12-inch nonstick skillet with nonstick cooking spray; heat over medium-high heat. Cook chicken and onion in skillet 3 to 5 minutes or until chicken is light brown.

2. Stir in water; heat to boiling. Stir in pasta. Cook 8 to 10 minutes, stirring occasionally, until pasta is almost tender (do not drain).

3. Stir in packet of sauce mix from stir-fry mix until well blended. Stir in vegetables.

4. Cover and cook 8 to 9 minutes, stirring occasionally, until vegetables are crisp-tender. Sprinkle with peanuts from stir-fry mix.

Preceding Page
Sichuan Chicken and Pasta

Pesto Turkey and Pasta ▶

Sausage Pesto Casserole

▼ 4 servings

To speed preparation time even more, cook sausage in another pan while the pasta cooks.

Prep: 5 min

Cook: 21 min

1 Serving: Calories 795 (Calories from Fat 515); Fat 57g (Saturated 17g); Cholesterol 100mg; Sodium 1290mg; Carbohydrate 38g (Dietary Fiber 2g); Protein 34g.

2 cups uncooked rainbow rotini pasta (6 ounces)
1 pound Italian sausage links, each cut into 6 pieces
1 container (7 ounces) refrigerated pesto
1/4 cup water
1/4 cup shredded Parmesan cheese (4 ounces)

1. Cook and drain pasta as directed on package in 3-quart saucepan; set aside.

2. Spray same saucepan with nonstick cooking spray; heat over medium heat. Cook sausage in saucepan about 6 minutes, stirring occasionally, until brown; drain.

3. Stir pesto sauce, water and pasta into sausage. Cover and cook over medium heat 5 to 8 minutes, stirring occasionally, until sausage is no longer pink in center.

4. Sprinkle with cheese.

Sausage Pesto Casserole ▶

Chicken–Green Bean Casserole

▼ 4 servings

Prep: 2 min

Cook: 5 min

1 Serving: Calories 485 (Calories from Fat 250); Fat 28g (Saturated 6g); Cholesterol 40mg; Sodium 1430mg; Carbohydrate 43g (Dietary Fiber 5g); Protein 20g.

3 cups frozen French-style green beans (from 16-ounce package)

1 can (10 3/4 ounces) condensed cream of chicken or cream of mushroom soup

2 cans (5 ounces each) chunk chicken, drained

1/2 cup sour cream

1 package (6 ounces) chow mein noodles

Paprika, if desired

1. Heat beans, soup and chicken to boiling in 2-quart saucepan over medium heat, stirring occasionally. Remove from heat; stir in sour cream.

2. Serve hot chicken mixture over noodles; sprinkle with paprika.

▼▼▼▼▼▼▼▼▼▼▼▼▼▼▼▼▼▼▼▼▼

Double Cheese Tortellini

▼ 4 servings

Prep: 2 min

Cook: 9 to 15 min

1 Serving: Calories 455 (Calories from Fat 110); Fat 12g (Saturated 7g); Cholesterol 55mg; Sodium 1820mg; Carbohydrate 71g (Dietary Fiber 4g); Protein 25g.

2 cans (15 ounces each) Italian-style or chunky garlic-and-herb tomato sauce

2 packages (9 ounces each) refrigerated cheese-filled tortellini

1/2 cup shredded or grated Parmesan cheese

1. Heat tomato sauce to boiling in 3-quart saucepan. Stir in tortellini. Heat to boiling; reduce heat to medium.

2. Simmer 3 to 7 minutes, stirring occasionally, until tortellini is tender. Serve with cheese.

Chicken–Green Bean Casserole ►

Alfredo Salmon and Noodles

▼ 4 servings

You'll like the creamy rich flavor of this saucepan casserole. If you like, substitute tuna for the salmon.

Prep: 5 min

Cook: 10 min

1 Serving: Calories 315 (Calories from Fat 125); Fat 14g (Saturated 6g); Cholesterol 80mg; Sodium 390mg; Carbohydrate 33g (Dietary Fiber 3g); Protein 17g.

3 cups uncooked wide egg noodles (6 ounces)
1 package (9 ounces) frozen cut broccoli
1/2 cup Alfredo sauce
1 can (about 6 ounces) skinless boneless salmon packed in water, drained and flaked
1/8 teaspoon pepper

1. Cook noodles as directed on package in 3-quart saucepan, adding broccoli the last 4 to 5 minutes of cooking. Drain and return to saucepan.

2. Stir in remaining ingredients. Cook over low heat 4 to 6 minutes, stirring occasionally, until hot.

▼▼▼▼▼▼▼▼▼▼▼▼▼▼▼▼▼▼▼▼▼▼▼▼▼▼▼

Ravioli with Tomatoes and Mushrooms

▼ 4 servings

Prep: 8 min

Cook: 15 min

1 Serving: Calories 275 (Calories from Fat 80); Fat 9g (Saturated 4g); Cholesterol 35mg; Sodium 1130mg; Carbohydrate 37g (Dietary Fiber 3g); Protein 15g.

1 package (9 ounces) refrigerated Italian sausage-filled ravioli
1 can (15 ounces) chunky garlic-and-herb tomato sauce
8 ounces whole mushrooms, cut into fourths
4 medium green onions, sliced (1/2 cup)
1/4 cup shredded Parmesan cheese

1. Cook and drain ravioli as directed on package in 3-quart saucepan; set aside.

2. Cook tomato sauce and mushrooms in same saucepan over medium heat 3 to 4 minutes, stirring occasionally, until mushrooms are tender.

3. Stir in onions and ravioli. Cook 2 to 4 minutes or until hot. Sprinkle each serving with cheese.

Betty Crocker's Top 10

Recipe Shortcuts for Super Express Cooking

1. Seasoned tomatoes—diced, pieces and stewed—and tomato sauces such as Italian and Mexican

2. Dry seasoning, sauce and salad dressing mixes—taco, sloppy joe, spaghetti, white sauce, gravy, hollandaise, Alfredo, pesto, honey-dijon and Caesar

3. Bottled sauces, marinades and salad dressings—teriyaki, stir-fry, sweet-and-sour, barbecue, mesquite and lemon-dill

4. Pre-shredded cheeses

5. Cut-up vegetables or stir-fry vegetable mixtures from the produce aisle

6. Bagged lettuce mixtures with or without the dressing and croutons included

7. Cold and hot foods from the deli

8. Meals in cans or shelf-stable packages such as soups, macaroni and cheese or other pasta mixtures

9. Frozen entrées from the freezer case in the grocery store

10. Instant or very quick-cooking foods such as instant rice, potatoes and couscous; hot dogs, minute steaks and frozen meatballs

Ramen Stir-Fry

▼ 4 servings

Serve this tangy lo mein–style dish with your favorite egg rolls.

Prep: 5 min

Cook: 12 min

1 Serving: Calories 245
(Calories from Fat 65);
Fat 7g (Saturated 3g);
Cholesterol 55mg;
Sodium 860mg;
Carbohydrate 25g
(Dietary Fiber 3g);
Protein 24g.

1   **pound beef boneless sirloin, cut into thin strips**
2   **cups water**
1   **package (3 ounces) Oriental-flavor ramen soup mix**
1   **package (16 ounces) fresh stir-fry vegetables**
1/4 **cup stir-fry sauce**

1. Spray 12-inch nonstick skillet with nonstick cooking spray; heat over medium-high heat. Cook beef in skillet 3 to 5 minutes, stirring occasionally, until brown. Remove beef from skillet.

2. Heat water to boiling in skillet. Break up noodles from soup mix into water; stir until slightly softened. Stir in vegetables.

3. Heat to boiling. Boil 5 to 7 minutes, stirring occasionally, until vegetables are crisp-tender. Stir in seasoning packet from soup mix, stir-fry sauce and beef. Cook 3 to 5 minutes, stirring frequently, until hot.

Thawing Meats in the Microwave

If you're like other busy people, you may sometimes forget to take meat out of the freezer to thaw. You can still make dinner—just use the handy chart below. Place wrapped meat in a microwavable dish. After half of the microwave defrosting time, remove from wrapper, separate pieces (if possible) and place in dish to catch any juice that may leak. As soon as possible, separate pieces and arrange thickest parts to outside edges of dish. Pierce packages of bacon, hot dogs and sausages with a fork. Microwave on Defrost setting as directed until few ice crystals remain in center. Let stand 5 to 10 minutes to complete thawing.

Timetable for Thawing Meats

Meat Type	Amount	Defrosting Time (Defrost setting)
Steak		
1/2-inch thick	1 pound	7 to 9 minutes, turning over after 4 minutes
1 inch thick	1 pound	8 to 11 minutes, turning over after 4 minutes
Chops		
1/2-inch thick	1 pound (about 4 chops)	6 to 9 minutes, rearranging after 4 minutes
Ribs, back	1 pound	7 to 9 minutes, rearranging after 4 minutes
Ground	1 pound	8 to 10 minutes, turning over after 4 minutes
Meatballs, cooked	1 pound (24 balls)	7 to 9 minutes, separating after 3 minutes
Patties, 3/4-inch thick	1 pound (4 patties)	8 to 10 minutes, turning over after 4 minutes
Bacon, sliced	1 pound	5 to 6 minutes
Hot Dogs	1 pound (about 10)	5 to 7 minutes, turning over after 3 minutes
	1/2 pound	2 to 4 minutes, turning over after 3 minutes
Sausages, cooked or uncooked (bratwurst, Italian, Polish)	1 pound (about 6)	6 to 8 minutes, turning over after 3 minutes

Oriental Turkey Patties and Vegetables

▼ 4 servings

Pre-seasoned turkey patties are combined with convenient prepared vegetables and sauce for this appealing main dish. Serve it with rice or noodles.

Prep: 5 min

Cook: 20 min

1 Serving: Calories 265 (Calories from Fat 100); Fat 11g (Saturated 3g); Cholesterol 70mg; Sodium 920mg; Carbohydrate 20g (Dietary Fiber 4g); Protein 25g.

1 orange
1/3 cup Hawaiian or regular stir-fry sauce
1 tablespoon packed brown sugar
1 package (1 pound) seasoned turkey patties
1 package (16 ounces) fresh stir-fry vegetables

1. Grate 1 teaspoon peel from orange. Peel orange; discard peel. Cut orange into thin wedges or slices. Mix stir-fry sauce, brown sugar and orange peel.

2. Spray 12-inch nonstick skillet with nonstick cooking spray; heat over medium-high heat. Cook turkey in skillet about 3 minutes on each side or until light brown.

3. Move turkey to one side of skillet. Add stir-fry sauce mixture and vegetables to other side of skillet; stir well to coat vegetables with sauce.

4. Heat to boiling; reduce heat to medium. Cover and cook 10 to 12 minutes, stirring occasionally, until vegetables are crisp-tender. Stir in orange wedges. Serve turkey topped with vegetable mixture.

Oriental Turkey Patties and Vegetables ▶

Glazed Turkey Tenderloins

▼ 4 servings

Prep: 5 min

Cook: 20 to 25 min

1 Serving: Calories 365 (Calories from Fat 90); Fat 10g (Saturated 3g); Cholesterol 135mg; Sodium 140mg; Carbohydrate 17g (Dietary Fiber 0g); Protein 52g.

	1 tablespoon vegetable oil
1 1/4	pounds turkey breast tenderloins
1/3	cup orange marmalade
1	teaspoon finely chopped gingerroot or 1/2 teaspoon ground ginger
1	teaspoon white or regular Worcestershire sauce

1. Heat oil in 10-inch skillet over medium heat. Cook turkey in oil about 5 minutes or until brown on one side; turn turkey. Stir in remaining ingredients; reduce heat to low.

2. Cover and simmer 15 to 20 minutes, stirring occasionally, until sauce is thickened and juice of turkey is no longer pink when center of thickest piece is cut. Cut turkey into thin slices. Spoon sauce over turkey.

▼ ▼ ▼ ▼ ▼ ▼ ▼ ▼ ▼ ▼ ▼ ▼ ▼ ▼ ▼ ▼ ▼ ▼

Bratwurst and Sauerkraut

▼ 6 servings

Prep: 5 min

Cook: 15 min

1 Serving: Calories 315 (Calories from Fat 215); Fat 24g (Saturated 9g); Cholesterol 55mg; Sodium 1100mg; Carbohydrate 16g (Dietary Fiber 2g); Protein 11g.

	1 tablespoon margarine, butter or spread
	1 pound fully cooked bratwurst
	2 cans (16 ounces each) sauerkraut, drained
1/3	cup packed brown sugar

1. Melt margarine in 10-inch skillet over medium heat. Cook bratwurst in margarine about 5 minutes, turning frequently, until brown.

2. Add sauerkraut. Sprinkle with brown sugar. Cover and cook over low heat about 10 minutes or until hot.

German Potato Salad with Bratwurst

▼ 4 servings

Serve this great busy-day meal with your favorite crusty loaf of bread and fresh fruit.

1 small red or green bell pepper, chopped (1/2 cup)
1 can (15 1/2 ounces) German potato salad
1 pound fully cooked bratwurst
2 tablespoons chopped fresh parsley

1. Spray 12-inch nonstick skillet with nonstick cooking spray; heat over medium heat. Cook bell pepper in skillet 2 to 3 minutes, stirring occasionally, until crisp-tender.

2. Stir in potato salad; add bratwurst. Cover and cook about 5 minutes, stirring occasionally, until hot. Sprinkle with parsley.

Prep: 5 min

Cook: 8 min

1 Serving: Calories 480 (Calories from Fat 335); Fat 37g (Saturated 14g); Cholesterol 85mg; Sodium 1550mg; Carbohydrate 20g (Dietary Fiber 1g); Protein 18g.

All-in-One Seasoning for Easy Cooking

Why store all those little spice and seasoning containers when just one would do? Although the name on the jar often suggests that a spice or seasoning be used only one way, such as apple pie spice, it doesn't mean you can't use them as creatively as you wish! If you can't find a specific seasoning blend at your store, don't worry; just use something similar or one of your favorites. Below, we've listed a sampling of seasoning blends and ways to spice up things:

Blends to Use for Savory Flavor:

- **Barbecue seasoning:** Mix with ground meats or poultry; sprinkle on meats before grilling; sprinkle on oil-coated, uncooked potatoes for oven-fries or on cooked French-fried potatoes; replace barbecue seasoning for the garlic salt or powder used for making "garlic toast."

- **Blackened steak seasoning:** This orange-colored powdery seasoning can be used for grilled steaks or roasts, or mix with ground beef.

- **Cajun/Creole seasoning:** Sprinkle this spicy salt-like seasoning on meats and poultry or add to marinades. Use in casseroles, stir-fries, vegetables, dips, spreads, soups, chili, stews and eggs.

- **Caribbean jerk:** Sprinkle on chicken, pork or fish or add to marinades and stir-fries. Sprinkle on vegetables or add to salsas.

- **Curry powder:** Use with chicken, seafood or fish in Indian or Thai recipes. Add to dips, spreads, rice, vegetables, sauces and eggs.

- **Fajita seasoning:** Use for chicken, beef or pork fajitas. Sprinkle on grilled meats and poultry or add to ground meats and poultry. Use in soups or chili for added zip!

- **Five-spice powder:** Use in any Chinese recipes, from stir-fries to egg roll filling. Because this is a strong, pungent spice, use sparingly at first and add more if desired.

- **Garlic bread sprinkle:** Sprinkle on garlic bread, pasta or vegetables.

- **Hamburger seasoning:** Add to ground beef or other ground meats. Sprinkle on burgers or other meats and poultry. Sprinkle on oil-coated, uncooked potato wedges for oven-fries or on cooked French-fried potatoes.

- **Herb chicken:** Sprinkle on chicken or turkey before roasting. Sprinkle on oil-coated, uncooked potato chunks for oven-roasted potatoes or sprinkle on cooked vegetables or garlic toast. Add to pasta, marinades, salad dressings, sauces, dips and spreads.

- **Italian seasoning:** Add to any Italian foods, from sauces and pizza, to meatballs, garlic bread and salad dressing. Add to soups, stews, sauces and marinades.

- **Lemon-pepper or garlic pepper:** Sprinkle on poultry, fish, meats and vegetables. Add to cooked pasta and grains.

- **Mesquite chicken:** Sprinkle on poultry, fish or meats before grilling.

- **Mexican:** Add to any Mexican or Tex-Mex foods, from tacos and burritos, to enchiladas, cheese dips and salsa. Or use as desired for instant "south-of-the-border" taste!

- **Rotisserie chicken:** Sprinkle on chicken or turkey before roasting. Sprinkle on oil-coated, uncooked potato wedges or chunks for oven-roasted potatoes.

- **Salt-free herb blends:** Use as a sprinkle for meats, fish, poultry, vegetables, pasta and grains. Use in soups, stews, casseroles, sauces, marinades, dips and spreads.

- **Thai:** Use in any Thai recipe or use in stir-fries, pasta dishes, rice or egg roll filling.

Blends to Use for Sweet Flavor:

- **Apple pie spice:** Use in apple or other fruit pies or in oatmeal cookie dough; sprinkle over fresh fruit, pudding, applesauce, yogurt or ice cream.

- **Pumpkin pie spice:** Use in pumpkin pie, bread, bars, cake and cookies. Sprinkle along with sugar on buttered toast. Use in mashed sweet potatoes or squash, or sprinkle on unmashed sweet potatoes or squash.

Skillet Pork Stew

▼ 4 servings

Serve this easy stew with bread, cornbread or biscuits.

Prep: 10 min

Cook: 25 min

1 Serving: Calories 380
(Calories from Fat 80);
Fat 9g (Saturated 4g);
Cholesterol 55mg;
Sodium 610mg;
Carbohydrate 54g
(Dietary Fiber 5g);
Protein 26g.

1 pound pork boneless loin, cut into 1/2-inch pieces
1 jar (12 ounces) pork gravy
2 tablespoons ketchup
8 unpeeled small red potatoes, cut into fourths
1 cup fresh or frozen cut green beans

1. Spray 12-inch nonstick skillet with nonstick cooking spray; heat over medium-high heat. Cook pork in skillet 3 to 5 minutes, stirring frequently, until light brown.

2. Stir in gravy, ketchup and potatoes. Heat to boiling; reduce heat to medium-low. Cover and cook 10 minutes.

3. Stir in beans. Cover and cook 5 to 10 minutes, stirring occasionally, until vegetables are tender.

Skillet Pork Stew ▶

Express Jambalaya

▼ 6 servings

This dish is especially easy when you buy chicken breasts that are already cut up.

Prep: 5 min

Cook: 25 to 30 min

1 Serving: Calories 260
(Calories from Fat 125);
Fat 14g (Saturated 5g);
Cholesterol 75mg;
Sodium 600mg;
Carbohydrate 11g
(Dietary Fiber 1g);
Protein 24g.

4 skinless boneless chicken breast halves (about 1 pound), cut into 3/4- to 1-inch pieces

1 package (6.8 ounces) rice and vermicelli mix with Spanish seasonings

2 cups water

1 can (14 ounces) chunky tomatoes with crushed red pepper, undrained

1/2 pound fully cooked Polish sausage, cut into 1/2-inch pieces

1. Spray 12-inch nonstick skillet with nonstick cooking spray; heat over medium-high heat. Cook chicken in skillet 3 to 5 minutes, stirring frequently, until light brown. Remove chicken from skillet.

2. Cook rice and vermicelli mix (without seasonings) in skillet over heat, stirring frequently, until golden brown. Gradually stir in water, tomatoes and seasonings from rice and vermicelli mix. Heat to boiling. Stir in sausage and chicken; reduce heat to low.

3. Cover and simmer 15 to 20 minutes, stirring occasionally, until liquid is absorbed and chicken is no longer pink in center.

Express Jambalaya ▶

Shrimp Creole

▼ 4 servings

Prep: 10 min

Cook: 14 min

1 Serving: Calories 100 (Calories from Fat 10); Fat 1g (Saturated 0g); Cholesterol 160mg; Sodium 350mg; Carbohydrate 7g (Dietary Fiber 2g); Protein 18g.

2 cups frozen stir-fry bell peppers and onions (from 16-ounce package)

1 can (14 ounces) chunky tomatoes with crushed red pepper, undrained

1 pound uncooked peeled and deveined medium shrimp, thawed if frozen

1 teaspoon chopped fresh or 1/4 teaspoon dried thyme leaves

1/8 teaspoon garlic powder

1. Spray 12-inch nonstick skillet with nonstick cooking spray; heat over medium-high heat. Cook stir-fry vegetables in skillet about 3 minutes, stirring occasionally, until crisp-tender.

2. Stir in remaining ingredients. Heat to boiling; reduce heat to low. Cover and simmer 8 to 10 minutes, stirring occasionally, until shrimp are pink and firm.

▼ ▼

Spicy Chicken Chili

▼ 4 servings

Prep: 5 min

Cook: 15 min

1 Serving: Calories 270 (Calories from Fat 80); Fat 9g (Saturated 4g); Cholesterol 80mg; Sodium 690mg; Carbohydrate 17g (Dietary Fiber 4g); Protein 34g.

4 skinless boneless chicken breast halves (about 1 pound), cut into 3/4-inch pieces

1 can (14 1/2 ounces) salsa-style chunky tomatoes, undrained

1 can (15 ounces) spicy chili beans

1/2 cup shredded Cheddar cheese (2 ounces)

1. Spray 12-inch nonstick skillet with nonstick cooking spray; heat over medium-high heat. Cook chicken in skillet 3 to 5 minutes, stirring frequently, until light brown.

2. Stir in tomatoes and beans; reduce heat to medium-low. Cook uncovered 8 to 10 minutes, stirring frequently, until chicken is no longer pink in center. Sprinkle each serving with cheese.

Smart Ways to Save

Monday through Friday, making dinner can seem overwhelming. Beat the stress by having some things ready-to-eat or ready-to-cook. You can prepare many items ahead to make weekday cooking a breeze. Convenience foods certainly help to shave time, but can be more expensive. When you'd rather save both time and money, try making some of your own convenience foods. We've started you off with some ideas—no doubt you'll come up with some savvy combinations of your own as well.

- **Frozen Vegetables:** Make your own frozen vegetable combinations by buying bags of individual vegetables and combining your favorites. Re-package in resealable plastic bags and freeze. Try adding chopped onion, garlic or cooked pasta to the vegetable mixture as well.

- **Salad Greens:** Make your own lettuce or coleslaw mixture and package in resealable plastic bags for up to 2 days. Wash and tear (cutting lettuce with a knife causes it to turn brown near where it was cut; tear by hand instead) lettuce making sure that leaves are dry before storing (they will stay crisper), using a salad spinner or paper towels.

- **Fresh Vegetables:** Wash and cut up vegetables for eating or cooking and store in cold water for up to 1 week or without water in resealable plastic bags for 2 to 3 days.

- **Coleslaw Mixtures:** Shred cabbage and carrots and package in resealable plastic bags for up 2 days.

- **Meat:** Cut up chicken breasts or beef steak into thin strips for stir-frying and freeze (partially frozen meat cuts more easily). To freeze, place desired amount in resealable plastic freezer bags or containers with lids, label and date. Freeze up to 9 months. Use partially frozen or thaw in refrigerator before using.

- **Pancakes and Waffles:** Don't throw out extra pancake or waffle batter. Instead, make the pancakes or waffles and freeze them for another time. Cool the pancakes or waffles completely before storing. Stack pancakes or waffles and wrap tightly; store in freezer no longer than 2 months. Pancakes can be re-heated in the microwave oven. A stack of two frozen pancakes will take about 2 to 3 minutes, and a stack of four will take 3 to 4 minutes. Waffles can be separated into sections and re-heated in the toaster.

Easy Picadillo

▼ 4 servings

Picadillo is a favorite dish of Spanish-speaking countries. Ingredients vary, but usually include ground meat, tomatoes and onions. This tasty version contains black beans, which are traditional with Cuban picadillo; it's very nice served over rice.

Prep: 5 min

Cook: 17 min

1 Serving: Calories 365 (Calories from Fat 155); Fat 17g (Saturated 7g); Cholesterol 65mg; Sodium 330mg; Carbohydrate 32g (Dietary Fiber 5g); Protein 26g.

1   pound lean ground beef

1   small green bell pepper, chopped (1/2 cup)

1   can (14 1/2 ounces) salsa-style chunky tomatoes, undrained

1   cup canned black beans, rinsed and drained

1/2 cup golden raisins

1. Cook beef and bell pepper in 12-inch nonstick skillet over medium heat 8 to 10 minutes, stirring occasionally, until beef is brown; drain.

2. Stir in remaining ingredients; reduce heat to low. Cover and simmer 5 to 7 minutes, stirring occasionally, until hot.

Easy Picadillo ▶

Apricot Fish

▼ 4 servings

Prep: 4 min

Broil: 9 min

1 Serving: Calories 305
(Calories from Fat 25);
Fat 3g (Saturated 1g);
Cholesterol 120mg;
Sodium 200mg;
Carbohydrate 26g
(Dietary Fiber 0g);
Protein 43g.

    1   pound halibut or other lean fish steaks
  1/2   cup apricot preserves
    2   tablespoons white vinegar
1 1/2   teaspoons chopped fresh or 1/2 teaspoon dried
        tarragon leaves

1. Set oven control to broil. Grease broiler pan rack. Place
    fish on rack in broiler pan.

2. Broil with top about 4 inches from heat 4 minutes; turn.
    Broil about 4 minutes longer, or until fish flakes easily with
    fork.

3. Meanwhile, mix remaining ingredients; spoon onto fish.
    Broil 1 minute longer.

Apricot Fish ▶

Spinach and Potatoes Alfredo

▼ 6 servings

Alfredo sauce can be purchased fresh in the refrigerated section or in jars near the pasta sauce section. Dry mixes to prepare Alfredo sauce are also available.

Prep: 5 min

Cook: 13 to 15 min

1 Serving: Calories 140 (Calories from Fat 25); Fat 3g (Saturated 2g); Cholesterol 10mg; Sodium 160mg; Carbohydrate 26g (Dietary Fiber 2g); Protein 4g.

- **6 unpeeled small red potatoes, sliced**
- **2 cups lightly packed spinach leaves**
- **1/2 cup Alfredo sauce**
- **Coarsely ground pepper**

1. Place potatoes in 2-quart saucepan. Add just enough water to cover potatoes. Heat to boiling; reduce heat to medium. Cover and cook 6 to 8 minutes or until potatoes are tender; drain.

2. Stir in spinach and Alfredo sauce. Cook, stirring frequently, until mixture is hot and spinach is wilted. Sprinkle with pepper.

▼ ▼ ▼ ▼ ▼ ▼ ▼ ▼ ▼ ▼ ▼ ▼ ▼ ▼ ▼ ▼ ▼ ▼ ▼ ▼

Green Enchiladas

▼ 5 servings

Prep: 15 min

Cook: 15 min

1 Serving: Calories 485 (Calories from Fat 235); Fat 26g (Saturated 14g); Cholesterol 135mg; Sodium 810mg; Carbohydrate 31g (Dietary Fiber 4g); Protein 36g.

- **1 cup sour cream**
- **1 jar (15 to 16 ounces) green salsa**
- **10 corn or flour tortillas (6 to 8 inches in diameter)**
- **2 1/2 cups shredded cooked chicken or refried beans**
- **1 cup shredded Monterey Jack cheese (4 ounces)**
- **Sour cream**

1. Heat oven to 350°.

2. Stir 1 cup sour cream into salsa. Dip each tortilla into sauce to coat both sides.

3. Spoon ¼ cup of the chicken onto each tortilla; roll up. Place seam sides down in ungreased rectangular baking dish, 13 x 9 x 2 inches. Pour remaining sauce over enchiladas. Sprinkle with cheese.

4. Bake uncovered about 15 minutes or until cheese is melted. Serve with sour cream.

Chili-Cheese Tortillas

▼ 4 servings

1 can (4 ounces) diced green chilies, drained
8 flour tortillas (8 or 10 inches in diameter)
1 cup shredded Cheddar cheese (4 ounces)

1. Heat oven to 350°.

2. Spread about 1 tablespoon chilies on each tortilla. Sprinkle each with 2 tablespoons cheese; roll up tightly (secure with toothpicks if necessary). Place seam sides down in ungreased square pan, 9 x 9 x 2 inches.

3. Cover and bake about 15 minutes or until warm.

Prep: 5 min

Bake: 15 min

1 Serving: Calories 380 (Calories from Fat 135); Fat 15g (Saturated 7g); Cholesterol 30mg; Sodium 870mg; Carbohydrate 49g (Dietary Fiber 2g); Protein 14g.

Salsa Chicken Sandwiches

▼ 4 sandwiches

These yummy sandwiches are great for a light lunch or snack. Look for the black bean dip in the snacks and chips or refrigerated dip sections of your store.

1 package (10 1/2 ounces) frozen breaded chicken breast patties
4 whole wheat sandwich buns, split
8 teaspoons purchased black bean dip
1/4 cup thick-and-chunky salsa
1/2 cup shredded lettuce

1. Cook chicken in oven as directed on package, adding buns, cut side up, the last 3 to 4 minutes of cooking time until lightly toasted.

2. Spread bottom half of each bun with 2 teaspoons dip. Top each with chicken patty; spread with 1 tablespoon salsa. Top each with 2 tablespoons lettuce and top of bun.

Prep: 5 min

Cook: 20 min

1 Sandwich: Calories 310 (Calories from Fat 155); Fat 17g (Saturated 4g); Cholesterol 45mg; Sodium 610mg; Carbohydrate 29g (Dietary Fiber 4g); Protein 14g.

Honey Ham Bagel Sandwiches

▼ 4 open-face sandwiches

It's a double honey treat when you add honey mustard to honey-baked ham in these tasty open-face sandwiches.

Prep: 5 min

Cook: 5 min

1 Open-face Sandwich:
Calories 185
(Calories from Fat 65);
Fat 7g (Saturated 4g);
Cholesterol 30mg;
Sodium 620mg;
Carbohydrate 18g
(Dietary Fiber 1g);
Protein 13g.

2 pumpernickel bagels, split and toasted

4 teaspoons honey mustard

4 slices (1 ounce each) fully cooked honey-baked ham

4 thin slices (1/2 ounce each) Swiss cheese

1. Heat oven to 400°.

2. Spread each bagel half with 1 teaspoon mustard. Top each with ham and cheese. Place on cookie sheet. Bake 3 to 5 minutes or until cheese is melted.

▼▼▼▼▼▼▼▼▼▼▼▼▼▼▼▼▼▼

Canadian Bacon and Spinach Sandwiches

▼ 4 open-face sandwiches

Fresh spinach is usually available prewashed and packaged in the produce section of large supermarkets—and it helps make it a snap to whip up these sandwiches.

Prep: 5 min

Cook: 7 min

1 Open-face Sandwich:
Calories 280
(Calories from Fat 135);
Fat 15g (Saturated 7g);
Cholesterol 55mg;
Sodium 1010mg;
Carbohydrate 15g
(Dietary Fiber 1g);
Protein 22g.

4 slices French bread, 1 inch thick

1 cup bite-size pieces spinach leaves

2 tablespoons ranch dressing

4 slices (2 ounces each) Canadian-style bacon

4 slices (1 ounce each) Swiss cheese

1. Set oven control to broil. Place bread on rack in broiler pan or cookie sheet. Broil with tops 4 to 6 inches from heat, 1 to 2 minutes on each side or until toasted.

2. Mix spinach and dressing. Spoon spinach onto bread. Broil about 2 minutes or until hot. Top with bacon and cheese. Broil about 1 minute or until cheese is melted.

Honey Ham Bagel Sandwiches ▶

Betty Crocker's Good and Easy Cookbook

Open-Face Garden Turkey Sandwiches

▼ 4 open-face sandwiches

Follow cooking times carefully on the package of turkey breast slices—cook just until no longer pink so they remain tender and juicy.

Prep: 5 min

Cook: 13 to 15 min

1 Open-face Sandwich:
Calories 330
(Calories from Fat 125);
Fat 14g (Saturated 5g);
Cholesterol 95mg;
Sodium 490mg;
Carbohydrate 21g
(Dietary Fiber 3g);
Protein 33g.

- 4 cups frozen stir-fry bell peppers and onions (from 16-ounce package)
- 1 pound uncooked turkey breast slices, about 1/4 inch thick
- 1/2 cup shredded Cheddar cheese (2 ounces)
- 4 tablespoons sandwich spread, mayonnaise or salad dressing
- 4 slices pumpernickel bread, toasted

1. Spray 12-inch nonstick skillet with nonstick cooking spray; heat over medium-high heat. Cook stir-fry vegetables in skillet 3 to 5 minutes, stirring frequently, until tender. Remove vegetables from skillet.

2. Cook turkey as directed on package in same skillet until light golden brown and no longer pink in center. Remove from heat.

3. Top each turkey slice with vegetables and cheese. Cover 1 to 2 minutes or until cheese is melted. Spread sandwich spread on bread. Top each slice bread with turkey topped with vegetables and cheese.

Open-Face Garden Turkey Sandwiches ▶

Super Shopper!

If walking down the aisles of a large grocery store makes you dizzy, we understand! With so many products and choices available, and the grocer's dilemma of limited shelf space, it can be downright confusing and sometimes maddening trying to find what you're looking for. To help in the search, the convenience products you need for our recipes fall into three basic categories:

1. **Shelf-stable:** Items needing no refrigeration or freezing
2. **Refrigerated:** Items in the produce, dairy or meat case
3. **Frozen:** Items in the freezer case

The table below gives you an idea of how to find many of the ingredients used in this book. Often items come in several forms: canned/jarred, frozen, dry or fresh. If critical to the success of a recipe, we've specifically listed what form of a product you need to use, otherwise, for example, one cup of Alfredo sauce can be homemade, from a jar, dry mix, refrigerated or frozen. This gives you the flexi-bility and choice to use whatever you prefer—or happen to have on hand!

Food Item	Store Location (aisle or food section)
Pesto	Usually sold fresh in the dairy aisle or deli section; can also purchase jarred pesto in the Italian foods or spaghetti sauce aisle, or a dry seasoning mix—sold with other seasoning mixes; usually in the pasta, rice or jarred sauce and gravy aisles
Chili oil, chili puree with garlic, fish sauce, hoisin sauce, sesame oil	Asian or Oriental aisle

Food Item	Store Location (aisle or food section)
Teriyaki baste and glaze (thicker and stickier) or teriyaki marinade and sauce (watery), stir-fry sauces	Asian or Oriental aisle or condiments aisle
Coconut milk (unsweetened)	Asian or Oriental aisle or in canned milk section
Chutney, marinated artichoke hearts, roasted red peppers	Condiments section near pickles and olives
Sun-dried tomatoes (oil-packed and dehydrated)	Condiments aisle, Italian foods section, spaghetti sauce section or in the produce section
Canned seasoned tomato products such as salsa or Mexican-style or Italian-style	Canned tomato products, spaghetti sauce or canned vegetable aisles
Couscous	Rice and pasta aisle
Instant grits	Rice and pasta aisle, baking ingredients aisle near the cornmeal or in the cereal aisle
Pork seasoning blend	Spice aisle
Original seasoning mix for oven-browned fresh potatoes	Coating mixes or potato mixes aisle
Black bean dip (refrigerated and shelf-stable)	Dairy or snacks and chips aisle
Italian bread shells or pizza crust	Deli, bread or dairy aisle
Flan sponge cake	A seasonal product, usually available in the produce section near the strawberries

Vegetable Patch Pita Sandwiches

▼ 4 sandwiches, 2 halves each

Prep: 10 min

1 Sandwich: Calories 345 (Calories from Fat 110); Fat 12g (Saturated 4g); Cholesterol 20mg; Sodium 970mg; Carbohydrate 51g (Dietary Fiber 3g); Protein 11g.

  3 cups bite-size pieces assorted fresh vegetables*

1/2 cup shredded Cheddar cheese (2 ounces)

1/2 cup creamy dressing (any flavor)

  4 pita breads (6 inches in diameter), cut crosswise in half

Mix vegetables, cheese and dressing. Spoon about 1/3 cup vegetable mixture into each pita bread pocket.

*Use vegetables such as broccoli, carrots, cauliflower, bell peppers, green onions, cherry tomatoes and zucchini.

▼ ▼ ▼ ▼ ▼ ▼ ▼ ▼ ▼ ▼ ▼ ▼ ▼ ▼ ▼ ▼ ▼ ▼ ▼

Salsa Sloppy Joe Pizza

▼ 6 servings

Prep: 12 min

Bake: 10 min

1 Serving: Calories 420 (Calories from Fat 200); Fat 22g (Saturated 10g); Cholesterol 65mg; Sodium 730mg; Carbohydrate 33g (Dietary Fiber 2g); Protein 23g.

  1 pound lean ground beef

  3 tablespoons taco seasoning mix

  1 Italian bread shell or purchased pizza crust (12 to 14 inches in diameter)

1/3 cup purchased black bean dip

  1 cup shredded Monterey Jack cheese with jalapeño peppers (4 ounces)

    Salsa and guacamole, if desired

1. Heat oven to 425°.

2. Cook beef in 10-inch nonstick skillet over medium heat 8 to 10 minutes, stirring occasionally, until brown; drain. Stir in taco seasoning.

3. Meanwhile, place bread shell on ungreased cookie sheet. Spread evenly with bean dip. Spoon beef over bean layer. Sprinkle with cheese.

4. Bake 8 to 10 minutes or until cheese is melted. Cut into wedges. Serve with salsa and guacamole.

Salsa Sloppy Joe Pizza ▶

Shrimp Salad Italiano

▼ 4 servings

Use your favorite Italian dressing to make this pretty salad, and buy the shrimp already cooked to make assembling the salad a snap.

Prep: 10 min

1 Serving: Calories 445 (Calories from Fat 205); Fat 23g (Saturated 5g); Cholesterol 255mg; Sodium 1030mg; Carbohydrate 28g (Dietary Fiber 1g); Protein 32g.

1 package (14 ounces) frozen precooked salad tortellini

3/4 to 1 pound cooked peeled and deveined medium shrimp, thawed if frozen

1/2 cup sliced ripe olives

1/4 cup chopped red onion

1/3 cup Italian dressing

1. Thaw tortellini as directed on package.

2. Toss tortellini and remaining ingredients until coated with dressing. Serve immediately, or refrigerate until serving time.

Shrimp Salad Italiano ▶

Southwestern Potato-Chicken Salad

▼ 4 servings

Prep: 5 min

1 Serving: Calories 635 (Calories from Fat 340); Fat 38g (Saturated 7g); Cholesterol 115mg; Sodium 1030mg; Carbohydrate 42g (Dietary Fiber 6g); Protein 37g.

1 pint deli potato salad (2 cups)

3 cups cubed cooked chicken (about 3/4 pound)

2 cans (11 ounces each) whole kernel corn with red and green peppers, drained

2/3 cup ranch dressing with tomato, onion and spicy peppers or regular ranch dressing

1 tablespoon canned chopped green chilies

1/8 teaspoon ground cumin

Gently mix all ingredients.

Potato-Corn Salad

▼ 4 servings

Prep: 1 min

1 Serving: Calories 270 (Calories from Fat 160); Fat 18g (Saturated 3g); Cholesterol 15mg; Sodium 500mg; Carbohydrate 26g (Dietary Fiber 2g); Protein 3g.

1 pint deli potato salad (2 cups)

1 can (11 ounces) whole kernel corn with red and green peppers, drained

1/8 teaspoon ground cumin or chili powder

Gently mix all ingredients.

Potato-Corn Salad ▶

Betty Crocker's Good and Easy Cookbook

Chutney-Salmon Salad

▼ 4 servings

Prep: 5 min

1 Serving: Calories 460
(Calories from Fat 340);
Fat 38g (Saturated 6g);
Cholesterol 60mg;
Sodium 660mg;
Carbohydrate 13g
(Dietary Fiber 2g);
Protein 18g.

2 cans (about 6 ounces each) skinless boneless salmon, drained and flaked

3 cups broccoli slaw or coleslaw mix

2/3 cup mayonnaise or salad dressing

1/3 cup chutney

1/4 cup dry-roasted peanuts, chopped

Mix salmon, broccoli slaw, mayonnaise and chutney in glass or plastic bowl. Stir in peanuts just before serving.

Fettuccine-Salmon Salad

▼ 4 servings

Prep: 15 min

1 Serving: Calories 460
(Calories from Fat 160);
Fat 18g (Saturated 8g);
Cholesterol 120mg;
Sodium 1000mg;
Carbohydrate 50g
(Dietary Fiber 6g);
Protein 31g.

1 package (8 ounces) spinach fettuccine

1 can (14 3/4 ounces) red or pink salmon

1 cup purchased dill dip

1 package (10 ounces) frozen green peas, thawed

4 medium green onions, thinly sliced (1/2 cup)

1. Cook and drain fettuccine as directed on package.

2. Drain salmon; remove skin and bones. Flake salmon.

3. Toss fettuccine, 1/2 cup of the dill dip, the peas and onions in large serving bowl. Top with salmon. Serve with remaining dill dip.

Fruity Coleslaw

▼ 4 servings

Prep: 1 min

1 Serving: Calories 225
(Calories from Fat 180);
Fat 20g (Saturated 3g);
Cholesterol 15mg;
Sodium 150mg;
Carbohydrate 12g
(Dietary Fiber 2g);
Protein 1g.

1 pint deli creamy coleslaw (2 cups)

1/4 cup diced dried fruit and raisin mixture

Mix ingredients.

Easy Chicken, Beef and Pork

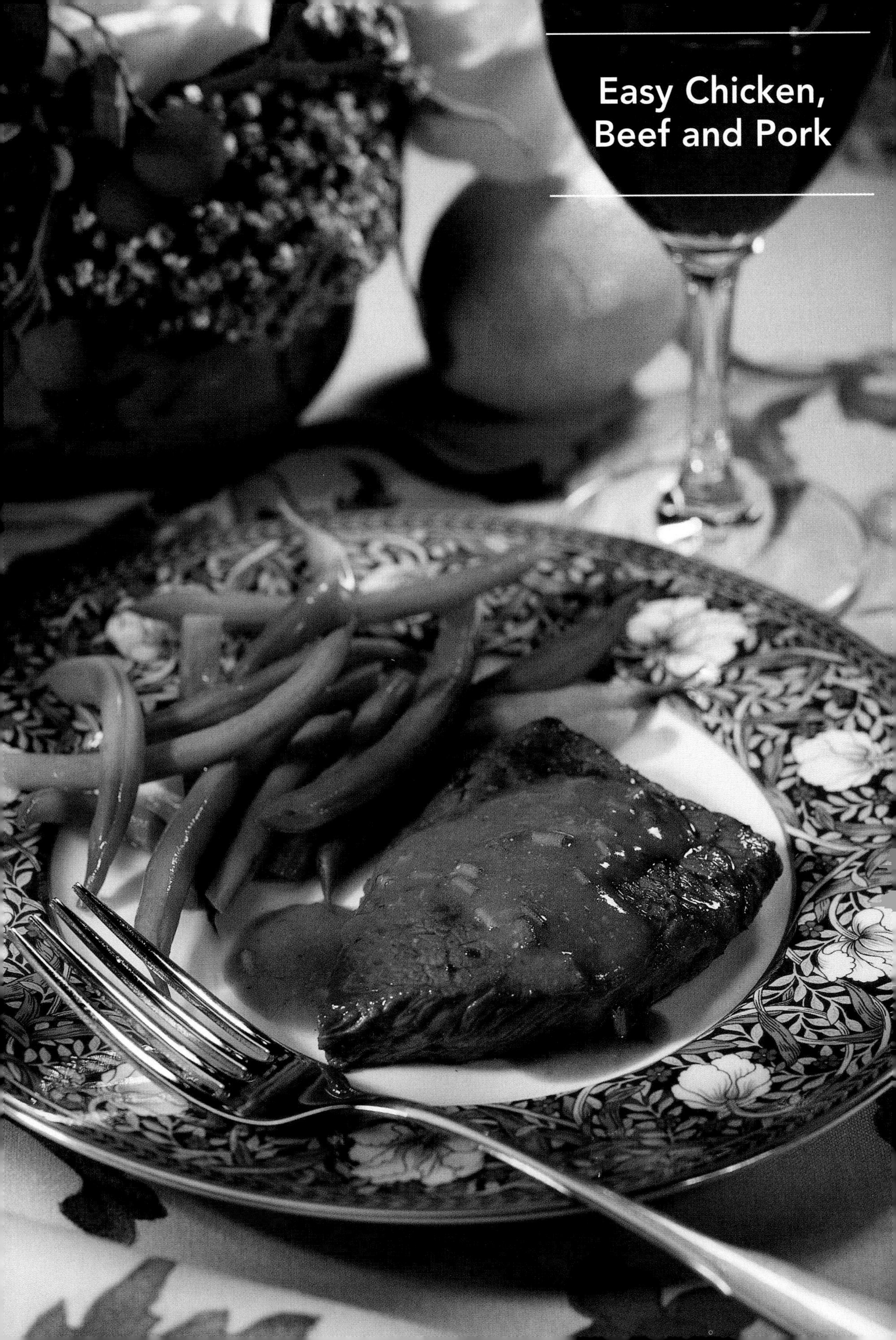

Gingered Orange and Peanut Chicken

▼ 6 servings

Prep: 12 min

Bake: 35 min

1 Serving: Calories 360 (Calories from Fat 200); Fat 22g (Saturated 4g); Cholesterol 60mg; Sodium 110mg; Carbohydrate 9g (Dietary Fiber 2g); Protein 34g.

1/3	cup orange juice
1/4	cup creamy peanut butter
1	tablespoon finely chopped gingerroot or 1/2 teaspoon ground ginger
6	skinless boneless chicken breast halves (about 1 1/2 pounds)
1 1/4	cups finely chopped salted peanuts

1. Heat oven to 400°. Grease rectangular pan, 13x9x2 inches.

2. Gradually stir orange juice into peanut butter in medium bowl. Stir in gingerroot. Dip chicken into peanut butter mixture, then coat with peanuts. Place in pan.

3. Bake uncovered 25 to 35 minutes, turning once, until juice of chicken is no longer pink when centers of thickest pieces are cut.

Ranch Chicken

▼ 4 servings

Prep: 5 min

Cook: 15 min

1 Serving: Calories 290 (Calories from Fat 145); Fat 16g (Saturated 3g); Cholesterol 70mg; Sodium 260mg; Carbohydrate 8g (Dietary Fiber 0g); Protein 28g.

These breaded chicken breasts are crispy and brown on the outside, tender and juicy on the inside. Serve the chicken with your favorite pasta and sauce.

4	skinless boneless chicken breast halves (about 1 pound)
1/4	cup ranch dressing
1/3	cup Italian-style dry bread crumbs
2	tablespoons olive or vegetable oil

1. Dip chicken into dressing, then coat with bread crumbs.

2. Heat oil in 12-inch nonstick skillet over medium-high heat. Cook chicken in oil 12 to 15 minutes, turning once, until outside is golden brown and juice is no longer pink when centers of thickest pieces are cut.

Preceding Page
Lemon Steak Diane (page 95)   Gingered Orange and Peanut Chicken

Mediterranean Skillet Chicken

▼ 4 servings

Prep: 5 min

Cook: 25 min

1 Serving: Calories 235 (Calories from Fat 110); Fat 12g (Saturated 2g); Cholesterol 65mg; Sodium 380mg; Carbohydrate 6g (Dietary Fiber 1g); Protein 27g.

2 tablespoons olive or vegetable oil

4 skinless boneless chicken breast halves (1 pound)

1 can (14 1/2 ounces) Italian-style stewed tomatoes, undrained

1/2 cup sliced ripe olives

1 teaspoon grated lemon peel

1. Heat oil in 12-inch nonstick skillet over medium-high heat. Cook chicken in oil 5 minutes, turning once, until brown.

2. Stir in remaining ingredients. Heat to boiling; reduce heat to low. Cover and simmer 15 to 20 minutes or until juice of chicken is no longer pink when centers of thickest pieces are cut.

▼▼▼▼▼▼▼▼▼▼▼▼▼▼▼▼▼▼▼▼▼

Chicken Piccata

▼ 4 servings

Prep: 8 min

Cook: 22 min

1 Serving: Calories 265 (Calories from Fat 135); Fat 15g (Saturated 4g); Cholesterol 60mg; Sodium 200mg; Carbohydrate 8g (Dietary Fiber 0g); Protein 25g.

4 skinless boneless chicken breast halves (about 1 pound)

1/4 cup all-purpose flour

1/4 cup (1/2 stick) margarine or butter

2 cloves garlic, finely chopped

1 cup dry white wine or chicken broth

2 tablespoons lemon juice

1/2 teaspoon pepper

1 tablespoon capers, if desired

1. Coat chicken with flour, shaking off excess.

2. Melt margarine in 12-inch skillet over medium-high heat. Cook chicken and garlic in margarine 15 to 20 minutes, turning once, until juice of chicken is no longer pink when centers of thickest pieces are cut.

3. Add wine and lemon juice; sprinkle with pepper. Heat until hot. Sprinkle with capers.

Mediterranean Skillet Chicken ▶

Broiling or Grilling Poultry

Broiling and direct-heat grilling are quick, low-fat methods for cooking poultry. Whole chicken and turkey can be grilled using the indirect method. Follow the guidelines that came with your grill for more information.

1. Marinate poultry, if desired.

2. **To Broil:** Brush rack of broiler pan with vegetable oil, or spray with nonstick cooking spray. Set oven to broil.

   To Grill: Brush grill rack with vegetable oil or spray with nonstick cooking spray. Start outdoor grill. If using charcoal grill, wait until coals are covered with ash (medium heat).

3. **To Broil:** Place poultry on rack in broiler pan. (For easy clean-up, line broiler pan with aluminum foil before placing poultry on rack.) For whole chicken, turkey or Rock Cornish hen, insert meat thermometer in thickest part of inside thigh muscle, not touching bone.

   To Grill: Place poultry on grill 4 to 6 inches from heat. For even cooking, place meatier poultry pieces in center of grill rack, smaller pieces on the edges. For whole chicken, turkey or Rock Cornish hen, insert meat thermometer in thickest part of inside thigh muscle, not touching bone.

4. Broil or grill as directed below in Timetable for Broiling or Grilling Poultry, turning frequently with tongs and, if desired, brushing with sauce during the last 15 to 20 minutes.

Timetable for Broiling or Grilling Poultry

Poultry Type	Weight (pounds)	Approximate Broiling Time	Approximate Grilling Time	Doneness
Chicken Cut-up chicken pieces	3 to 3 1/2	Skin sides down 30 minutes; turn. Broil 15 to 25 minutes longer. (7 to 9 inches from heat)	35 to 40 minutes (dark meat may take longer to cook)	Cook until juice of chicken is no longer pink when centers of thickest pieces are cut.

Timetable for Broiling or Grilling Poultry

Poultry Type	Weight (pounds)	Approximate Broiling Time	Approximate Grilling Time	Doneness
Chicken breast halves (bone in)	1	25 to 35 minutes (7 to 9 inches from heat)	20 to 25 minutes	Cook until juice of chicken is no longer pink when centers of thickest pieces are cut.
Breast halves (boneless)	1	15 to 20 minutes; turning once (4 to 6 inches from heat)	15 to 20 minutes	Cook until juice of chicken is no longer pink when centers of thickest pieces are cut.
Wings	3 to 3 1/2	10 minutes; turning once (5 to 7 inches from heat)	12 to 18 minutes	Cook until juice of chicken is no longer pink when centers of thickest pieces are cut.
Ground chicken or turkey patties (1/2 inch thick)	1	6 minutes on each side (3 inches from heat)	15 to 20 minutes	Cook until no longer pink.
Turkey Tenderloins	1 to 1 1/2		20 to 30 minutes	Cook until juice of turkey is no longer pink when centers of thickest pieces are cut.
Breast slices	1 to 1 1/2	7 minutes; turning once (4 inches from heat)	8 to 10 minutes	Cook until turkey is no longer pink in center.
Rock Cornish Hens*	2 to 3 (two hens)	30 to 40 minutes (4 to 6 inches from heat)	30 to 40 minutes	Cook until meat thermometer reads 180° and juice of hen is no longer pink when center of thigh is cut.

*For best results, cut hens in half before broiling or grilling.

Spicy Mexicali Drumsticks

▼ 4 servings

Prep: 10 min

Bake: 45 min

1 Serving: Calories 350 (Calories from Fat 155); Fat 17g (Saturated 5g); Cholesterol 95mg; Sodium 190mg; Carbohydrate 20g (Dietary Fiber 1g); Protein 30g.

1/3 cup buttermilk*

1/4 teaspoon red pepper sauce

2/3 cup cornmeal

2 teaspoons taco seasoning mix

8 chicken drumsticks (about 1 3/4 pounds)

2 teaspoons vegetable oil

Salsa, if desired

1. Heat oven to 400°. Grease rectangular pan, 13 x 9 x 2 inches.

2. Mix buttermilk and pepper sauce in medium bowl. Mix cornmeal and seasoning mix in large plastic bag.

3. Dip chicken into buttermilk mixture, then shake in bag to coat with cornmeal mixture. Place in pan. Drizzle with oil.

4. Bake uncovered 40 to 45 minutes, turning once, until juice of chicken is no longer pink when centers of thickest pieces are cut. Serve with salsa.

*One-third cup milk mixed with 1 teaspoon lemon juice can be substituted for the buttermilk. Let stand 5 minutes.

Spicy Mexicali Drumsticks ▶

Lemon-Dill Chicken

▼ 6 servings

Prep: 5 min

Cook: 16 to 24 min

1 Serving: Calories 200
(Calories from Fat 100);
Fat 11g (Saturated 3g);
Cholesterol 60mg;
Sodium 240mg;
Carbohydrate 1g
(Dietary Fiber 0g);
Protein 24g.

1/4 cup (1/2 stick) margarine or butter

  6 skinless boneless chicken breast halves (about
     1 1/2 pounds)

1/2 cup dry white wine or chicken broth

  1 tablespoon chopped fresh or 1/2 teaspoon dried dill
     weed

  1 tablespoon lemon juice

1/4 teaspoon salt

  1 medium green onion, sliced (2 tablespoons)

1. Melt margarine in 10-inch skillet over medium-high heat. Cook chicken in margarine about 6 minutes, turning once, until light brown.

2. Mix wine, dill weed, lemon juice and salt; pour over chicken. Heat to boiling; reduce heat to low. Cover and simmer 10 to 15 minutes or until juice of chicken is no longer pink when centers of thickest pieces are cut. Remove chicken from skillet; keep warm.

3. Meanwhile, heat wine mixture to boiling. Boil about 3 minutes or until reduced to about half; pour over chicken. Sprinkle with onion.

Lemon-Dill Chicken ▶

Parmesan-Dijon Chicken

▼ 6 servings

Prep: 10 min

Bake: 30 min

1 Serving: Calories 300
(Calories from Fat 135);
Fat 15g (Saturated 5g);
Cholesterol 85mg;
Sodium 350mg;
Carbohydrate 11g
(Dietary Fiber 0g);
Protein 30g.

3/4 cup dry bread crumbs

1/4 cup grated Parmesan cheese

1/4 cup (1/2 stick) margarine, butter or spread, melted

2 tablespoons Dijon mustard

6 skinless boneless chicken breast halves (about
1 1/2 pounds)

1. Heat oven to 375°.

2. Mix bread crumbs and cheese in large plastic bag. Combine margarine and mustard. Dip chicken in margarine mixture. Shake chicken in bag to coat with crumb mixture.

3. Bake uncovered 20 to 30 minutes, turning once, until juice of chicken is no longer pink when centers of thickest pieces are cut.

Quick Coatings for Chicken and Fish

Try these quick coatings for chicken or fish. Dip chicken or fish in melted margarine, salad dressing, mayonnaise or mustard; then coat with desired crumbs and bake or cook in skillet.

- Bread crumbs mixed with dry salad dressing mix
- Bread crumbs mixed with Parmesan cheese
- Bread crumbs mixed with dry seasoning mixes
- Cornmeal mixed with chili powder, Cajun or Creole seasoning
- Crushed cereal
- Crushed corn chips
- Crushed crackers
- Crushed potato chips
- Crushed tortilla chips
- Seasoned bread crumbs

Chicken Breasts in Mustard Sauce

▼ 4 servings

2 tablespoons margarine or butter

4 skinless boneless chicken breast halves (about 1 pound)

1 small onion, finely chopped (1/4 cup)

2 tablespoons apple juice

1 cup whipping (heavy) cream

2 tablespoons chopped fresh parsley

2 tablespoons Dijon mustard

Prep: 5 min

Cook: 20 to 25 min

1 Serving: Calories 415 (Calories from Fat 290); Fat 32g (Saturated 14g); Cholesterol 130mg; Sodium 240mg; Carbohydrate 6g (Dietary Fiber 1g); Protein 27g.

1. Melt margarine in 10-inch skillet over medium heat. Cook chicken in margarine 15 to 20 minutes, turning once, until juice of chicken is no longer pink when centers of thickest pieces are cut. Remove chicken from skillet; keep warm.

2. Add onion and apple juice to skillet. Heat to boiling; reduce heat to low.

3. Stir in whipping cream, parsley and mustard. Cook over medium heat 5 minutes, stirring frequently. Add chicken; heat until hot.

Thai Chicken with Basil

▼ 4 servings

Serve this Thai-inspired dish over rice and offer chopped peanuts and shredded coconut to sprinkle on top.

Prep: 10 min

Cook: 8 to 10 min

1 Serving: Calories 210 (Calories from Fat 90); Fat 10g (Saturated 2g); Cholesterol 60mg; Sodium 230mg; Carbohydrate 5g (Dietary Fiber 0g); Protein 25g.

4   skinless boneless chicken breast halves (about 1 pound)

2   tablespoons vegetable oil

3   cloves garlic, finely chopped

2   red or green jalapeño chilies, seeded and finely chopped

1   tablespoon fish sauce

1   teaspoon sugar

1/4   cup chopped fresh basil leaves

1   tablespoon chopped fresh mint leaves

1. Cut each chicken breast half into 4 pieces.

2. Heat oil in wok or 12-inch skillet over medium-high heat. Cook garlic and chilies in oil, stirring constantly, until garlic is golden brown.

3. Add chicken; stir-fry 8 to 10 minutes or until chicken is no longer pink in center. Stir in fish sauce and sugar. Sprinkle with basil and mint.

Thai Chicken with Basil ▶

Betty Crocker's Top 10

Recipe Shortcuts for Easy Chicken, Beef and Pork

1. Fried, roasted or broasted chicken pieces from a grocery store or restaurant

2. Pre-cooked ribs from a grocery store or restaurant

3. Seasoned or marinated chicken or turkey pieces from the meat counter or deli case, such as fajita mixtures and kabobs

4. Minute steaks and pre-formed hamburger patties from the meat or freezer case

5. Skinless, boneless chicken breasts

6. Thinly cut pieces of beef or pork

7. Pre-cooked shrimp

8. Canned tuna, clams and shrimp

9. Thickly sliced deli meats

10. Ham slices from the meat case

Oriental Barbecued Chicken

▼ 4 servings

  4 skinless boneless chicken breast halves (about
    1 pound)
1/2 cup hoisin sauce
  1 tablespoon sesame oil
  1 tablespoon tomato paste
1/2 teaspoon ground ginger
  2 cloves garlic, finely chopped

Prep: 5 min

Broil: 11 to 14 min

1 Serving: Calories 230
(Calories from Fat 70);
Fat 8g (Saturated 2g);
Cholesterol 60mg;
Sodium 90mg;
Carbohydrate 12g
(Dietary Fiber 1g);
Protein 28g.

1. Set oven control to broil.

2. Place chicken on rack in broiler pan. Mix remaining ingredients; brush some of sauce over chicken. Broil with tops
   about 4 to 6 inches from heat 7 to 8 minutes or until
   brown; turn. Brush with sauce. Broil 4 to 5 minutes longer
   or until juice of chicken is no longer pink when centers of
   thickest pieces are cut.

3. Meanwhile, heat remaining sauce to boiling; boil 1 minute.
   Serve with chicken.

Turkey Patty Melts

▼ 4 open-face sandwiches

You'll like this updated version of the patty melt, made with ground turkey flavored with chili sauce. Instead of ketchup, serve with extra chili sauce.

Prep: 10 min

Cook: 20 min

1 Open-face Sandwich:
Calories 380 (Calories from Fat 190); Fat 21g (Saturated 8g); Cholesterol 95mg; Sodium 510mg; Carbohydrate 21g (Dietary Fiber 3g); Protein 30g.

1	medium onion, thinly sliced
1	medium bell pepper, thinly sliced
1	pound lean ground turkey
1/4	cup chili sauce
1/2	teaspoon garlic powder
1/2	cup shredded Cheddar cheese (2 ounces)
4	teaspoons mayonnaise or salad dressing
4	slices whole-grain bread, toasted

1. Spray 12-inch nonstick skillet with nonstick cooking spray; heat over medium heat. Cook onion and bell pepper in skillet 6 to 8 minutes, stirring frequently, until tender. Remove from skillet; keep warm.

2. Mix turkey, chili sauce and garlic powder. Shape mixture into 4 patties, each 5 inches in diameter. Cook patties in skillet over medium heat 4 to 5 minutes on each side or until turkey is no longer pink in center.

3. Top each patty with about ¼ cup onion mixture; sprinkle with 2 tablespoons cheese. Cover and cook 1 to 2 minutes or until cheese is melted.

4. Spread 1 teaspoon mayonnaise on each slice toast. Top each with patty.

Maple-Glazed Turkey

▼ 4 servings

        1   package (6 ounces) long grain and wild rice mix
 1 1/2   cups water
        1   pound turkey breast tenderloins
        3   tablespoons maple-flavored syrup
     1/2   cup chopped walnuts
     1/2   teaspoon ground cinnamon

1. Heat oven to 350°.

2. Mix rice mix with seasoning packet and water in ungreased square baking dish, 8 x 8 x 2 inches. Place turkey on rice mixture. Drizzle with maple syrup. Sprinkle with walnuts and cinnamon.

3. Cover and bake about 45 minutes or until turkey is no longer pink in center and rice is tender.

Prep: 8 min

Bake: 45 min

1 Serving: Calories 305 (Calories from Fat 110); Fat 12g (Saturated 2g); Cholesterol 55mg; Sodium 350mg; Carbohydrate 25g (Dietary Fiber 1g); Protein 25g.

▼ ▼

Southwestern Turkey Tenderloins

▼ 6 servings

        1   tablespoon olive or vegetable oil
 1 1/4   pounds turkey breast tenderloins
        1   can (14 1/2 ounces) salsa-style chunky tomatoes, undrained
     1/2   medium green bell pepper, thinly sliced
        1   teaspoon chili powder
        1   teaspoon sugar
        2   tablespoons lime juice
        2   tablespoons chopped fresh cilantro

1. Heat oil in 12-inch nonstick skillet over medium-high heat. Cook turkey in oil 4 to 6 minutes, turning once, until brown.

2. Stir in tomatoes, bell pepper, chili powder, sugar and lime juice; reduce heat to medium-low. Cover and simmer 25 to 30 minutes or until juice of turkey is no longer pink when centers of the thickest pieces are cut.

3. Slice turkey. Serve with sauce. Sprinkle with cilantro.

Prep: 5 min

Cook: 30 min

1 Serving: Calories 155 (Calories from Fat 45); Fat 5g (Saturated 2g); Cholesterol 55mg; Sodium 170mg; Carbohydrate 5g (Dietary Fiber 1g); Protein 23g.

Mustard Marinated Steak

▼ 4 servings

Prep: 5 min

Marinate: 4 hr

Broil: 12 min

Cook: 2 min

1 Serving: Calories 145
(Calories from Fat 65);
Fat 7g (Saturated 2g);
Cholesterol 55mg;
Sodium 85mg;
Carbohydrate 1g
(Dietary Fiber 0g);
Protein 20g.

1 tablespoon lemon juice
1 tablespoon olive or vegetable oil
1 tablespoon coarse brown or Dijon mustard
1/8 teaspoon pepper
1 pound beef sirloin steak, about 3/4-inch thick
1 tablespoon water

1. Mix lemon juice, oil, mustard and pepper in shallow glass or plastic dish. Add beef; turn to coat with marinade. Cover and refrigerate at least 4 hours but no longer than 24 hours, turning occasionally.

2. Set oven control to broil. Remove beef from marinade; reserve marinade. Place beef on rack in broiler pan. Broil with top 4 to 6 inches from heat about 12 minutes for medium doneness, turning once.

3. Meanwhile, heat marinade and water to boiling in 1-quart saucepan; boil 1 minute. Serve with beef.

No-Mess Marinating

Ditch the dishes! Marinate meats, poultry, fish and vegetables in a resealable plastic bag instead of a dish. It's quick to use and convenient for turning the food while marinating. Best of all, there's no clean-up—just throw away the bag!

Saucy Italian Steak

2 tablespoons all-purpose flour

1/4 teaspoon pepper

1 1/2 pound beef round steak, 3/4- to 1-inch thick

1 tablespoon olive or vegetable oil

1 jar (14 ounces) spaghetti sauce (any variety)

1 package (9 ounces) frozen Italian or regular cut green beans

1/4 cup sliced ripe olives

Prep: 8 min

Bake: 1 1/2 hr

1 Serving: Calories 205 (Calories from Fat 80); Fat 9g (Saturated 2g); Cholesterol 55mg; Sodium 540mg; Carbohydrate 11g (Dietary Fiber 2g); Protein 22g.

1. Heat oven to 375°.

2. Mix flour and pepper; rub over beef, shaking off excess. Cut beef into 6 serving pieces.

3. Heat oil in 12-inch skillet over medium heat. Cook beef in oil 5 minutes, turning once, until brown.

4. Place beef in ungreased rectangular baking dish, 11½ x 7½ x 1½ inches. Pour spaghetti sauce over beef. Cover and bake 45 minutes.

5. Place frozen green beans in sauce around beef. Cover and bake about 45 minutes or until beef is tender. Sprinkle with olives.

Mexican Flank Steak

▼ 6 servings

Prep: 8 min

Marinate: 8 hr

Broil: 14 min

Cook: 2 min

1 Serving: Calories 125 (Calories from Fat 55); Fat 6g (Saturated 2g); Cholesterol 40mg; Sodium 410mg; Carbohydrate 3g (Dietary Fiber 0g); Protein 15g.

1 pound beef flank steak, 1/2-inch thick
1/3 cup lime juice
1 teaspoon vegetable oil
1/2 teaspoon salt
1 small onion, chopped (1/4 cup)
2 cloves garlic, finely chopped
1 can (4 ounces) chopped green chilies, undrained

1. Place beef in shallow glass or plastic dish.

2. Mix remaining ingredients; pour over beef. Turn beef to coat both sides. Cover and refrigerate at least 8 hours but no longer than 24 hours, turning beef occasionally.

3. Set oven control to broil. Remove beef from marinade; reserve marinade. Place beef on rack in broiler pan. Broil with top 4 to 6 inches from heat about 14 minutes for medium doneness, turning once. Meanwhile, heat marinade to boiling in 1-quart saucepan; boil 1 minute.

4. Cut beef across grain at slanted angle into thin slices. Serve with marinade.

Lemon Steak Diane

▼ 4 servings

Steak Diane typically consists of individual steaks served with a sauce of pan drippings, lemon juice, chives and Worcestershire sauce. You'll like this tasty version. (Photograph on page 73.)

1	pound beef top sirloin steak, about 3/4-inch thick
1/4	teaspoon coarsely ground pepper
1	cup beef broth
1	tablespoon all-purpose flour
2	teaspoons Dijon mustard
2	teaspoons Worcestershire sauce
1/2	teaspoon grated lemon peel
2	tablespoons chopped fresh chives

Prep: 5 min

Cook: 13 min

1 Serving: Calories 125 (Calories from Fat 25); Fat 3g (Saturated 1g); Cholesterol 55mg; Sodium 250mg; Carbohydrate 3g (Dietary Fiber 0g); Protein 22g.

1. Cut steak into 4 pieces.

2. Spray 12-inch skillet with nonstick cooking spray; heat over medium heat. Sprinkle both sides of beef with pepper. Cook beef in skillet 9 to 11 minutes for medium doneness, turning once. Remove beef from skillet; keep warm.

3. Mix remaining ingredients except chives until smooth; add to skillet. Heat to boiling. Boil 1 minute, stirring constantly. Stir in chives. Serve over beef.

Broiled Santa Fe Steaks

▼ 4 servings

If you are a cilantro lover, increase the amount of cilantro in the salsa until you have just the amount you like.

Prep: 10 min

Cook: 11 min

1 Serving: Calories 330 (Calories from Fat 125); Fat 14g (Saturated 6g); Cholesterol 110mg; Sodium 250mg; Carbohydrate 9g (Dietary Fiber 2g); Protein 44g.

1/2 cup thick-and-chunky salsa

1/2 cup canned black beans, rinsed and drained

2 tablespoons finely chopped red onion

2 tablespoons chopped fresh cilantro

1 tablespoon lime juice

1 1/2 teaspoons chili powder

4 beef boneless New York strip steaks (about 1 1/2 pounds)

2 teaspoons chopped fresh or 1/2 teaspoon dried oregano leaves

1. Mix salsa, beans, onion, cilantro, lime juice and 1/2 teaspoon of the chili powder. Cover and refrigerate while preparing beef steaks.

2. Set oven control to broil. Sprinkle both sides of beef with remaining 1 teaspoon chili powder and the oregano; gently press into beef. Place beef on rack in broiler pan. Broil with tops 4 to 6 inches from heat 6 minutes; turn. Broil 2 to 5 minutes longer for medium doneness. Serve with salsa.

Broiled Santa Fe Steaks ▶

Broiling or Grilling Beef

Broiling and direct-heat grilling are quick, low-fat methods for cooking tender cuts, such as steaks, or ground beef patties. For less-tender cuts, marinate beef before cooking. The directions below are for broiling or for grilling over direct heat. Other beef cuts can be cooked over indirect heat. Refer to the instructions that came with your grill for more information.

1. Select beef cut from those listed in Timetable for Broiling or Grilling Beef.

2. Marinate beef, if desired.

3. **To Broil:** Set oven to broil.

   To Grill: Start outdoor grill. If using charcoal grill, wait until coals are covered with ash (medium heat).

4. Slash outer edge of fat on beef diagonally at 1-inch intervals to prevent curling (do not cut into meat).

5. **To Broil:** Place beef on rack in broiler pan. (For easy clean-up, line the broiler pan with aluminum foil before placing beef on rack.) Place in oven with top of beef the inches from heat listed in chart for beef cut chosen.

   To Grill: Place beef on grill the inches from heat listed in chart for beef cut chosen.

6. Broil or grill about half the time shown in chart for beef cut or until beef is brown on one side.

7. Turn beef and continue cooking until desired doneness. (To check doneness, cut a small slit in the center of boneless cuts or in the center near the bone of bone-in cuts. Medium-rare is very pink in center and slightly brown toward exterior. Medium is light pink in center and brown toward exterior.) Season each side after cooking, if desired.

Timetable for Broiling or Grilling Beef

Beef Cut	Approximate Thickness or Weight	Inches from Heat	Approximate Total Broiling Time (minutes)		Approximate Total Grilling Time (minutes)	
			145° (medium-rare)	160° (medium)	145° (medium-rare)	160° (medium)
Rib and Rib Eye Steaks	3/4 to 1 inch	2 to 4	8	15	7	12
Top Loin Steak (boneless)	3/4 to 1 inch	2 to 4	8	17	7	12
Porterhouse and T-Bone Steaks	1 inch	3 to 4	10	15	10	14
Sirloin Steak (boneless)	3/4 to 1 inch	2 to 4	10	21	12	16
Sirloin Cubes (kabobs)	1 to 1 1/4 inches	3 to 4	9	12	8	11
Tenderloin Steak	1 inch	2 to 3	10	15	11	13
Tri-Tip Roast* (bottom sirloin)	1 1/2 to 2 pounds	4 to 5	25	30	30	35
Chuck Shoulder Steak** (boneless)	1 inch	3 to 4	14	18	14	20
Eye Round Steak	1 inch	2 to 3	9	11	9	12
Top Round Steak**	1 inch	3 to 4	15	18	12	14
Flank Steak**	1 to 1 1/2 pounds	2 to 3	12	14	12	15
Ground Beef Patties	1/2 inch	3/4 inch	3 to 4	‡	10	13

*For food safety reasons, cook patties until beef is no longer pink in center and juice is clear.

**Cover roast with tent of aluminum foil and let stand 15 to 20 minutes before carving. Temperature will continue to rise about 5°, and roast will be easier to carve as juices set up.

†Marinate beef 6 to 8 hours to tenderize.

‡USDA recommends cooking ground beef to 160°.

Hungarian Swiss Steak

▼ 4 servings

Prep: 5 min

Cook: 28 min

1 Serving: Calories 195 (Calories from Fat 80); Fat 9g (Saturated 5g); Cholesterol 70mg; Sodium 390mg; Carbohydrate 8g (Dietary Fiber 1g); Protein 22g.

1 **pound beef boneless sirloin steak, about 3/4-inch thick**
1/4 **teaspoon peppered seasoned salt**
1 **can (14 1/2 ounces) stewed tomatoes, undrained**
1 **tablespoon paprika**
2 **tablespoons ketchup**
1/4 **teaspoon caraway seeds**
1/2 **cup sour cream**
   Chopped fresh chives, if desired

1. Cut beef into 4 serving pieces. Sprinkle both sides of beef with seasoned salt.

2. Spray 12-inch nonstick skillet with nonstick cooking spray; heat over medium-high heat. Cook beef in skillet 4 to 8 minutes, turning once, until brown.

3. Stir in tomatoes, paprika, ketchup and caraway seeds; reduce heat to low. Cover and simmer 15 to 20 minutes or until beef is tender. Top each serving with sour cream and chives.

Salsa Salisbury Steak

▼ 4 servings

Prep: 10 min

Cook: 15 min

1 Serving: Calories 255 (Calories from Fat 145); Fat 16g (Saturated 7g); Cholesterol 65mg; Sodium 280mg; Carbohydrate 7g (Dietary Fiber 1g); Protein 22g.

1 **pound lean ground beef**
1 **medium onion, finely chopped (1/2 cup)**
1/2 **teaspoon chili powder**
1/4 **teaspoon garlic salt**
1 **can (14 1/2 ounces) salsa-style chunky tomatoes, undrained**

1. Mix beef, onion, chili powder and garlic salt. Shape mixture into 4 oblong patties.

2. Spray 12-inch nonstick skillet with nonstick cooking spray; heat over medium-high heat. Cook patties in skillet 3 to 5 minutes, turning once, until brown; drain.

3. Stir in tomatoes; reduce heat to low. Cover and simmer about 10 minutes, stirring tomatoes occasionally and turning patties once, until patties are no longer pink in center and juice is clear.

Hungarian Swiss Steak ▶

Italian Burgers

▼ 4 servings

Prep: 15 min

Broil: 13 min

1 Serving: Calories 450 (Calories from Fat 235); Fat 26g (Saturated 12g); Cholesterol 90mg; Sodium 690mg; Carbohydrate 23g (Dietary Fiber 1g); Protein 32g.

1 pound ground beef
1/3 cup spaghetti sauce
3 tablespoons finely chopped onion
4 slices (1 ounce each) provolone cheese
8 slices Italian bread

1. Mix beef, spaghetti sauce and onion. Shape mixture into 4 patties, each about 3/4-inch thick.

2. Set oven control to broil. Place patties on rack in broiler pan. Broil with tops about 3 inches from heat 12 minutes, turning once.

3. Top each patty with cheese slice. Broil about 1 minute longer or until beef is no longer pink in center and juice is clear. Serve between bread slices. Serve with additional spaghetti sauce, if desired.

Easy Stroganoff Meatballs

▼ 4 servings

Prep: 5 min

Cook: 8 min

1 Serving: Calories 400 (Calories from Fat 225); Fat 25g (Saturated 11g); Cholesterol 140mg; Sodium 990mg; Carbohydrate 19g (Dietary Fiber 1g); Protein 26g.

1 1/4 cups beef broth
2 tablespoons flour
2 teaspoons Worcestershire sauce
16 frozen cooked meatballs (about 1 1/2 inches in diameter)
1 jar (4 1/2 ounces) sliced mushrooms, drained
1/2 cup sour cream
1 tablespoon chopped fresh parsley

1. Beat broth, flour and Worcestershire sauce in small bowl with wire whisk.

2. Place frozen meatballs, mushrooms and broth mixture in 10-inch skillet. Heat to boiling; reduce heat to low. Cover and simmer 4 to 6 minutes or until meatballs are hot.

3. Remove meatballs from heat. Stir in sour cream and parsley.

Italian Burgers ▶

Sauerbraten Burgers

▼ 4 servings

Sauerbraten is a traditional German specialty that takes two to three days to make. Our super-quick version uses ground beef and purchased gravy and keeps all the great taste. This was a taste panel favorite!

Prep: 10 min

Cook: 15 min

1 Serving: Calories 385 (Calories from Fat 170); Fat 19g (Saturated 8g); Cholesterol 65mg; Sodium 590mg; Carbohydrate 29g (Dietary Fiber 1g); Protein 25g.

1	pound ground beef
6	gingersnap cookies, finely crushed
1	small onion, finely chopped (1/4 cup)
1/4	teaspoon ground ginger
1	jar (12 ounces) brown gravy
1/4	cup red wine vinegar
2	tablespoons packed brown sugar
1/4	cup raisins

1. Mix beef, 2 tablespoons of the cookie crumbs, the onion and ginger. Shape mixture into 4 patties, each about ¹/₂-inch thick.

2. Spray 12-inch nonstick skillet with nonstick cooking spray; heat over medium-high heat. Cook patties in skillet 5 minutes, turning once, until brown; drain.

3. Meanwhile, mix gravy, vinegar and brown sugar in small bowl. Stir in remaining cookie crumbs and the raisins. Pour over patties in skillet; reduce heat to medium-low. Cook uncovered about 10 minutes, stirring occasionally, until gravy is desired consistency, beef is no longer pink in center and juice is clear.

Southwestern Cheeseburgers

▼ 4 servings

1 1/2   **pounds ground beef**

   2   **tablespoons finely chopped onion**

   2   **tablespoons canned chopped green chilies, drained**

   1   **can (4 ounces) mushroom stems and pieces, well drained and finely chopped**

   8   **slices Monterey Jack cheese with jalapeño peppers, 2 x 1 x 1/4 inch (4 ounces)**

   4   **kaiser rolls or hamburger buns, split**

1/4   **cup taco sauce or salsa**

     Sliced onions, if desired

Prep: 12 min

Broil: 16 min

1 Serving: Calories 610 (Calories from Fat 315); Fat 35g (Saturated 16g); Cholesterol 125mg; Sodium 830mg; Carbohydrate 33g (Dietary Fiber 2g); Protein 43g.

1. Mix beef, chopped onion and chilies. Shape mixture into 8 thin patties.

2. Top centers of 4 patties with mushrooms. Top each with 2 slices cheese. Place remaining patties on top; pinch edges to seal securely. Place patties on rack in broiler pan.

3. Set oven control to broil. Broil patties with tops 4 to 6 inches from heat 14 to 16 minutes, turning once, until beef is no longer pink in center and juice is clear. Serve on rolls with taco sauce and sliced onions.

Mexican Pork Chops

▼ 4 servings

Prep: 10 min

Cook: 1 hr

1 Serving: Calories 230 (Calories from Fat 70); Fat 8g (Saturated 3g); Cholesterol 65mg; Sodium 210mg; Carbohydrate 15g (Dietary Fiber 1g); Protein 25g.

4 pork loin or rib chops, 1-inch thick (about 1 1/2 pounds)

1 medium green bell pepper, cut into 4 rings

1/4 cup uncooked instant rice

1 can (14 1/2 ounces) Mexican-style stewed or regular stewed tomatoes, undrained

1. Spray 10-inch skillet with nonstick cooking spray; heat over medium heat. Cook pork in skillet 5 minutes, turning once, until brown. Top each pork chop with bell pepper ring; fill each ring with 1 tablespoon uncooked rice.

2. Carefully pour 1/4 cup of the tomatoes over rice in each pepper ring. Pour remaining tomatoes into skillet. Cover tightly and simmer over low heat about 1 hour, spooning sauce over pork occasionally, until pork is slightly pink in center. (Add a small amount of water during simmer time if necessary.)

▼ ▼ ▼ ▼ ▼ ▼ ▼ ▼ ▼ ▼ ▼ ▼ ▼ ▼ ▼ ▼ ▼ ▼ ▼

Yummy Pork Chops

▼ 4 servings

Prep: 5 min

Bake: 50 min

1 Serving: Calories 190 (Calories from Fat 70); Fat 8g (Saturated 3g); Cholesterol 65mg; Sodium 940mg; Carbohydrate 7g (Dietary Fiber 0g); Protein 23g.

4 pork loin chops, 1/2-inch thick (about 1 1/4 pounds)

3 tablespoons soy sauce

3 tablespoons ketchup

2 teaspoons honey

1. Heat oven to 350°.

2. Place pork in ungreased square baking dish, 8 x 8 x 2 inches.

3. Mix remaining ingredients; pour over pork.

4. Cover and bake about 45 minutes or until pork is slightly pink in center. Uncover and bake 5 minutes longer.

Pork Chop Dinner

▼ 4 servings

4 pork loin or rib chops, 1-inch thick (about
1 1/2 pounds)

1/4 cup water, beef broth or chicken broth

4 medium potatoes, peeled and cut into fourths

4 small carrots, cut into 1-inch pieces

4 medium onions, cut into fourths

3/4 teaspoon salt

1/4 teaspoon pepper

Prep: 8 min

Cook: 35 min

1 Serving: Calories 310
(Calories from Fat 70);
Fat 8g (Saturated 3g);
Cholesterol 65mg;
Sodium 600mg;
Carbohydrate 39g
(Dietary Fiber 6g);
Protein 27g.

1. Spray 12-inch skillet with nonstick cooking spray; heat over medium heat. Cook pork about 5 minutes, turning once, until brown.

2. Add water, potatoes, carrots and onions to skillet. Sprinkle with salt and pepper. Heat to boiling; reduce heat to low. Cover and simmer about 30 minutes or until pork is slightly pink in center and vegetables are tender.

Pork Chops and Apples

▼ 6 servings

Prep: 10 min

Cook: 5 min

Bake: 1 hr

1 Serving: Calories 295 (Calories from Fat 125); Fat 12g (Saturated 4g); Cholesterol 65mg; Sodium 90mg; Carbohydrate 20g (Dietary Fiber 1g); Protein 23g.

6 pork rib chops, 1/2-inch thick (about 1 1/2 pounds)
3 or 4 unpeeled apples, sliced
1/4 cup firmly packed brown sugar
1/2 teaspoon ground cinnamon
2 tablespoons margarine or butter

1. Heat oven to 350°. Grease rectangular baking dish, 13 x 9 x 2 inches.

2. Spray 10-inch skillet with nonstick cooking spray; heat over medium heat. Cook pork in skillet about 5 minutes, turning once, until brown.

3. Place apple slices in baking dish. Sprinkle with brown sugar and cinnamon; dot with margarine. Top with pork. Cover and bake about 1 hour or until pork is slightly pink in center and apples are tender.

Stuffing-Topped Pork Chops

▼ 6 servings

Prep: 12 min

Bake: 1 1/4 hr

1 Serving: Calories 275 (Calories from Fat 115); Fat 13g (Saturated 4g); Cholesterol 65mg; Sodium 290mg; Carbohydrate 16g (Dietary Fiber 1g); Protein 25g.

6 pork loin or rib chops, 1-inch thick (about 1 1/2 pounds)
1/2 cup water
1/4 cup finely chopped celery
2 tablespoons finely chopped onion
2 cups herb-seasoned stuffing crumbs
1 can (8 1/2 ounces) cream-style corn

1. Heat oven to 350°.

2. Place pork in ungreased rectangular baking dish, 13 x 9 x 2 inches. Add water to baking dish. Bake uncovered 45 minutes.

3. Meanwhile, mix celery, onion, stuffing and corn; set aside.

4. Spoon 1/3 cup stuffing mixture onto each pork chop. Bake uncovered 30 minutes longer or until pork is slightly pink in center.

Skillet Barbecue Pork Chops

▼ 4 servings

This simple sauce turns pork chops into something special!

4   pork loin or rib chops, 1/2-inch thick (about
    1 1/4 pounds)

1/4 teaspoon salt

1/8 teaspoon pepper

1   can (15 ounces) chunky tomato sauce with onions,
    celery and green bell peppers

2   tablespoons packed brown sugar

2   tablespoons vinegar

2   tablespoons Worcestershire sauce

1   teaspoon ground mustard (dry)

Prep: 5 min

Cook: 20 min

1 Serving: Calories 230
(Calories from Fat 70);
Fat 8g (Saturated 3g);
Cholesterol 65mg;
Sodium 900mg;
Carbohydrate 16g
(Dietary Fiber 1g);
Protein 24g.

1. Spray 12-inch nonstick skillet with nonstick cooking spray; heat over medium heat. Sprinkle both sides of pork with salt and pepper. Cook pork in skillet about 5 minutes, turning once, until brown.

2. Mix remaining ingredients; add to skillet. Heat to boiling; reduce heat to low. Cover and simmer 10 to 15 minutes, stirring occasionally, until pork is slightly pink in center.

Parmesan Breaded Pork Chops

▼ 4 servings

Parmesan cheese highlights the flavors in these tasty pork chops. Try serving them with pasta, couscous or rice.

Prep: 5 min

Cook: 17 min

1 Serving: Calories 245 (Calories from Fat 90); Fat 10g (Saturated 5g); Cholesterol 110mg; Sodium 680mg; Carbohydrate 16g (Dietary Fiber 2g); Protein 25g.

1/3 cup Italian-style dry bread crumbs

2 tablespoons grated Parmesan cheese

4 pork boneless butterfly loin chops, 1/2-inch thick (about 1 1/4 pounds)

1 egg, beaten

1 can (14 1/2 ounces) chunky tomatoes with olive oil, garlic and spices, undrained

1 can (8 ounces) tomato sauce

1 small green bell pepper, chopped (1/2 cup)

1. Mix bread crumbs and cheese. Dip pork in egg, then coat with crumb mixture.

2. Spray 12-inch nonstick skillet with nonstick cooking spray; heat over medium heat. Cook pork in skillet about 5 minutes, turning once, until brown.

3. Stir in remaining ingredients. Heat to boiling; reduce heat to low. Cover and simmer 10 to 12 minutes, stirring occasionally, until pork is slightly pink in center.

Parmesan Breaded Pork Chops ▶

Pork with Sweet Mustard Gravy

▼ 4 servings

Serve this 15-minute meal with rice and fresh broccoli spears.

Prep: 5 min

Cook: 10 min

1 Serving: Calories 205 (Calories from Fat 55); Fat 6g (Saturated 3g); Cholesterol 70mg; Sodium 610mg; Carbohydrate 11g (Dietary Fiber 0g); Protein 27g.

1	pound pork tenderloin, cut into 1/4-inch slices
1/4	teaspoon peppered seasoned salt
1	jar (12 ounces) pork gravy
2	tablespoons red currant jelly
1	teaspoon ground mustard (dry)
1	medium green onion, sliced (2 tablespoons)

1. Spray 12-inch nonstick skillet with nonstick cooking spray; heat over medium heat. Sprinkle both sides of pork with seasoned salt. Cook pork in skillet about 5 minutes, turning once, until brown.

2. Stir in gravy, jelly, mustard and onion. Heat to boiling; reduce heat to medium. Cook 3 to 4 minutes, stirring occasionally, until sauce is desired consistency and pork is slightly pink in center.

Zesty Pork Tenderloin

▼ 6 servings

Prep: 5 min

Marinate: 1 hr

Roast: 29 min

1 Serving: Calories 155 (Calories from Fat 35); Fat 4g (Saturated 2g); Cholesterol 65mg; Sodium 170mg; Carbohydrate 6g (Dietary Fiber 0g); Protein 24g.

1/4	cup ketchup
1	tablespoon sugar
1	tablespoon dry white wine or water
1	tablespoon hoisin sauce
1	clove garlic, finely chopped
2	pork tenderloins (about 3/4 pound each)

1. Mix all ingredients except pork in shallow glass or plastic dish. Add pork; turn to coat with marinade. Cover and refrigerate at least 1 hour but no longer than 24 hours, turning pork occasionally.

2. Heat oven to 425°. Place pork on rack in shallow roasting pan. Insert meat thermometer horizontally so tip is in thickest part of pork.

3. Roast uncovered 27 to 29 minutes or until thermometer reads 160° or pork is slightly pink in center.

Spicy Oriental Pork Ribs

▼ 4 to 6 servings

    4 pounds pork loin back ribs
1/4 cup orange marmalade
    2 tablespoons hoisin sauce
    1 tablespoon soy sauce
1/4 teaspoon ground mustard (dry)

1. Heat oven to 350°.

2. Place pork in ungreased rectangular pan, 13 x 9 x 2 inches. Mix remaining ingredients in 1-quart saucepan. Brush pork generously with some of the marmalade mixture.

3. Cover and bake 1 hour. Brush with marmalade mixture. Cover and bake 15 to 30 minutes longer or until pork is tender.

4. Heat remaining marmalade mixture to boiling; boil 1 minute. Serve with pork.

Prep: 5 min

Bake: 1 1/2 hr

Cook: 2 min

1 Serving: Calories 925 (Calories from Fat 605); Fat 67g (Saturated 25g); Cholesterol 260mg; Sodium 470mg; Carbohydrate 16g (Dietary Fiber 0g); Protein 64g.

Easy Mustard Spareribs

▼ 6 servings

    Mustard Sauce (below)
4 1/2 pounds pork spareribs

1. Heat oven to 325°.

2. Cut pork into serving pieces. Place meaty sides up on rack in shallow roasting pan. Roast uncovered 1 hour.

3. Meanwhile, prepare Mustard Sauce; set aside.

4. Brush sauce over pork. Roast about 45 minutes longer, turning and brushing frequently with sauce, until tender. Discard any remaining sauce.

Prep: 10 min

Bake: 1 3/4 hr

1 Serving: Calories 605 (Calories from Fat 370); Fat 41g (Saturated 15g); Cholesterol 160mg; Sodium 300mg; Carbohydrate 20g (Dietary Fiber 0g); Protein 39g.

Mustard Sauce

1/2 cup molasses or maple-flavored syrup
1/3 cup Dijon mustard
1/3 cup cider vinegar

Mix all ingredients.

Sesame Pork with Garlic Cream Sauce

▼ 6 servings

Prep: 5 min

Broil: 11 min

Cook: 4 min

1 Serving: Calories 240 (Calories from Fat 125); Fat 14g (Saturated 6g); Cholesterol 85mg; Sodium 120mg; Carbohydrate 2g (Dietary Fiber 0g); Protein 26g.

1 1/2 pounds pork tenderloin
1 tablespoon vegetable oil
1 tablespoon sesame seeds
1 tablespoon margarine, butter or spread
2 cloves garlic, finely chopped
1 package (3 ounces) cream cheese, cut into cubes
1/3 cup milk
1 tablespoon chopped fresh or 1 teaspoon freeze-dried chives

1. Cut pork into 1/2-inch slices.

2. Set oven control to broil. Brush oil over pork. Place pork on rack in broiler pan. Sprinkle with half of the sesame seeds. Broil pork with tops 4 to 6 inches from heat 6 minutes; turn. Sprinkle with remaining sesame seeds. Broil about 5 minutes longer or until pork is slightly pink in center.

3. Meanwhile, melt margarine in 10-inch skillet over medium heat. Cook garlic in margarine about 2 minutes, stirring occasionally, until softened; reduce heat to low.

4. Stir cream cheese and milk into garlic mixture. Cook about 1 minute, stirring constantly, until smooth and hot. Stir in chives. Serve with pork.

Sesame Pork with Garlic Cream Sauce ▶

Broiling or Grilling Pork

Broiling and direct-heat grilling are quick, low-fat methods for chops and other small pieces. Other pork cuts, such as ribs or roasts, can be grilled over indirect heat. Refer to the instructions that came with your grill for more information.

1. Select pork cut from those listed in Timetable for Broiling or Grilling Pork.

2. Marinate pork if desired.

3. **To Broil:** Set oven to broil.

   To Grill: Start outdoor grill. If using charcoal grill, wait until coals are covered with ash (medium heat).

4. **To Broil:** Place pork on rack in broiler pan. (For easy clean-up, line the broiler pan with aluminum foil before placing pork on rack.) Place in oven with top of pork the inches from heat listed in chart for pork cut chosen.

   To Grill: Place pork on grill at the number of inches from heat listed in chart for pork cut chosen.

5. Broil or grill about half the time shown in chart for pork cut chosen or until pork is brown on one side.

6. Turn pork and continue cooking until doneness shown in chart for pork cut chosen.* (To check doneness, cut a small slit in the center of boneless cuts or in the center near the bone of bone-in cuts. Medium pork is slightly pink in center. Well-done pork is no longer pink in center.) Season each side after cooking, if desired.

*Well-done pork, although a little less juicy, is recommended for some cuts because the pork will be more flavorful.

Timetable for Broiling or Grilling Pork

Pork Cut	Approximate Thickness or Weight	Inches from Heat	Meat Doneness	Approximate Total Broiling Time (minutes)	Approximate Total Grilling Time (minutes)
Loin or Rib Chops (bone-in)	3/4 inch	3 to 4	160° (medium)	8 to 11	6 to 8
	1 1/2 inches	3 to 4	160° (medium)	19 to 22	12 to 16
Loin Chop (boneless)	1 inch	3 to 4	160° (medium)	11 to 13	8 to 10
Blade Chop (bone-in)	3/4 inch	3 to 4	170° (well)	13 to 15	11 to 13
	1 1/2 inches	3 to 4	170° (well)	26 to 29	19 to 22
Arm Chop (bone-in)	3/4 inch	3 to 4	170° (well)	16 to 18	13 to 15
	1 inch	3 to 4	170° (well)	18 to 20	15 to 18
Cubes for Kabobs					
Loin or Leg	1-inch pieces	3 to 4	160° (medium)	9 to 11	10 to 20
Tenderloin	1-inch pieces	3 to 4	160° (medium)	12 to 14	13 to 21
Ground Pork Patties	1/2 inch thick	3 to 4	170° (well)	7 to 9	7 to 9
Country-Style Ribs	1-inch slices	5	160° (medium)	45 to 60	1 1/2 to 2 hours*
Spareribs		5	160° (medium)	45 to 60	1 1/2 to 2 hours*
Backribs		5	160° (medium)	45 to 55	1 1/2 to 2 hours*

*Grill over indirect heat.

Ham with Cabbage and Apples

▼ 4 servings

Prep: 6 min

Cook: 15 min

1 Serving: Calories 195
(Calories from Fat 65);
Fat 7g (Saturated 2g);
Cholesterol 45mg;
Sodium 1100mg;
Carbohydrate 18g
(Dietary Fiber 3g);
Protein 18g.

4 cups shredded cabbage or coleslaw mix
1 tablespoon packed brown sugar
1 tablespoon cider vinegar
1/8 teaspoon pepper
1 large onion, chopped (1 cup)
1 large green cooking apple, sliced
1 pound fully cooked ham slice, about 1/2-inch thick

1. Spray 10-inch nonstick skillet with nonstick cooking spray; heat over medium heat.

2. Cook all ingredients except ham in skillet about 5 minutes, stirring frequently, until apple is crisp-tender.

3. Place ham on cabbage mixture; reduce heat to low. Cover and cook about 10 minutes or until ham is hot.

▼ ▼ ▼ ▼ ▼ ▼ ▼ ▼ ▼ ▼ ▼ ▼ ▼ ▼ ▼ ▼ ▼ ▼

Honey Mustard Ham

▼ 4 servings

Prep: 5 min

Cook: 12 min

1 Serving: Calories 235
(Calories from Fat 115);
Fat 13g (Saturated 6g);
Cholesterol 65mg;
Sodium 1290mg;
Carbohydrate 10g
(Dietary Fiber 0g);
Protein 19g.

1 pound fully cooked ham slice, about 1-inch thick
1/4 cup water
3 tablespoons honey mustard
1/2 cup sour cream
1 medium green onion, sliced (2 tablespoons)

1. Cut ham into 4 serving pieces. Mix water and honey mustard in 10-inch skillet. Add ham.

2. Cover and heat to boiling; reduce heat to low. Simmer about 10 minutes, turning ham once, until ham is hot. Remove ham from skillet; keep warm.

3. Stir sour cream into mixture in skillet; heat 1 minute (do not boil). Pour over ham. Sprinkle with onion.

Honey Mustard Ham ▶

Caramelized Pork Slices

▼ 4 servings

Serve these slightly sweet pork slices over noodles, rice or with baked or mashed sweet potatoes.

Prep: 10 min

Cook: 10 min

1 Serving: Calories 175 (Calories from Fat 35); Fat 4g (Saturated 1g); Cholesterol 65mg; Sodium 320mg; Carbohydrate 11g (Dietary Fiber 0g); Protein 24g.

1 pound pork tenderloin, cut into 1/2-inch slices
2 cloves garlic, finely chopped
2 tablespoons packed brown sugar
1 tablespoon orange juice
1 tablespoon molasses
1/2 teaspoon salt
1/4 teaspoon pepper

1. Spray 10-inch nonstick skillet with nonstick cooking spray; heat over medium-high heat.

2. Cook pork and garlic in skillet 6 to 8 minutes, turning occasionally, until pork is light brown and slightly pink in center. Drain if necessary.

3. Stir in remaining ingredients; cook until mixture thickens and coats pork.

Broiled Ham and Sweet Potatoes

▼ 4 servings

Prep: 5 min

Broil: 10 min

1 Serving: Calories 360 (Calories from Fat 80); Fat 9g (Saturated 3g); Cholesterol 55mg; Sodium 1500mg; Carbohydrate 49g (Dietary Fiber 2g); Protein 23g.

1 pound fully cooked ham slice, about 1/2-inch thick
1 can (18 ounces) sweet potatoes, drained
4 slices canned pineapple, well drained
1/4 cup orange marmalade

1. Set oven control to broil.

2. Cut outer edge of fat on ham slice diagonally at 1-inch intervals to prevent curling (do not cut into ham). Place ham on rack in broiler pan. Broil with top 4 to 6 inches from heat about 5 minutes or until light brown.

3. Turn ham; place potatoes and pineapple on rack. Brush marmalade on potatoes and pineapple. Broil about 5 minutes or until potatoes and pineapple are hot and ham is light brown.

Stir-Fry and
Skillet Suppers

Southwestern Chicken Stir-Fry

▼ 4 servings

Prep: 15 min

Marinate: 1 hr

Cook: 11 min

1 Serving: Calories 205
(Calories from Fat 100);
Fat 11g (Saturated 2g);
Cholesterol 60mg;
Sodium 210mg;
Carbohydrate 4g
(Dietary Fiber 2g);
Protein 25g.

2 tablespoons lime juice

2 teaspoons chili powder

1 pound skinless boneless chicken breast halves, cut into 1/2-inch strips

2 tablespoons vegetable oil

1 small zucchini, thinly sliced

1 small yellow summer squash, thinly sliced

1/3 cup picante sauce or salsa

2 tablespoons chopped fresh cilantro

1. Mix lime juice and chili powder in medium glass or plastic bowl. Stir in chicken until well coated. Cover and refrigerate 1 hour.

2. Heat wok or 12-inch skillet over high heat. Add 1 tablespoon of the oil; rotate wok to coat side.

3. Add chicken and marinade; stir-fry 5 to 6 minutes or until chicken is no longer pink in center. Remove chicken from wok.

4. Add remaining 1 tablespoon oil to wok; rotate wok to coat side. Add zucchini and yellow squash; stir-fry about 4 minutes or until vegetables are crisp-tender. Stir in chicken, picante sauce and cilantro.

Preceding Page
Meatballs with Orzo and Zucchini (page 142)

Southwestern Chicken Stir-Fry ▶

Teriyaki Chicken Stir-Fry

▼ 4 servings

Prep: 5 min

Cook: 11 min

1 Serving: Calories 245
(Calories from Fat 65);
Fat 7g (Saturated 2g);
Cholesterol 60mg;
Sodium 1480mg;
Carbohydrate 21g
(Dietary Fiber 3g);
Protein 28g.

1 tablespoon vegetable oil

1 pound cut-up chicken breast for stir-fry

1/2 cup teriyaki baste and glaze

3 tablespoons lemon juice

1 package (16 ounces) frozen broccoli, carrots, water chestnuts and red peppers

Hot cooked couscous, rice or noodles, if desired

1. Heat wok or 12-inch skillet over high heat. Add oil; rotate wok to coat side. Add chicken; stir-fry 3 to 4 minutes or until chicken is no longer pink in center.

2. Stir in remaining ingredients except couscous. Heat to boiling, stirring constantly; reduce heat to low. Cover and simmer about 6 minutes or until vegetables are crisp-tender. Serve with couscous.

Chicken-Chutney Stir-Fry

▼ 4 servings

Prep: 10 min

Cook: 10 min

1 Serving: Calories 295
(Calories from Fat 100);
Fat 11g (Saturated 2g);
Cholesterol 60mg;
Sodium 360mg;
Carbohydrate 23g
(Dietary Fiber 3g);
Protein 29g.

1 tablespoon cornstarch

1 tablespoon soy sauce

1/2 cup chutney

1 tablespoon vegetable oil

1 pound skinless boneless chicken breast halves, cut into 1-inch pieces

1 package (16 ounces) frozen cauliflower, carrots and snap pea pods, thawed

Hot cooked rice or noodles, if desired

1/4 cup chopped peanuts

1. Mix cornstarch, soy sauce and chutney.

2. Heat oil in 10-inch skillet or wok over medium-high heat. Add chicken and vegetables; stir-fry 5 to 7 minutes or until chicken is no longer pink in center.

3. Stir in chutney mixture. Cook over medium heat, stirring constantly, until slightly thickened. Serve over rice. Sprinkle with peanuts.

Teriyaki Chicken Stir-Fry

Sweet-and-Sour Chicken

▼ 4 servings

Prep: 15 min

Cook: 7 min

1 Serving: Calories 290 (Calories from Fat 65); Fat 7g (Saturated 2g); Cholesterol 60mg; Sodium 200mg; Carbohydrate 36g (Dietary Fiber 6g); Protein 27g.

   1 **tablespoon vegetable oil**

   1 **pound skinless boneless chicken breast halves, cut into 1-inch pieces**

   3 **cups assorted cut-up vegetables (bell peppers, tomatoes, carrots)**

   1 **can (8 ounces) pineapple chunks in juice, drained**

1/2 **cup sweet-and-sour sauce**

     Chow mein noodles, if desired

1. Heat wok or 12-inch skillet over high heat. Add oil; rotate wok to coat side.

2. Add chicken; stir-fry about 3 minutes or until no longer pink in center. Add vegetables; stir-fry about 2 minutes or until crisp-tender. Stir in pineapple and sweet-and-sour sauce; cook and stir 1 minute. Serve with chow mein noodles.

▼ ▼ ▼ ▼ ▼ ▼ ▼ ▼ ▼ ▼ ▼ ▼ ▼ ▼ ▼ ▼ ▼ ▼

Sichuan Cashew Chicken

▼ 4 servings

Prep: 5 min

Cook: 7 min

1 Serving: Calories 260 (Calories from Fat 100); Fat 11g (Saturated 2g); Cholesterol 60mg; Sodium 1050mg; Carbohydrate 13g (Dietary Fiber 2g); Protein 29g.

   1 **tablespoon chili oil or vegetable oil**

   1 **pound skinless boneless chicken breast halves, cut into 1-inch pieces**

   1 **package (16 ounces) frozen cauliflower, carrots and asparagus**

1/3 **cup stir-fry sauce**

     Hot cooked rice or noodles, if desired

1/4 **cup cashew halves**

1. Heat wok or 12-inch skillet over high heat. Add oil; rotate wok to coat side.

2. Add chicken; stir-fry 1 minute. Add cauliflower mixture; stir-fry about 4 minutes or until vegetables are crisp-tender and chicken is no longer pink in center. Stir in stir-fry sauce; cook and stir about 30 seconds or until hot.

3. Serve over rice. Sprinkle with cashews.

Sweet-and-Sour Chicken ▶

Turkey Ratatouille

▼ 4 servings

Prep: 15 min

Cook: 16 min

1 Serving: Calories 190
(Calories from Fat 65);
Fat 7g (Saturated 2g);
Cholesterol 45mg;
Sodium 310mg;
Carbohydrate 16g
(Dietary Fiber 5g);
Protein 21g.

3/4 pound turkey breast tenderloin, cut into 3/4-inch pieces

1/8 teaspoon pepper

1 tablespoon olive or vegetable oil

2 cups frozen stir-fry bell peppers and onions (from 16-ounce package)

1 small eggplant, cubed (2 cups)

1 medium zucchini, cubed (1 cup)

1 can (14 1/2 ounces) Italian-style stewed tomatoes, undrained

1/4 cup shredded Parmesan cheese

1. Sprinkle turkey with pepper.

2. Heat oil in 12-inch nonstick skillet over medium-high heat. Cook turkey in oil 3 to 5 minutes, stirring occasionally, until brown.

3. Stir in stir-fry vegetables. Cook 2 minutes, stirring occasionally. Stir in eggplant and zucchini. Cook 2 to 4 minutes, stirring occasionally, until vegetables are tender.

4. Stir in tomatoes; reduce heat to low. Cover and simmer 3 to 5 minutes, stirring occasionally, until sauce is desired consistency. Sprinkle each serving with cheese.

Turkey Ratatouille ▶

Quick Chicken Risotto

▼ 4 servings

Risotto is a wonderful Italian rice dish made by slowly stirring broth into cooking rice. This supper dish has a similar creamy texture, but we've eliminated the constant stirring.

Prep: 10 min

Cook: 25 min

1 Serving: Calories 335 (Calories from Fat 65); Fat 7g (Saturated 3g); Cholesterol 50mg; Sodium 880mg; Carbohydrate 42g (Dietary Fiber 1g); Protein 27g.

1/2 pound skinless boneless chicken breast halves, cut into 1/2-inch pieces

1 can (14 1/2 ounces) ready-to-serve chicken broth

1 cup uncooked regular medium or long grain rice

1/2 pound asparagus, cut into 1 1/2-inch pieces

1/4 pound fully cooked ham, diced

1 teaspoon chopped fresh or 1/4 teaspoon dried basil leaves

1/4 cup shredded Parmesan cheese

1. Spray 12-inch nonstick skillet with nonstick cooking spray; heat over medium-high heat. Cook chicken in skillet 3 to 5 minutes, stirring frequently, until light brown.

2. Stir in broth; heat to boiling. Stir in rice; reduce heat to low. Cover and simmer 10 minutes without stirring.

3. Stir in asparagus, ham and basil. Cover and simmer without stirring 8 to 10 minutes or until chicken is no longer pink in center and rice is tender; remove from heat. Stir in cheese.

Quick Chicken Risotto ▶

Turkey Creole

▼ 4 servings

Prep: 10 min

Cook: 21 min

1 Serving: Calories 410
(Calories from Fat 100);
Fat 11g (Saturated 3g);
Cholesterol 90mg;
Sodium 440mg;
Carbohydrate 46g
(Dietary Fiber 4g);
Protein 36g.

1 tablespoon olive or vegetable oil
1 medium onion, thinly sliced
1 small green bell pepper, cut into strips
1/4 cup thinly sliced celery
2 cans (15 ounces each) Mexican-style tomatoes, undrained
3 cups cut-up cooked turkey
Hot cooked rice or spaghetti

1. Heat oil in 10-inch skillet over medium-high heat. Cook onion, bell pepper and celery in oil about 5 minutes, stirring frequently, until vegetables are tender.

2. Stir in tomatoes; reduce heat to low. Simmer uncovered 10 minutes. Stir in turkey. Cover and simmer about 5 minutes or until turkey is hot. Serve over rice.

▼▼▼▼▼▼▼▼▼▼▼▼▼▼▼▼▼▼▼▼▼▼▼▼▼

Chicken Curry

▼ 4 servings

Prep: 10 min

Cook: 10 min

1 Serving: Calories 410
(Calories from Fat 135);
Fat 15g (Saturated 4g);
Cholesterol 65mg;
Sodium 720mg;
Carbohydrate 45g
(Dietary Fiber 2g);
Protein 26g.

2 tablespoons margarine, butter or spread
1 teaspoon curry powder
1 small onion, chopped (1/4 cup)
2 cups cut-up cooked chicken or turkey
1 unpeeled small red apple, coarsely chopped
1 can (10 3/4 ounces) condensed cream of chicken soup
1 soup can of milk
Hot cooked rice

1. Melt margarine in 3-quart saucepan over medium heat. Cook curry powder and onion in margarine about 5 minutes, stirring occasionally, until onion is tender.

2. Stir in remaining ingredients except rice. Cook, stirring occasionally, until hot. Serve over rice.

Chicken-Noodle Paprikash

▼ 4 servings

2 slices bacon, cut into 1/2-inch pieces
1 pound skinless boneless chicken breast halves, cut into 3/4-inch pieces
1 jar (12 ounces) chicken gravy
1 can (14 1/2 ounces) ready-to-serve chicken broth
1 tablespoon paprika
1 medium green bell pepper, sliced
2 cups uncooked wide egg noodles
1/2 cup sour cream

Prep: 10 min

Cook: 20 min

1 Serving: Calories 340 (Calories from Fat 125); Fat 14g (Saturated 7g); Cholesterol 105mg; Sodium 930mg; Carbohydrate 21g (Dietary Fiber 1g); Protein 34g.

1. Cook bacon in 12-inch nonstick skillet over medium heat, stirring occasionally, until crisp; remove all but 1 tablespoon drippings from skillet.

2. Add chicken to bacon and drippings. Cook 3 to 5 minutes, stirring occasionally, until chicken is brown.

3. Stir in gravy, broth, paprika and bell pepper. Heat to boiling; stir in noodles. Heat to boiling; reduce heat to medium. Cover and cook 8 to 10 minutes, stirring occasionally, until noodles are tender; remove from heat. Stir in sour cream.

Italian White Beans with Chicken

▼ 4 servings

1 tablespoon olive or vegetable oil
1 tablespoon chopped fresh or 1 teaspoon dried basil leaves
1 clove garlic, finely chopped
2 cups cut-up cooked chicken or turkey
1/2 cup chopped, drained, oil-packed sun-dried tomatoes
1/4 cup sliced ripe olives
2 cans (15 to 16 ounces each) great northern beans, rinsed and drained

Prep: 10 min

Cook: 5 min

1 Serving: Calories 425 (Calories from Fat 100); Fat 11g (Saturated 2g); Cholesterol 60mg; Sodium 630mg; Carbohydrate 52g (Dietary Fiber 11g); Protein 40g.

1. Heat oil in 10-inch skillet over medium heat. Cook basil and garlic in oil 3 minutes, stirring frequently.

2. Stir in remaining ingredients. Cook, stirring frequently, until hot.

Tortellini with Fresh Vegetables

▼ 4 servings

We used chicken- and prosciutto-filled tortellini, but feel free to use any flavor—it's just as tasty.

Prep: 10 min

Cook: 15 min

1 Serving: Calories 270 (Calories from Fat 90); Fat 10g (Saturated 4g); Cholesterol 25mg; Sodium 400mg; Carbohydrate 35g (Dietary Fiber 2g); Protein 12g.

1 package (9 ounces) refrigerated chicken- and prosciutto-filled tortellini

1 tablespoon olive or vegetable oil

1 medium bell pepper, cut into 1-inch pieces (1 cup)

6 to 8 medium roma (plum) tomatoes, chopped (2 cups)

1 medium yellow summer squash, cut lengthwise in half and sliced (1 1/2 cups)

1/2 teaspoon Italian seasoning

1/2 teaspoon garlic salt

1/4 cup shredded Parmesan cheese

1. Cook and drain tortellini as directed on package in 3-quart saucepan. Wipe out saucepan with paper towel; wipe dry with paper towel.

2. Heat oil in same saucepan over medium-high heat. Cook bell pepper in oil 2 to 3 minutes, stirring occasionally, until crisp-tender.

3. Stir in tomatoes, squash, Italian seasoning and garlic salt. Cover and cook 3 to 5 minutes, stirring occasionally, until squash is tender.

4. Stir in tortellini. Cook 2 to 3 minutes, stirring occasionally, until hot. Sprinkle each serving with cheese.

Cassoulet Supper

▼ 4 servings

A cassoulet traditionally simmers many hours, but this version can be on your table in just 30 minutes!

1/2 pound skinless boneless chicken breast halves, cut into 1/2-inch pieces

1/2 pound fully cooked Polish sausage, cut into 1/2-inch slices

1 can (15 to 16 ounces) great northern beans, rinsed and drained

1 can (15 to 16 ounces) dark red kidney beans, rinsed and drained

1 can (14 1/2 ounces) chunky tomatoes with olive oil, garlic and spices, undrained

1 tablespoon packed brown sugar

4 medium green onions, sliced (1/2 cup)

Prep: 10 min

Cook: 20 min

1 Serving: Calories 485 (Calories from Fat 170); Fat 19g (Saturated 7g); Cholesterol 70mg; Sodium 1370mg; Carbohydrate 54g (Dietary Fiber 12g); Protein 37g.

1. Spray 12-inch nonstick skillet with nonstick cooking spray; heat over medium-high heat. Cook chicken 3 to 5 minutes, stirring occasionally, until brown.

2. Stir in remaining ingredients except onions. Cook uncovered over medium-low heat 8 to 10 minutes, stirring occasionally, until chicken is no longer pink in center.

3. Stir in onions. Cook 3 to 5 minutes, stirring occasionally, until onions are crisp-tender.

Spicy Pepper Steak

▼ 4 servings

Prep: 10 min

Cook: 5 min

1 Serving: Calories 185
(Calories from Fat 65);
Fat 7g (Saturated 2g);
Cholesterol 55mg;
Sodium 40mg;
Carbohydrate 9g
(Dietary Fiber 1g);
Protein 23g.

1 tablespoon chili oil or vegetable oil
1 pound cut-up beef for stir-fry
1 medium bell pepper, cut into 3/4-inch squares
1 medium onion, sliced
1/4 cup hoisin sauce
   Hot cooked noodles or rice, if desired

1. Heat wok or 12-inch skillet over high heat. Add oil; rotate wok to coat side.

2. Add beef; stir-fry about 2 minutes or until brown. Add bell pepper and onion; stir-fry about 1 minute or until vegetables are crisp-tender. Stir in hoisin sauce; cook and stir about 30 seconds or until hot. Serve with noodles.

▼▼▼▼▼▼▼▼▼▼▼▼▼▼▼▼▼▼▼

Beef and Leeks in Spicy Chili Sauce

▼ 4 servings

Prep: 15 min

Cook: 8 min

1 Serving: Calories 185
(Calories from Fat 65);
Fat 7g (Saturated 2g);
Cholesterol 55mg;
Sodium 125mg;
Carbohydrate 11g
(Dietary Fiber 4g);
Protein 23g.

1 tablespoon chili oil or vegetable oil
1 pound beef boneless sirloin steak, cut into 1/4-inch strips
2 leeks, thinly sliced (2 cups)
1 package (16 ounces) frozen broccoli, carrots, water chestnuts and red peppers
1 tablespoon chili purée with garlic
   Hot cooked rice or noodles, if desired

1. Heat wok or 12-inch skillet over high heat. Add oil; rotate wok to coat side.

2. Add beef and leeks; stir-fry 2 minutes. Add broccoli mixture; stir-fry about 4 minutes or until beef is brown and vegetables are crisp-tender. Stir in chili purée; cook and stir about 30 seconds or until hot. Serve with rice.

Spicy Pepper Steak ▶

Sesame Beef

▼ 4 servings

Prep: 10 min

Marinate: 30 min

Cook: 5 min

1 Serving: Calories 385 (Calories from Fat 70); Fat 8g (Saturated 2g); Cholesterol 55mg; Sodium 1420mg; Carbohydrate 52g (Dietary Fiber 1g); Protein 27g.

1	pound beef boneless sirloin steak
1/2	cup teriyaki marinade or sauce
3	medium green onions, finely chopped (3 tablespoons)
2	cloves garlic, finely chopped
1	tablespoon vegetable oil
4	cups hot cooked rice
1	tablespoon sesame seeds, toasted if desired

1. Cut beef diagonally across grain into $1/8$-inch slices. (Beef is easier to cut if partially frozen, about $1^1/2$ hours.)

2. Mix teriyaki marinade, onions and garlic in medium glass or plastic bowl. Stir in beef until well coated. Cover and refrigerate 30 minutes.

3. Remove beef mixture from marinade; reserve marinade. Heat oil in 10-inch skillet over medium-high heat. Cook beef mixture in oil, stirring occasionally, until beef is brown. Stir in marinade. Heat to boiling; boil and stir 1 minute.

4. Serve beef mixture over rice. Sprinkle with sesame seeds.

Sweet-and-Sour Beef with Cabbage

▼ 4 servings

2 tablespoons vegetable oil
1 pound cut-up beef for stir-fry
3 cups cut-up cabbage or coleslaw mix
1/2 cup sweet-and-sour sauce
Hot cooked couscous, rice or noodles, if desired

1. Heat wok or 12-inch skillet over high heat. Add 1 tablespoon of the oil; rotate wok to coat side.

2. Add beef; stir-fry 2 minutes or until brown. Remove beef from wok.

3. Add remaining 1 tablespoon oil to wok; rotate wok to coat side. Add cabbage; stir-fry about 3 minutes or until crisptender. Add beef and sweet-and-sour sauce; cook and stir about 2 minutes or until hot. Serve with couscous.

Prep: 10 min

Cook: 9 min

1 Serving: Calories 225 (Calories from Fat 90); Fat 10g (Saturated 2g); Cholesterol 55mg; Sodium 150mg; Carbohydrate 13g (Dietary Fiber 1g); Protein 22g.

Skillet Goulash

▼ 4 servings

1 pound ground beef
1 1/2 cups uncooked fine egg noodles (3 ounces)
1/2 cup water
1 medium onion, chopped (1/2 cup)
1 medium stalk celery, chopped (1/2 cup)
1 can (15 ounces) Italian-style tomato sauce

1. Cook beef in 10-inch skillet over medium heat 8 to 10 minutes, stirring occasionally, until brown; drain.

2. Stir in remaining ingredients. Heat to boiling; reduce heat to low. Cover and simmer 15 to 20 minutes, stirring occasionally, until noodles are tender. (Add a small amount of water if necessary.)

Prep: 5 min

Cook: 30 min

1 Serving: Calories 375 (Calories from Fat 190); Fat 21g (Saturated 8g); Cholesterol 85mg; Sodium 440mg; Carbohydrate 24g (Dietary Fiber 3g); Protein 25g.

Chunky Hash with Eggs

▼ 4 servings

To keep the eggs in a nice round shape, break each egg into a custard cup, then slide it into the pan.

Prep: 10 min

Cook: 21 min

1 Serving: Calories 430 (Calories from Fat 235); Fat 26g (Saturated 9g); Cholesterol 280mg; Sodium 1350mg; Carbohydrate 29g (Dietary Fiber 3g); Protein 23g.

    2 tablespoons vegetable oil
    1 package (1 pound 4 ounces) refrigerated diced
      potatoes with onions
  1/2 pound cooked corned beef, diced
    1 small green bell pepper, chopped (1/2 cup)
    4 eggs
  1/2 teaspoon peppered seasoned salt
  1/2 cup shredded Swiss cheese (2 ounces)

1. Heat oil in 12-inch nonstick skillet over medium-high heat. Cover and cook potatoes in oil 5 to 7 minutes, stirring occasionally, until light brown; reduce heat to medium-low.

2. Stir in corned beef and bell pepper. Cover and cook 5 to 6 minutes, stirring occasionally, until vegetables are crisp-tender.

3. Make 4 wells in potato mixture with back of spoon. Break 1 egg into each well; sprinkle with seasoned salt. Cover and cook 3 to 5 minutes or until eggs are firm.

4. Sprinkle with cheese. Cover and cook 2 to 3 minutes or until melted.

Mexican Beef and Black Beans

▼ 4 servings

1   pound ground beef
1   tablespoon chopped fresh parsley or 1 teaspoon dried parsley flakes
1   tablespoon white wine vinegar
1   teaspoon grated lime or lemon peel
1/4 teaspoon red pepper sauce
1   medium red or green bell pepper, chopped (1 cup)
2   medium green onions, thinly sliced (1/4 cup)
2   cans (15 ounces each) black beans, rinsed and drained

Prep: 10 min

Cook: 15 min

1 Serving: Calories 465 (Calories from Fat 155); Fat 17g (Saturated 7g); Cholesterol 65mg; Sodium 530mg; Carbohydrate 54g (Dietary Fiber 14g); Protein 38g.

1. Cook beef in 10-inch skillet over medium heat 8 to 10 minutes, stirring occasionally, until brown; drain.

2. Stir in remaining ingredients. Cook about 5 minutes, stirring frequently, until hot.

▼▼▼▼▼▼▼▼▼▼▼▼▼▼▼▼▼▼▼▼▼▼▼▼▼▼▼▼

Sloppy Joes with Potatoes and Onion

▼ 4 servings

1   pound extra-lean ground beef
1   medium onion, sliced
2   medium potatoes, thinly sliced
1   can (15 1/2 ounces) sloppy joe sauce

Prep: 10 min

Cook: 30 min

1 Serving: Calories 340 (Calories from Fat 155); Fat 17g (Saturated 6g); Cholesterol 70mg; Sodium 800mg; Carbohydrate 25g (Dietary Fiber 3g); Protein 25g.

1. Crumble beef into 10-inch skillet. Layer onion and potatoes on beef; pour sloppy joe sauce over top.

2. Cover and cook over low heat about 30 minutes or until beef is brown and potatoes are tender.

Korean Barbecued Beef

▼ 4 servings

Prep: 10 min

Marinate: 30 min

Cook: 4 min

1 Serving: Calories 260 (Calories from Fat 125); Fat 14g (Saturated 4g); Cholesterol 55mg; Sodium 1080mg; Carbohydrate 12g (Dietary Fiber 0g); Protein 22g.

   1 pound beef boneless top loin or sirloin steak
1/4 cup soy sauce
   3 tablespoons sugar
   2 tablespoons sesame or vegetable oil
1/4 teaspoon pepper
   3 medium green onions, finely chopped (3 tablespoons)
   2 cloves garlic, chopped
      Hot cooked rice, if desired

1. Cut beef diagonally across grain into 1/8-inch slices. (Beef is easier to cut if partially frozen, about 1 1/2 hours.)

2. Mix remaining ingredients except rice in medium glass or plastic bowl. Stir in beef until well coated. Cover and refrigerate 30 minutes.

3. Drain beef; discard marinade. Heat 10-inch skillet over medium heat. Cook beef in skillet 2 to 3 minutes, stirring frequently, until brown. Serve beef with rice.

Meatballs with Orzo and Zucchini

▼ 4 servings

(Photograph on page 121)

Prep: 10 min

Cook: 20 min

1 Serving: Calories 475 (Calories from Fat 180); Fat 20g (Saturated 8g); Cholesterol 125mg; Sodium 1150mg; Carbohydrate 47g (Dietary Fiber 3g); Protein 30g.

16 frozen cooked meatballs (about 1 1/2 inches in diameter)
 1 can (14 1/2 ounces) ready-to-serve beef broth
 1 cup uncooked rosamarina (orzo) pasta (6 ounces)
 1 can (14 1/2 ounces) chunky tomatoes with olive oil, garlic and spices, undrained
 1 medium zucchini, cut into julienne strips

1. Place frozen meatballs and broth in 10-inch skillet; heat to boiling. Stir in pasta; reduce heat to low. Cover and simmer about 12 minutes or until pasta is tender.

2. Stir in tomatoes and zucchini. Cook about 5 minutes, stirring occasionally, until zucchini is tender.

Sichuan Pork Fried Rice

▼ 4 servings

1 tablespoon vegetable oil
1 pound pork boneless loin, cut into thin strips
2 medium carrots, chopped (1 cup)
1 medium onion, chopped (1/2 cup)
1 small green or red bell pepper, chopped (1/2 cup)
3 cups cold cooked rice
1/4 cup Sichuan spicy or regular stir-fry sauce
1 cup bean sprouts

Prep: 15 min

Cook: 18 min

1 Serving: Calories 350 (Calories from Fat 100); Fat 11g (Saturated 3g); Cholesterol 50mg; Sodium 360mg; Carbohydrate 44g (Dietary Fiber 2g); Protein 21g.

1. Heat oil in 10-inch skillet over medium-high heat. Cook pork in oil 3 to 5 minutes, stirring occasionally, until brown.

2. Stir in carrots, onion and bell pepper. Cook about 5 minutes, stirring occasionally, until vegetables are crisp-tender.

3. Stir in rice and stir-fry sauce until well mixed. Stir in bean sprouts. Cook 5 to 7 minutes, stirring occasionally, until hot.

Honeyed Pork and Chinese Cabbage

▼ 4 servings

1 tablespoon chili oil or vegetable oil
1 pound pork tenderloin, cut into 1/2-inch slices
1 cup fresh pineapple chunks or 1 can (8 ounces) pineapple chunks in juice, drained
3 tablespoons honey
4 cups shredded napa (Chinese) cabbage (1 pound)
Hot cooked rice, if desired

Prep: 12 min

Cook: 7 min

1 Serving: Calories 245 (Calories from Fat 70); Fat 8g (Saturated 2g); Cholesterol 65mg; Sodium 95mg; Carbohydrate 19g (Dietary Fiber 1g); Protein 25g.

1. Heat wok or 12-inch skillet over high heat. Add oil; rotate wok to coat side.

2. Add pork; stir-fry 4 to 5 minutes or until no longer pink. Add pineapple and honey; cook and stir 1 minute. Add cabbage; stir-fry about 30 seconds or until hot. Serve with rice.

Curried Pork and Sweet Potatoes

▼ 4 servings

Prep: 20 min

Cook: 20 min

1 Serving: Calories 240
(Calories from Fat 55);
Fat 6g (Saturated 2g);
Cholesterol 50mg;
Sodium 190mg;
Carbohydrate 29g
(Dietary Fiber 2g);
Protein 19g.

1	tablespoon all-purpose flour
1	tablespoon curry powder
1/4	teaspoon salt
1	pound pork boneless loin, cut into thin strips
2	medium sweet potatoes, cut into thin strips (2 cups)
3/4	cup apple juice
1	medium green bell pepper, cut into thin strips (1 cup)
2	tablespoons apple jelly

1. Mix flour, curry powder and salt in medium bowl. Add pork; toss to coat.

2. Spray 12-inch nonstick skillet with nonstick cooking spray; heat over medium-high heat. Cook pork in skillet 3 to 5 minutes, stirring occasionally, until brown.

3. Stir in sweet potatoes and apple juice; reduce heat to low. Cover and simmer 5 minutes. Stir in bell pepper. Cover and simmer 3 to 5 minutes or until bell pepper is crisp-tender. Stir in jelly until melted.

If You Don't Have It, Try This!

The recipes in this book call for many different types of frozen vegetable combinations such as broccoli, carrots and cauliflower or newer blends like bell pepper strips and onions. The vegetable combinations in the recipes were selected to complement the other ingredients and to offer variety. In some cases, we just called for frozen mixed vegetables—you can pick your favorite. If you are not able to find the particular vegetable combination we have specified in a recipe, go ahead and use your favorite vegetables instead.

Curried Pork and Sweet Potatoes ▶

Apricot-Glazed Pork

▼ 4 servings

Prep: 8 min

Cook: 9 min

1 Serving: Calories 235 (Calories from Fat 70); Fat 8g (Saturated 2g); Cholesterol 65mg; Sodium 270mg; Carbohydrate 18g (Dietary Fiber 3g); Protein 26g.

1 tablespoon chili oil or vegetable oil

1 pound pork tenderloin, cut into 1/2-inch slices

1 package (16 ounces) frozen broccoli, cauliflower and carrots

3 tablespoons apricot preserves

1 tablespoon oyster sauce or hoisin sauce

Hot cooked rice or noodles, if desired

1. Heat wok or 12-inch skillet over high heat. Add oil; rotate wok to coat side.

2. Add pork; stir-fry 4 to 5 minutes or until no longer pink. Add broccoli mixture; stir-fry 2 minutes. Stir in preserves and oyster sauce; cook and stir about 30 seconds or until hot. Serve with rice.

▼▼▼▼▼▼▼▼▼▼▼▼▼▼▼▼▼▼

Sausage Skillet Supper

▼ 6 servings

Prep: 10 min

Cook: 26 min

1 Serving: Calories 500 (Calories from Fat 270); Fat 30g (Saturated 11g); Cholesterol 45mg; Sodium 1750mg; Carbohydrate 47g (Dietary Fiber 4g); Protein 15g.

3 tablespoons vegetable oil

1 package (24 ounces) frozen diced potatoes with onions and peppers

1/2 teaspoon dried oregano or basil leaves

1/2 teaspoon pepper

2 cups broccoli flowerets

1 ring (about 3/4 pound) bologna or smoked sausage

3 slices processed American cheese, cut diagonally in half

1. Heat oil in 10-inch skillet over medium-high heat.

2. Add potatoes, oregano and pepper. Cover and cook 8 to 10 minutes, stirring occasionally, until potatoes are light brown.

3. Stir in broccoli; add bologna. Cover and cook about 15 minutes or until bologna is hot. Top with cheese. Cover and heat until cheese is melted.

Apricot-Glazed Pork ▶

Ham, Vegetables and Bows

▼ 4 servings

For speedier preparation, the pasta can be cooking in one pot while the ham and vegetables are cooking in another.

Prep: 5 min

Cook: 25 min

1 Serving: Calories 315 (Calories from Fat 125); Fat 14g (Saturated 3g); Cholesterol 40mg; Sodium 1040mg; Carbohydrate 30g (Dietary Fiber 4g); Protein 21g.

2 cups uncooked farfalle (bow-tie) pasta (4 ounces)

2 tablespoons olive or vegetable oil

1 medium red onion, cut into thin wedges

1 package (16 ounces) frozen cauliflower, carrots and asparagus

2 cups julienne strips fully cooked ham

1/2 teaspoon fennel seed, crushed

1/4 teaspoon coarsely ground pepper

1. Cook and drain pasta as directed on package in 3-quart saucepan; set aside. Wipe saucepan dry with paper towel.

2. Heat oil in same saucepan over medium-high heat. Cook onion in oil 3 to 5 minutes, stirring occasionally, until crisp-tender; reduce heat to medium. Stir in cauliflower mixture. Cover and cook 3 to 5 minutes, stirring occasionally, until cauliflower mixture is crisp-tender.

3. Stir in ham, fennel seed, pepper and pasta. Cook 5 to 8 minutes, stirring occasionally, until hot.

Ham, Vegetables and Bows ▶

Kielbasa-Vegetable Stew

▼ 4 servings

Fresh can be fast! Leaving the peel on potatoes and cutting vegetables into large pieces speeds the preparation time.

Prep: 12 min

Cook: 23 min

1 Serving: Calories 375 (Calories from Fat 155); Fat 17g (Saturated 6g); Cholesterol 40mg; Sodium 700mg; Carbohydrate 49g (Dietary Fiber 7g); Protein 13g.

1	medium red onion, cut into thin wedges
1	can (14 1/2 ounces) stewed tomatoes, undrained
6	small red potatoes, cut into fourths (2 cups)
2	medium carrots, cut into 2 1/4-inch strips (1 cup)
1/2	pound fully cooked Polish sausage or kielbasa, cut into 1/2- to 3/4-inch slices
1	teaspoon chopped fresh or 1/4 teaspoon dried marjoram leaves
1/8	teaspoon pepper
2	cups coarsely chopped cabbage or coleslaw mix (8 ounces)

1. Spray 12-inch nonstick skillet with nonstick cooking spray; heat over medium heat. Cook onion in skillet 2 to 3 minutes, stirring occasionally, until crisp-tender.

2. Stir in tomatoes, potatoes, carrots, sausage, marjoram and pepper. Heat to boiling; reduce heat to medium-low. Cover and cook 10 minutes.

3. Stir in cabbage. Cover and cook 5 to 10 minutes, stirring occasionally, until vegetables are tender.

Kielbasa-Vegetable Stew ▶

Betty Crocker's Top 10

Recipe Shortcuts for Stir-fry and Skillet Suppers

1. Pre-cut stir-fry meat, poultry and seafood from the meat case

2. Fresh stir-fry vegetable mixtures from the produce case or pick and choose vegetables from a grocery salad bar—try pea pods, Chinese cabbage, bok choy, bean sprouts, baby carrots, celery and miniature corn cobs

3. Frozen vegetable combinations

4. Dry stir-fry sauce and seasoning mixes

5. Bottled stir-fry and sweet-and-sour sauces

6. Take-out food from a restaurant or deli

7. Couscous (plain and flavored)—it's ready in 5 minutes

8. Instant white or brown rice

9. Canned tomato products; plain, chunky and seasoned

10. Jarred minced garlic

Sweet and Spicy Spanish Rice

▼ 4 servings

Serve this southwestern-inspired main dish with rolled-up tortillas and pass with extra salsa, lime wedges and avocado.

3/4	pound pork boneless loin, cut into 1/2-inch pieces
1/2	cup coarsely chopped red onion
2	cups water
1	cup uncooked regular long grain rice
3/4	cup thick-and-chunky salsa
1/4	cup peach or apricot preserves
1	to 2 tablespoons lime juice
	Chopped avocado, if desired

Prep: 10 min

Cook: 30 min

1 Serving: Calories 335 (Calories from Fat 45); Fat 5g (Saturated 2g); Cholesterol 35mg; Sodium 160mg; Carbohydrate 57g (Dietary Fiber 2g); Protein 18g.

1. Spray 12-inch nonstick skillet with nonstick cooking spray; heat over medium-high heat. Cook pork and onion in skillet 3 to 5 minutes, stirring occasionally, until pork is brown.

2. Stir in water; heat to boiling. Stir in rice; reduce heat to low. Cover and simmer 15 to 20 minutes, stirring occasionally, until liquid is absorbed.

3. Stir in salsa, preserves and lime juice; heat until hot. Serve topped with avocado.

Quick Tip: For step 2, substitute 2 cups instant rice for the regular rice. Stir instant rice into boiling water. Cover and remove from heat, let stand 5 minutes. Continue with step 3.

Shrimp Florentine Stir-Fry

▼ 4 servings

Prep: 10 min

Cook time: 8 min

1 Serving: Calories 165
(Calories from Fat 45);
Fat 5g (Saturated 1g);
Cholesterol 160mg;
Sodium 510mg;
Carbohydrate 12g
(Dietary Fiber 2g);
Protein 20g.

1	tablespoon olive or vegetable oil
1	pound uncooked peeled and deveined medium shrimp, thawed if frozen
4	cups lightly packed spinach leaves
1	can (14 ounces) baby corn nuggets, drained
1/4	cup coarsely chopped roasted red bell peppers (from 7-ounce jar)
1 1/2	teaspoons chopped fresh or 1/2 teaspoon dried tarragon leaves
1/2	teaspoon garlic salt
	Lemon wedges

1. Heat oil in 12-inch nonstick skillet over medium-high heat. Add shrimp; stir-fry 2 to 3 minutes or until shrimp are pink and firm.

2. Add spinach, corn, bell peppers, tarragon and garlic salt; stir-fry 2 to 4 minutes or until spinach is wilted. Serve with lemon wedges.

Garlic Shrimp

▼ 4 servings

Prep: 15 min

Cook: 6 min

1 Serving: Calories 120
(Calories from Fat 35);
Fat 4g (Saturated 1g);
Cholesterol 160mg;
Sodium 200mg;
Carbohydrate 4g
(Dietary Fiber 1g);
Protein 18g.

1	tablespoon vegetable oil
3	large cloves garlic, finely chopped
1	pound uncooked medium shrimp, peeled and deveined
1	large carrot, cut into julienne strips (1 cup)
2	tablespoons chopped fresh cilantro
	Hot cooked noodles or rice, if desired

1. Heat wok or 12-inch skillet over medium-high heat. Add oil; rotate wok to coat side.

2. Add garlic; stir-fry 1 minute. Add shrimp; stir-fry 1 minute. Add carrot; stir-fry about 3 minutes or until shrimp are pink and firm and carrot is crisp-tender. Stir in cilantro. Serve over noodles.

Shrimp Florentine Stir-Fry ▶

Scallops in Cream Sauce

▼ 6 servings

Prep: 5 min

Cook: 10 min

1 Serving: Calories 385 (Calories from Fat 170); Fat 19g (Saturated 8g); Cholesterol 90mg; Sodium 420mg; Carbohydrate 31g (Dietary Fiber 2g); Protein 25g.

1	pound scallops
1/4	cup (1/2 stick) margarine, butter or spread
1	medium green onion, thinly sliced (2 tablespoons)
1/4	teaspoon salt
1/4	cup dry white wine or chicken broth
2	teaspoons cornstarch
1/2	cup whipping (heavy) cream
1/2	cup finely shredded Swiss cheese (2 ounces)

1. If scallops are large, cut in half.

2. Melt margarine in 10-inch skillet over medium-high heat. Cook onion in margarine, stirring occasionally, until tender. Stir in scallops and salt. Cook 3 to 4 minutes, stirring frequently, until scallops are white.

3. Mix wine and cornstarch; stir into scallop mixture. Heat to boiling, stirring constantly. Boil and stir 1 minute; reduce heat to medium. Stir in whipping cream. Heat 1 to 2 minutes or until hot; remove from heat. Stir in cheese until melted.

4. Spoon scallop mixture over hot cooked noodles or rice if desired. Serve with regular or freshly ground pepper if desired.

Lemon-Dill Salmon and Potatoes

▼ 4 servings

Sweet, flavorful salmon is enhanced with butter, lemon and dill in this quick supper.

- 1 pound salmon fillets, cut into 3/4-inch pieces
- 1/2 teaspoon lemon pepper
- 1 tablespoon margarine, butter or spread
- 6 to 8 small red potatoes, cut into fourths (2 cups)
- 1/4 cup water
- 1/2 cup frozen green peas
- 2 tablespoons lemon juice
- 1 tablespoon chopped fresh or 1 teaspoon dried dill weed

1. Sprinkle salmon pieces with 1/4 teaspoon of the lemon pepper.

2. Melt margarine in 12-inch nonstick skillet over medium-high heat. Cook salmon in margarine 3 to 5 minutes, stirring occasionally, until salmon flakes easily with fork. Remove salmon from skillet.

3. Heat potatoes and water to boiling in same skillet; reduce heat to medium-low. Cover and cook 5 to 8 minutes or until potatoes are tender. Stir in peas. Cook 3 minutes.

4. Stir in lemon juice, dill weed, remaining 1/4 teaspoon lemon pepper and the salmon. Cook 3 to 5 minutes, stirring occasionally, until hot.

Prep: 10 min

Cook: 24 min

1 Serving: Calories 315 (Calories from Fat 80); Fat 9g (Saturated 2g); Cholesterol 65mg; Sodium 160mg; Carbohydrate 38g (Dietary Fiber 4g); Protein 24g.

Red Snapper Teriyaki

▼ 4 servings

Prep: 10 min

Cook: 7 min

1 Serving: Calories 185 (Calories from Fat 45); Fat 5g (Saturated 1g); Cholesterol 60mg; Sodium 1480mg; Carbohydrate 11g (Dietary Fiber 2g); Protein 26g.

    1 tablespoon vegetable oil
    1 pound red snapper or other lean fish fillets, cut into 1-inch pieces
    3 cups 1-inch pieces asparagus
    1 medium red bell pepper, cut into strips
 1/2 cup teriyaki baste and glaze
       Hot cooked noodles or rice, if desired

1. Heat wok or 12-inch skillet over medium-high heat. Add oil; rotate wok to coat side.

2. Add fish; stir-fry 2 minutes. Add asparagus and bell pepper; stir-fry 2 to 3 minutes or until vegetables are crisp-tender. Stir in teriyaki baste and glaze; cook 30 seconds or until hot. Serve with noodles.

Halibut and Vegetable Lo Mein

▼ 4 servings

Prep: 5 min

Cook: 15 min

1 Serving: Calories 310 (Calories from Fat 80); Fat 9g (Saturated 2g); Cholesterol 80mg; Sodium 1270mg; Carbohydrate 32g (Dietary Fiber 4g); Protein 29g.

       1 tablespoon vegetable oil
       1 pound halibut, snapper or salmon fillets, cut into 3/4-inch pieces
       1 medium onion, cut into thin wedges
       1 can (14 1/2 ounces) ready-to-serve chicken broth
   1 1/2 cups uncooked fine egg noodles (3 ounces)
       1 package (16 ounces) refrigerated chopped vegetables for stir-fry
     1/3 cup stir-fry sauce
       1 tablespoon packed brown sugar

1. Heat oil in 12-inch nonstick skillet over medium-high heat. Add fish; stir-fry 3 to 5 minutes or until fish flakes with fork. Remove fish from skillet.

2. Add onion to skillet; stir-fry 2 minutes. Add broth; heat to boiling. Stir in noodles and vegetables; heat to boiling. Cover and boil about 10 minutes or until noodles and vegetables are tender.

3. Stir in fish, stir-fry sauce and brown sugar. Cook 2 to 4 minutes, stirring occasionally.

Do Ahead

Super-Easy Chicken Manicotti

▼ 7 servings

Just say "no" to the time-consuming task of cooking and stuffing mani-cotti shells and use our clever new technique: simply insert chicken breast tenders into uncooked manicotti shells! Smother with sauce, olives and cheese; cover and refrigerate 24 hours to help "soften" the pasta.

Prep: 12 min

Chill: 24 hr, freeze up to 1 month

Bake: 1 hr from refrigerator, 1 1/2 hrs from freezer

1 Serving: Calories 405 (Calories from Fat 145); Fat 16g (Saturated 7g); Cholesterol 30mg; Sodium 1430mg; Carbohydrate 43g (Dietary Fiber 4g); Protein 26g.

1	jar (30 ounces) spaghetti sauce
1	teaspoon garlic salt
1 1/2	pounds chicken breast tenders
14	uncooked manicotti shells (8 ounces)
1	can (2 1/2 ounces) sliced ripe olives, drained
2	cups shredded mozzarella cheese (8 ounces)

1. Spread about one-third of the spaghetti sauce in ungreased rectangular baking dish, 13 x 9 x 2 inches.

2. Sprinkle garlic salt on chicken. Insert chicken into uncooked manicotti shells, stuffing from each end of shell to fill if necessary. Place shells on spaghetti sauce in dish.

3. Pour remaining spaghetti sauce evenly over shells, covering completely. Sprinkle with olives and cheese. STOP HERE—see *To Store* and *To Cook* below.

TO STORE

Refrigerator: Cover unbaked manicotti tightly with aluminum foil and refrigerate no longer than 24 hours.

Freezer: Wrap unbaked manicotti tightly with aluminum foil and label. Freeze no longer than 1 month.

TO COOK FROM REFRIGERATOR

Oven: About 1 hour before serving, heat oven to 350°. Bake in covered baking dish about 1 hour or until shells are tender.

TO COOK FROM FREEZER

Oven: About 1 1/2 hours before serving, heat oven to 350°. Bake in covered baking dish about 1 1/2 hours or until shells are tender.

Preceding Page
Brisket with Cranberry Gravy (page 169)   Super-Easy Chicken Manicotti

Gingered Apricot Chicken Breasts

▼ 4 servings

Prep: 5 min

Chill: 24 hr, freeze up to 2 months

Bake: 20 min from refrigerator and 30 min from freezer

1 Serving: Calories 195 (Calories from Fat 65); Fat 7g (Saturated 2g); Cholesterol 60mg; Sodium 570mg; Carbohydrate 8g (Dietary Fiber 0g); Protein 25g.

1 can (5 1/2 ounces) apricot nectar

2 tablespoons dry white wine or apricot nectar

2 tablespoons soy sauce

1 tablespoon vegetable oil

1 teaspoon grated gingerroot or 1/4 teaspoon ground ginger

4 skinless boneless chicken breast halves (about 1 pound)

TO COMPLETE RECIPE:

2 teaspoons cornstarch

1. Mix all ingredients except chicken and cornstarch in heavy-duty plastic food-storage bag.

2. Add chicken to bag, turning to coat. See *To Store* and *To Cook* below.

TO STORE

Refrigerator: Seal bag tightly and refrigerate at least 1 hour but no longer than 24 hours.

Freezer: Label bag. Freeze no longer than 2 months.

TO COOK FROM REFRIGERATOR

Oven: Heat oven to 375°. Grease square pan, 8 x 8 x 2 inches. Remove chicken from marinade; reserve marinade. Place chicken in pan. Bake uncovered about 20 minutes or until juice is no longer pink when centers of thickest pieces are cut. Mix marinade and cornstarch in 1-quart saucepan. Heat to boiling; boil and stir 1 minute. Serve over chicken.

TO COOK FROM FREEZER

At least 12 hours before serving or overnight, place frozen chicken in refrigerator to thaw. Follow *To Cook from Refrigerator* directions.

Italian Turkey Rolls

▼ 4 servings

2 slices provolone cheese (2 1/2 ounces), cut in half
4 thin slices pastrami
4 uncooked turkey breast slices, about 1/4 inch thick
1/3 cup Italian-style dry bread crumbs
1/4 cup grated Romano or Parmesan cheese
2 tablespoons finely chopped fresh parsley
1/4 cup milk

Prep: 15 min

Chill: 24 hr, freeze up to 2 months

Bake: 45 min from refrigerator, 50 min from freezer

1 Serving: Calories 245 (Calories from Fat 115); Fat 13g (Saturated 6g); Cholesterol 70mg; Sodium 550mg; Carbohydrate 8g (Dietary Fiber 0g); Protein 24g.

1. Grease square pan, 8 x 8 x 2 inches.

2. Place piece of provolone cheese and slice of pastrami on each turkey slice. Fold long sides of each turkey slice over pastrami. Roll up turkey from short side; secure with toothpick.

3. Mix bread crumbs, Romano or Parmesan cheese and parsley. Dip turkey rolls into milk, then coat evenly with bread crumb mixture. Place seam sides down in pan. STOP HERE—see *To Store* and *To Cook* below.

To serve now, heat oven to 425°. Bake uncovered about 30 minutes or until turkey is no longer pink in center.

TO STORE

Refrigerator: Cover tightly and refrigerate at least 8 hours but no longer than 24 hours.

Freezer: Freeze unbaked turkey rolls uncovered about 1 hour or until firm. Wrap tightly and label. Freeze no longer than 2 months.

TO COOK FROM REFRIGERATOR

Oven: About 1 hour before serving, heat oven to 375°. Bake turkey roll uncovered about 45 minutes or until turkey is no longer pink in center.

TO COOK FROM FREEZER

Oven: About 1 1/4 hours before serving, heat oven to 375°. Bake frozen turkey rolls uncovered about 50 minutes or until turkey is no longer pink in center.

Tarragon-Pimiento Turkey Rolls

▼ 4 servings

A great party dish! This recipe is easy to double or triple.

Prep: 12 min

Chill: 8 hr

Bake: 25 min from refrigerator, 50 min from freezer

1 Serving: Calories 255 (Calories from Fat 125); Fat 14g (Saturated 6g); Cholesterol 90mg; Sodium 190mg; Carbohydrate 4g (Dietary Fiber 0g); Protein 28g.

1 pound uncooked turkey breast slices, about 1/4-inch thick

1 package (3 ounces) cream cheese, softened

2 tablespoons chopped fresh or 2 teaspoons dried tarragon leaves

1 jar (2 ounces) diced pimientos, drained

1/2 teaspoon garlic pepper

1 tablespoon margarine, butter or spread, melted

2 tablespoons dry bread crumbs

1. Spread each turkey slice with cream cheese. Sprinkle with tarragon, pimientos and garlic pepper.

2. Roll up each slice from short side; secure with toothpicks. Brush rolls with margarine. Sprinkle with bread crumbs. See *To Store* and *To Cook*.

TO STORE

Refrigerator: Grease square pan, 8 x 8 x 2 inches. Place unbaked rolls, seam sides down, in pan. Cover tightly and refrigerate at least 8 hours but no longer than 24 hours.

Freezer: Wrap unbaked rolls individually in plastic wrap. Place in labeled airtight 1-quart freezer container. Freeze no longer than 1 month.

TO COOK FROM REFRIGERATOR

Oven: About 35 minutes before serving, heat oven to 425°. Bake rolls uncovered about 25 minutes or until turkey is no longer pink in center.

TO COOK FROM FREEZER

Oven: About 1 hour before serving, heat oven to 375°. Grease square pan, 8 x 8 x 2 inches. Remove plastic wrap from turkey rolls. Place rolls, seam sides down, in pan. Bake uncovered about 50 minutes or until turkey is no longer pink in center.

Tarragon-Pimiento Turkey Rolls

Asian Turkey Tenderloins

▼ 6 servings

Fresh gingerroot is a gnarled tan-colored root. Gingerroot adds a distinctive pungency and aroma to foods and is used extensively in dishes of the Far East.

Prep: 12 min

Chill: 24 hr, freeze up to 2 months

Cook: 40 min from refrigerator or freezer

1 Serving: Calories 295 (Calories from Fat 160); Fat 18g (Saturated 8g); Cholesterol 80mg; Sodium 360mg; Carbohydrate 6g (Dietary Fiber 0g); Protein 27g.

1	cup coconut milk
1/2	cup French dressing
2	tablespoons lime juice
1 1/2	teaspoons grated gingerroot or 1/2 teaspoon ground ginger
3/4	teaspoon ground cumin
1/8	teaspoon ground red pepper (cayenne)
4	medium green onions, chopped (1/4 cup)
2	turkey breast tenderloins (about 3/4 pound each)

1. Mix all ingredients except turkey in heavy-duty plastic food-storage bag.

2. Add turkey to bag, turning to coat. See *To Store* and *To Cook* below.

TO STORE

Refrigerator: Seal bag tightly and refrigerate at least 4 hours but no longer than 24 hours.

Freezer: Label bag. Freeze no longer than 2 months.

TO COOK FROM REFRIGERATOR

Stovetop: About 45 minutes before serving, cover and heat turkey and sauce to boiling in 10-inch skillet over medium heat; reduce heat to low. Simmer 30 to 40 minutes, turning turkey occasionally, until juice of turkey is no longer pink when centers of thickest pieces are cut. Slice turkey. Serve with sauce.

TO COOK FROM FREEZER

Stovetop: At least 12 hours before serving or overnight, place frozen turkey in refrigerator to thaw. Follow *To Cook from Refrigerator* directions.

Layered Chicken Salad

1 package (10 ounces) salad mix
1 small zucchini, thinly sliced
1 can (10 ounces) chunk chicken, drained
1/4 cup chopped red onion
1/2 cup pimiento-stuffed salad olives
3/4 cup mayonnaise or salad dressing
1/2 cup shredded Cheddar cheese (2 ounces)
1/2 cup frozen green peas, rinsed and drained

Prep: 10 min

Chill: 24 hr

1 Serving: Calories 470 (Calories from Fat 380); Fat 42g (Saturated 9g); Cholesterol 70mg; Sodium 820mg; Carbohydrate 8g (Dietary Fiber 2g); Protein 17g.

TO COMPLETE RECIPE:

Tomato wedges, if desired
Parsley sprigs, if desired

1. Layer salad mix, zucchini, chicken, onion and olives in large bowl.

2. Spread mayonnaise over olives, sealing to edge of bowl. Sprinkle with cheese and peas. See *To Store* and *To Serve* below.

TO STORE

Refrigerator: Cover tightly and refrigerate no longer than 24 hours.

TO SERVE FROM REFRIGERATOR

Toss just before serving. Garnish with tomato wedges and parsley sprigs.

Robust London Broil

▼ 4 servings

Prep: 10 min

Chill: 24 hr

Broil: 10 min

1 Serving: Calories 190 (Calories from Fat 70); Fat 8g (Saturated 3g); Cholesterol 60mg; Sodium 1090mg; Carbohydrate 6g (Dietary Fiber 0g); Protein 24g.

  1 pound high-quality beef flank steak, 1-inch thick
1/2 cup dry white wine or beef broth
1/4 cup soy sauce
1/4 cup water
  1 tablespoon molasses
  2 cloves garlic, finely chopped

1. Cut both sides of beef in diamond pattern ⅛-inch deep. Place beef in shallow baking dish.

2. Mix remaining ingredients; pour over beef. See *To Store* and *To Cook* below.

TO STORE

Refrigerator: Cover tightly and refrigerate at least 6 hours but no longer than 24 hours, turning beef occasionally.

TO COOK FROM REFRIGERATOR

Broiler: About 15 minutes before serving, set oven control to broil. Remove beef from marinade; discard marinade. Place beef on rack in broiler pan. Broil with top 2 to 3 inches from heat about 5 minutes or until brown; turn. Broil about 5 minutes longer for medium (160°). Cut beef across grain at slanted angle into thin slices.

Brisket with Cranberry Gravy

▼ 6 to 8 servings

Cranberries are a native North American food. Pilgrims noticed that cranes flew to the cranberry bogs in great flocks and feasted on the sour red berries. Thus the berries got the name "craneberries," which later became cranberries.

2-	to 2 1/2-pound fresh beef brisket (not corned beef)
1/2	teaspoon salt
1	can (16 ounces) whole berry cranberry sauce
1	can (15 ounces) tomato sauce
1	medium onion, chopped (1/2 cup)

1. Rub surface of beef with salt. Place beef in 10-inch skillet.

2. Mix cranberry sauce, tomato sauce and onion; pour over beef. Heat to boiling over medium-high heat. Stir; reduce heat to low. Cover and simmer 1½ to 2 hours or until beef is tender. STOP HERE—see *To Store* and *To Reheat* below.

To serve now, cut beef across grain into thin slices. Serve with gravy.

Prep: 5 min

Chill: 48 hr, freeze up to 2 months

Cook: 2 hr

Reheat: 30 min from refrigerator, 50 min from freezer

1 Serving: Calories 310 (Calories from Fat 70); Fat 8g (Saturated 3g); Cholesterol 65mg; Sodium 690mg; Carbohydrate 36g (Dietary Fiber 2g); Protein 26g.

TO STORE

Refrigerator: Cover tightly and refrigerate cooked beef in gravy no longer than 48 hours.

Freezer: Cool beef 30 minutes. Cut beef across grain into thin slices. Place beef and gravy in labeled airtight 1½-quart freezer container. Freeze no longer than 2 months.

TO REHEAT FROM REFRIGERATOR

Stovetop: About 30 minutes before serving, cover and heat beef and gravy in 10-inch skillet over medium-low heat, stirring occasionally, until hot. Cut beef across grain into thin slices. Serve with gravy.

TO REHEAT FROM FREEZER

Stovetop: About 50 minutes before serving, dip container into hot water to loosen; remove container. Cover and heat beef and gravy in 10-inch skillet over medium-low heat, stirring occasionally, until hot.

Applesauce Meat Squares and Spaghetti

▼ 6 servings

Applesauce makes these "meat squares" very tender without imparting a sweet taste. Cutting the meat into squares is much quicker than forming individual meatballs.

Prep: 10 min

Bake: 15 min

Chill: 24 hr, freeze up to 2 months

Reheat: 20 min from refrigerator, 35 min from freezer

1 Serving: Calories 395 (Calories from Fat 155); Fat 17g (Saturated 6g); Cholesterol 45mg; Sodium 1070mg; Carbohydrate 43g (Dietary Fiber 3g); Protein 20g.

1 pound lean ground beef
1/2 cup dry bread crumbs
1/2 cup applesauce
1 tablespoon instant minced onion
3/4 teaspoon garlic salt
1/4 teaspoon pepper

TO COMPLETE RECIPE:

1 jar (26 to 28 ounces) spaghetti sauce
3 cups hot cooked spaghetti

1. Heat oven to 400°.

2. Mix all ingredients except spaghetti sauce and spaghetti. Press mixture evenly in ungreased rectangular pan, 11 x 7 x 1½ inches. Cut into 1¼-inch squares.

3. Bake uncovered about 15 minutes or until no longer pink in center and juice is clear; drain. Separate squares. STOP HERE—see *To Store* and *To Reheat* below.

To complete recipe and serve now, mix meat squares and spaghetti sauce in 3-quart saucepan. Heat to boiling; reduce heat to low. Simmer uncovered about 15 minutes, stirring occasionally, until hot. Serve over spaghetti.

TO STORE

Refrigerator: Cover meat squares tightly and refrigerate no longer than 2 days.

Freezer: Cool meat squares 5 minutes. Place on cookie sheet. Freeze uncovered 15 minutes. Place meat squares in labeled airtight 1½-quart freezer container. Freeze no longer than 2 months.

TO REHEAT FROM REFRIGERATOR

Stovetop: Heat meat squares and spaghetti sauce to boiling in 3-quart saucepan; reduce heat to low. Simmer uncovered about 15 minutes, stirring occasionally, until hot. Serve over spaghetti.

TO REHEAT FROM FREEZER

Stovetop: Heat meat squares and spaghetti sauce to boiling in 3-quart saucepan; reduce heat to low. Simmer uncovered about 25 minutes, stirring occasionally, until hot. Serve over spaghetti.

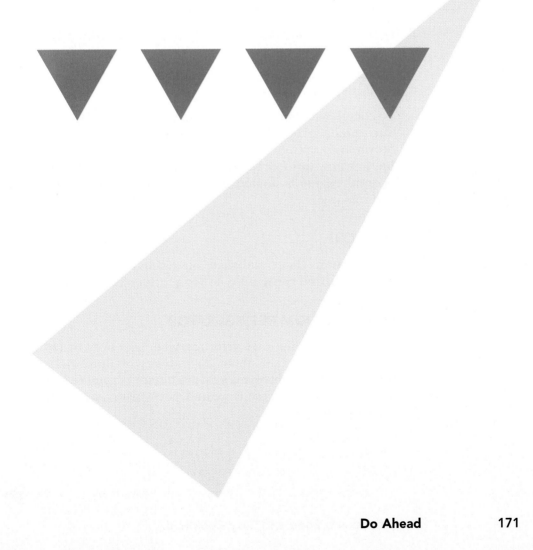

Baked Taco Sandwich

▼ 4 servings

Prep: 8 min

Cook: 10 min

Chill: 24 hr

Bake: 25 min

1 Serving: Calories 485
(Calories from Fat 270);
Fat 30g (Saturated 14g);
Cholesterol 95mg;
Sodium 980mg;
Carbohydrate 26g
(Dietary Fiber 1g);
Protein 29g.

1   pound ground beef
1   envelope (1 1/4 ounces) taco seasoning mix
1   cup Bisquick® Original baking mix
1/3   cup cold water

TO COMPLETE RECIPE:

3/4   cup shredded Cheddar cheese (3 ounces)
     Sour cream, if desired
     Shredded lettuce, if desired
     Chopped tomatoes, if desired

1. Grease square pan, 8 x 8 x 2 inches.

2. Cook beef as directed on envelope of taco seasoning mix.

3. Mix baking mix and cold water until smooth; spread in pan. Spread beef mixture over dough. STOP HERE—see *To Store* and *To Cook* below.

To complete recipe and serve now, heat oven to 450°. Bake uncovered 25 to 30 minutes or until edges are golden brown and toothpick inserted in center comes out clean. Immediately sprinkle with cheese. Let stand 1 to 2 minutes or until cheese is melted. Serve with sour cream, lettuce and tomatoes.

TO STORE

Refrigerator: Cover unbaked sandwich tightly with aluminum foil and refrigerate no longer than 24 hours.

TO COOK FROM REFRIGERATOR

Oven: About 45 minutes before serving, heat oven to 450°. Bake in covered pan about 25 minutes or until golden brown. Immediately sprinkle with cheese. Let stand 1 to 2 minutes or until cheese is melted. Serve with sour cream, lettuce and tomatoes.

Betty Crocker's Top 10

Recipe Shortcuts for Do-Ahead Cooking

1. Plain, chunky, diced and seasoned canned tomatoes
2. Rice and pasta—white, brown and wild rice and pasta shapes such as rigatoni, penne, ziti, rotini and wagon wheels
3. Ground meats—beef, chicken, turkey, lamb
4. Canned soups
5. Heavy-duty aluminum foil
6. Freezer paper
7. Re-sealable plastic freezer bags
8. Disposable aluminum cooking trays and pans
9. Plastic freezer containers with lids
10. Freezer-proof tape or labels on which to write food contents and storage dates

Chili con Queso Casserole

▼ 6 servings

2 cans (4 ounces each) mild chopped green chilies, drained
2 large tomatoes, seeded and chopped (2 cups)
2 cups shredded Cheddar cheese (8 ounces)
1 cup Bisquick® Original baking mix
1/2 cup sour cream
3 eggs

1. Grease square pan, 8 x 8 x 2 inches.

2. Sprinkle chilies and tomato evenly in pan.

3. Beat remaining ingredients with wire whisk or hand beater until smooth; pour over top. STOP HERE—see *To Store* and *To Cook* below.

To serve now, heat oven to 375°. Bake uncovered 35 to 40 minutes or until knife inserted in center comes out clean.

TO STORE

Refrigerator: Cover unbaked casserole tightly and refrigerate no longer than 24 hours.

TO COOK FROM REFRIGERATOR

Oven: About 45 minutes before serving, heat oven to 375°. Bake uncovered 35 to 40 minutes or until knife inserted in center comes out clean.

Prep: 8 min

Chill: 24 hr

Bake: 40 min

1 Serving: Calories 325 (Calories from Fat 200); Fat 22g (Saturated 12g); Cholesterol 160mg; Sodium 890mg; Carbohydrate 18g (Dietary Fiber 1g); Protein 15g.

Easy Lasagna

▼ 8 to 10 servings

　2　cups ricotta or small curd creamed cottage cheese

1/2　cup grated Parmesan cheese

　2　tablespoons chopped fresh parsley

　1　tablespoon chopped fresh or 1 1/2 teaspoons dried oregano leaves

　2　jars (28 ounces each) spaghetti sauce

12　uncooked lasagna noodles

　2　cups shredded mozzarella cheese (8 ounces)

1/4　cup grated Parmesan cheese

Prep: 20 min

Chill: 24 hr, freeze up to 2 months

Bake: 65 min from refrigerator, 90 min from freezer

---

1 Serving: Calories 455 (Calories from Fat 190); Fat 21g (Saturated 9g); Cholesterol 40mg; Sodium 1710mg; Carbohydrate 47g (Dietary Fiber 4g); Protein 24g.

TO COMPLETE RECIPE:

Shredded mozzarella cheese, if desired

1. Mix ricotta cheese, 1/2 cup Parmesan cheese, the parsley and oregano.

2. Spread 2 cups spaghetti sauce in ungreased rectangular pan, 13 x 9 x 2 inches; top with 4 noodles. Spread cheese mixture over noodles. Spread with 2 cups spaghetti sauce and top with 4 noodles; repeat with 2 cups spaghetti sauce and 4 noodles. Sprinkle with 2 cups mozzarella cheese. Spread with remaining spaghetti sauce. Sprinkle with 1/4 cup Parmesan cheese. STOP HERE—see *To Store* and *To Cook* below.

To complete recipe and serve now, heat oven to 350°. Cover with aluminum foil and bake 30 minutes. Uncover and bake about 30 minutes longer or until hot and bubbly. Sprinkle with mozzarella cheese. Let stand 15 minutes before cutting.

TO STORE

Refrigerator: Cover unbaked lasagna tightly with aluminum foil and refrigerate no longer than 24 hours.

Freezer: Wrap unbaked lasagne tightly with aluminum foil and label. Freeze no longer than 2 months.

Easy Lasagne

TO COOK FROM REFRIGERATOR

Oven: About 1½ hours before serving, heat oven to 350°. Bake in covered pan 45 minutes. Uncover and bake 15 to 20 minutes longer or until hot and bubbly. Sprinkle with mozzarella cheese. Let stand 15 minutes before cutting.

TO COOK FROM FREEZER

Oven: About 2 hours before serving, heat oven to 350°. Bake in covered pan 45 minutes. Uncover and bake 35 to 45 minutes longer or until hot and bubbly. Sprinkle with mozzarella cheese. Let stand 15 minutes before cutting.

Almond-Stuffed Pork Chops

▼ 4 servings

1/2 cup chicken broth

1/4 cup uncooked quick-cooking brown rice

2 tablespoons finely chopped dried apricots

2 tablespoons slivered almonds, toasted

2 teaspoons chopped fresh or 3/4 teaspoon dried marjoram leaves

2 tablespoons chopped fresh parsley

4 pork loin chops, 1-inch thick (about 2 pounds)

TO COMPLETE RECIPE:

1/4 cup apricot preserves

1. Mix broth, rice, apricots, almonds and marjoram in 1¹/₂-quart saucepan. Heat to boiling; reduce heat to low. Cover and simmer about 10 minutes or until rice is tender. Stir in parsley.

2. Cut a 3-inch pocket in each pork chop, cutting from fat side almost to bone. Spoon about 2 tablespoons rice mixture into each pocket. Secure pockets with toothpicks.

3. Set oven control to broil. Place pork on rack in broiler pan. Broil with tops 5 to 6 inches from heat 10 minutes; turn. Broil 10 to 15 minutes longer for medium doneness (160°). STOP HERE—see *To Store* and *To Reheat* below.

To complete recipe and serve now, heat preserves; brush over pork.

Prep: 15 min

Broil: 25 min

Chill: 48 hr, freeze up to 2 months

Reheat: 40 min from refrigerator, 1 hr from freezer

1 Serving: Calories 285 (Calories from Fat 90); Fat 10g (Saturated 3g); Cholesterol 65mg; Sodium 150mg; Carbohydrate 25g (Dietary Fiber 1g); Protein 25g.

TO STORE

Refrigerator: Place broiled pork in square baking dish, 8 x 8 x 2 inches. Cover tightly with aluminum foil and refrigerate no longer than 48 hours.

Freezer: Place broiled pork in square baking dish, 8 x 8 x 2 inches. Wrap tightly with aluminum foil and label. Freeze no longer than 2 months.

TO REHEAT FROM REFRIGERATOR

Oven: About 50 minutes before serving, heat oven to 375°. Bake in covered baking dish 35 to 40 minutes or until stuffing is hot in center and meat thermometer in stuffing reads 160°. Heat preserves; brush over pork.

TO REHEAT FROM FREEZER

Oven: About $1^1/_4$ hours before serving, heat oven to 375°. Bake in covered baking dish about 1 hour or until stuffing is hot in center and meat thermometer in stuffing reads 160°. Heat preserves; brush over pork.

Almond-Stuffed Pork Chops ▶

Curried Ham Salad

▼ 4 servings

Curry powder is a blend of spices including turmeric, cardamom, cumin, pepper, cloves, cinnamon, nutmeg and sometimes ginger. Chilies give it heat, and garlic intensifies the flavor.

Prep: 15 min

Chill: 48 hr

1 Serving: Calories 400 (Calories from Fat 260); Fat 29g (Saturated 6g); Cholesterol 60mg; Sodium 1240mg; Carbohydrate 20g (Dietary Fiber 2g); Protein 17g.

2 cups cubed fully cooked ham

1 can (8 ounces) pineapple tidbits, drained

2 medium stalks celery, sliced (1 cup)

4 medium green onions, sliced (1/2 cup)

1/3 cup raisins

3/4 teaspoon curry powder

1/2 cup mayonnaise or salad dressing

TO COMPLETE RECIPE:

Coconut, toasted, if desired

1. Mix ham, pineapple, celery, onions and raisins in medium glass bowl.
2. Stir curry powder into mayonnaise; fold into ham mixture. See *To Store* and *To Serve* below.

TO STORE

Refrigerator: Cover tightly and refrigerate at least 4 hours but no longer than 48 hours.

TO SERVE FROM REFRIGERATOR

Stir salad. Sprinkle with coconut.

Curried Ham Salad ▶

Sausage and Cheese Squares

▼ 8 servings

Prep: 12 min

Chill: 24 hr, freeze up to 1 month

Bake: 45 min

1 Serving: Calories 350 (Calories from Fat 215); Fat 24g (Saturated 10g); Cholesterol 150mg; Sodium 1070mg; Carbohydrate 19g (Dietary Fiber 1g); Protein 15g.

1	can (8 ounces) refrigerated crescent rolls
16	refrigerated smoked cocktail sausage links
1	large bell pepper, coarsely chopped (1 1/2 cups)
1 1/2	cups shredded Monterey Jack cheese (6 ounces)
1	can (10 3/4 ounces) condensed cream of onion soup
4	eggs

1. Unroll crescent roll dough. Place dough in bottom of ungreased rectangular baking dish, 11 x 7 x 1 1/2 inches. Press seams closed and push dough 1 inch up sides of baking dish.

2. Arrange sausage evenly on dough. Sprinkle with bell pepper and 1 cup of the cheese.

3. Beat soup and eggs until blended; pour over ingredients in baking dish. Sprinkle with remaining cheese. STOP HERE—see *To Store* and *To Cook* and *To Reheat* below.

To serve now, heat oven to 350°. Bake uncovered 30 to 35 minutes or until knife inserted in center comes out clean.

TO STORE

Refrigerator: Cover unbaked casserole tightly and refrigerate no longer than 24 hours.

Freezer: Bake casserole as directed above. Cool 30 minutes. Cut into 16 squares, about 3 1/2 x 1 1/2 inches. Place squares in labeled airtight 2-quart freezer container. Freeze no longer than 1 month.

TO COOK FROM REFRIGERATOR

Oven: About 50 minutes before serving, heat oven to 350°. Bake uncovered 40 to 45 minutes or until knife inserted in center comes out clean. Cut into squares.

TO REHEAT FROM FREEZER

Oven: About 40 minutes before serving, heat oven to 325°. Place squares on ungreased cookie sheet. Bake about 30 minutes or until hot.

Ham and Potato Bake

▼ 8 servings

If you'd like a spicier dish, increase red pepper sauce to $^1/_2$ teaspoon.

Prep: 10 min

Chill: 24 hr

Bake: 1 hr

1 Serving: Calories 190
(Calories from Fat 70);
Fat 8g (Saturated 4g);
Cholesterol 125mg;
Sodium 680mg;
Carbohydrate 20g
(Dietary Fiber 1g);
Protein 11g.

- 1 package (1 pound 4 ounces) refrigerated shredded hash brown potatoes
- 1 cup chopped fully cooked ham
- 1 cup seasoned croutons
- 1 can (11 ounces) condensed Cheddar cheese soup
- 4 eggs
- 1/2 cup milk
- 1/4 teaspoon red pepper sauce

1. Grease rectangular baking dish, 11 x 7 x 1½ inches. Spread potatoes in baking dish. Sprinkle with ham and croutons.

2. Beat soup, eggs, milk and pepper sauce until blended. Pour over ingredients in baking dish. See *To Store* and *To Cook* below.

TO STORE

Refrigerator: Cover unbaked mixture tightly and refrigerate at least 4 hours but no longer than 24 hours.

TO COOK FROM REFRIGERATOR

Oven: About 1¼ hours before serving, heat oven to 350°. Bake uncovered 50 to 60 minutes or until top is light brown and center is set.

Seafood Casserole

▼ 4 servings

The frozen vegetable mixture used in this recipe is a great time-saver for soups, stews and casseroles.

> 4 cups herb-seasoned stuffing cubes
> 1/2 pound frozen uncooked peeled and deveined medium shrimp, thawed if frozen
> 1 package (8 ounces) refrigerated imitation crabmeat chunks
> 1 cup frozen onions, celery, bell pepper and parsley (from 16-ounce package)
> 1 1/4 cups vegetable or chicken broth
> 2 tablespoons margarine, butter or spread, melted

1. Mix stuffing cubes, shrimp, crabmeat and vegetables in 2-quart casserole.

2. Stir in broth and margarine. See *To Store* and *To Cook* below.

Prep: 10 min

Chill: 24 hr

Bake: 45 min

1 Serving: Calories 270 (Calories from Fat 80); Fat 9g (Saturated 2g); Cholesterol 90mg; Sodium 900mg; Carbohydrate 30g (Dietary Fiber 2g); Protein 19g.

TO STORE

Refrigerator: Cover unbaked casserole tightly and refrigerate at least 8 hours but no longer than 24 hours.

TO COOK FROM REFRIGERATOR

Oven: About 1 hour before serving, heat oven to 350°. Bake covered casserole about 45 minutes or until center is hot.

Blueberry Breakfast Bake

▼ 8 servings

It's easy to cut the calories and fat in this recipe without losing the delicious flavor. Simply substitute reduced-fat cream cheese (Neufchâtel) for the regular cream cheese and fat-free cholesterol-free egg product for the eggs.

Prep: 10 min

Chill: 24 hr

Bake: 45 min from refrigerator

1 Serving: Calories 425 (Calories from Fat 205); Fat 23g (Saturated 10g); Cholesterol 50mg; Sodium 1410mg; Carbohydrate 31g (Dietary Fiber 3g); Protein 27g.

8   slices white bread, cut into 1-inch pieces (about 6 cups)

1   package (8 ounces) cream cheese, chilled and cut into 1/2-inch pieces

1   cup fresh blueberries

8   eggs

1 1/2   cups milk

TO COMPLETE RECIPE:

1   cup blueberry syrup

1. Grease rectangular baking dish, 11 x 7 x 1½ inches. Spread half of the bread pieces evenly in baking dish. Top with cream cheese. Sprinkle with blueberries. Spread remaining bread over blueberries.

2. Beat eggs and milk in medium bowl until blended; pour over bread. See *To Store* and *To Cook* below.

TO STORE

Refrigerator: Cover unbaked mixture tightly with aluminum foil and refrigerate at least 8 hours but no longer than 24 hours.

TO COOK FROM REFRIGERATOR

Oven: About 1¼ hours before serving, heat oven to 350°. Bake in covered baking dish 30 minutes. Uncover and bake 25 to 30 minutes longer or until top is puffed and center is set. Serve with blueberry syrup.

Blueberry Breakfast Bake ▶

One-Crust Tuna-Vegetable Pie

▼ 4 servings

Prep: 10 min

Chill: 8 hr

Bake: 1 hr

1 Serving: Calories 395 (Calories from Fat 155); Fat 17g (Saturated 9g); Cholesterol 245mg; Sodium 350mg; Carbohydrate 49g (Dietary Fiber 0g); Protein 12g.

    2 cups frozen mixed vegetables
    1 can (9 1/4 ounces) tuna, drained
    4 medium green onions, sliced (1/2 cup)
1/2 cup sour cream
    1 can (11 ounces) condensed Cheddar cheese soup
    1 cup Bisquick® Original baking mix
1/4 cup cold water

1. Layer frozen vegetables, tuna and onions in ungreased square baking dish, 8 x 8 x 2 inches. Mix sour cream and soup; spread over top.

2. Mix baking mix and cold water; beat vigorously 20 strokes. On lightly floured surface, pat dough into 9-inch square. Place on soup mixture; cut slits to allow steam to escape. STOP HERE—see *To Store* and *To Cook* below.

To serve now, heat oven to 375°. Bake uncovered 25 to 30 minutes or until hot and bubbly and crust is golden brown. Let stand at least 5 minutes before cutting.

TO STORE

Refrigerator: Cover unbaked pie tightly and refrigerate no longer than 24 hours.

TO COOK FROM REFRIGERATOR

Oven: About 50 minutes before serving, heat oven to 375°. Bake uncovered 40 to 45 minutes or until hot and bubbly and crust is golden brown. Let stand at least 5 minutes before cutting.

Casseroles and Oven Dinners

Zesty Roasted Chicken and Potatoes

▼ 6 servings

Serve this family favorite with a super-quick salad. Simply pick up prepared salad greens at your local fast-food restaurant or supermarket, toss them with your favorite dressing, and you'll have a meal on the table in a snap!

Prep: 10 min

Bake: 35 min

1 Serving: Calories 380 (Calories from Fat 200); Fat 22g (Saturated 5g); Cholesterol 90mg; Sodium 240mg; Carbohydrate 17g (Dietary Fiber 1g); Protein 29g.

6 **skinless boneless chicken breast halves**

1 **pound small red potatoes, cut in quarters**

1/3 **cup mayonnaise or salad dressing**

3 **tablespoons Dijon mustard**

1/2 **teaspoon pepper**

2 **cloves garlic, crushed**

Chopped fresh chives, if desired

1. Heat oven to 350°. Grease jelly roll pan, $15^1/_2$ x $10^1/_2$ x 1 inch.

2. Place chicken and potatoes in pan. Mix remaining ingredients except chives; brush over chicken and potatoes.

3. Bake uncovered 30 to 35 minutes or until potatoes are tender and juice of chicken is no longer pink when centers of thickest pieces are cut. Sprinkle with chives.

Preceding Page
Shrimp Supreme (page 216)

Chicken with Orange-Pecan Rice

▼ 4 servings

This is the dish for easy entertaining. Complete the meal with aspara-
gus spears, sliced tomatoes and your favorite dinner rolls.

Prep: 5 min

Bake: 45 min

1 Serving: Calories 285
(Calories from Fat 70);
Fat 8g (Saturated 2g);
Cholesterol 60mg;
Sodium 60mg;
Carbohydrate 27g
(Dietary Fiber 1g);
Protein 27g.

> 1 package (6.25 ounces) fast-cooking long grain and wild rice
> 2 cups orange juice
> 1/4 cup chopped pecans
> 1 jar (2 ounces) diced pimientos, drained
> 4 skinless boneless chicken breast halves (about 1 pound)
> Chopped fresh parsley, if desired

1. Heat oven to 350°. Grease square pan, 8 x 8 x 2 inches.

2. Mix rice, seasoning packet included in rice mix, orange juice, pecans and pimientos in pan. Place chicken on rice.

3. Cover and bake 35 to 45 minutes or until liquid is absorbed and juice of chicken is no longer pink when centers of thickest pieces are cut. Sprinkle with parsley.

▼ ▼ ▼ ▼ ▼ ▼ ▼ ▼ ▼ ▼ ▼ ▼ ▼ ▼ ▼ ▼ ▼ ▼

Chicken-Linguine Casserole

▼ 6 servings

Prep: 10 min

Bake: 43 min

1 Serving: Calories 340
(Calories from Fat 90);
Fat 10g (Saturated 4g);
Cholesterol 55mg;
Sodium 630mg;
Carbohydrate 39g
(Dietary Fiber 1g);
Protein 24g.

> 1 package (9 ounces) refrigerated linguine
> 2 cups cut-up cooked chicken
> 1 cup frozen onions, celery, bell pepper and parsley (from 16-ounce package)
> 1 can (10 3/4 ounces) condensed cream of chicken soup
> 1 cup chicken broth
> 1/2 cup shredded Cheddar cheese (2 ounces)

1. Heat oven to 350°. Grease square pan, 8 x 8 x 2 inches.

2. Place uncooked linguine in large colander and rinse with hot water 15 seconds; drain. Mix linguine, chicken, vegetables, soup and broth in pan.

3. Bake uncovered 35 to 40 minutes or until bubbly around edges. Sprinkle with cheese. Bake uncovered about 3 minutes longer or until cheese is melted.

Chicken with Orange-Pecan Rice ▶

Saturday Night Supper

▼ 4 servings

An easy casserole that both kids—and adults—would like. Try serving with milk and fresh fruit.

Prep: 15 min

Bake: 30 min

1 Serving: Calories 370 (Calories from Fat 125); Fat 14g (Saturated 5g); Cholesterol 80mg; Sodium 1020mg; Carbohydrate 35g (Dietary Fiber 5g); Protein 31g.

    1   pound ground turkey
    2   cups frozen mixed vegetables
    1   can (15 ounces) Italian-style tomato sauce
1 1/2   cups cooked small pasta shells or elbow macaroni
  3/4   teaspoon garlic salt
  1/4   teaspoon pepper
  1/4   cup grated Parmesan cheese

1. Heat oven to 400°.

2. Cook turkey in 10-inch skillet over medium heat 8 to 10 minutes, stirring occasionally, until no longer pink; drain.

3. Spoon turkey into ungreased 2-quart casserole. Stir in vegetables, tomato sauce, pasta, garlic salt and pepper. Cover and bake about 30 minutes or until vegetables are tender; stir. Sprinkle with cheese.

Rice and Onion Chicken Casserole

▼ 4 servings

Prep: 10 min

Bake: 1 hr

1 Serving: Calories 405 (Calories from Fat 100); Fat 11g (Saturated 4g); Cholesterol 70mg; Sodium 1710mg; Carbohydrate 46g (Dietary Fiber 2g); Protein 32g.

1 can (10 3/4 ounces) condensed cream of mushroom soup

1 soup can of milk

3/4 cup uncooked regular long grain rice

1 can (4 ounces) mushroom stems and pieces, undrained

1 envelope (about 1 1/2 ounces) onion soup mix

4 skinless boneless chicken breast halves (about 1 pound)

1. Heat oven to 350°.

2. Mix mushroom soup and milk; reserve 1/2 cup soup mixture. Mix remaining soup mixture, the rice, mushrooms and half of the dry onion soup mix; spoon into ungreased rectangular baking dish, 11 x 7 x 1 1/2 inches.

3. Place chicken on rice mixture. Pour reserved soup mixture over chicken. Sprinkle with remaining dry onion soup mix.

4. Cover and bake 45 minutes. Uncover and bake about 15 minutes longer or until chicken is no longer pink when centers of thickest pieces are cut.

Quick Fix-Ups

Jazzing up purchased products to create something special that your family will love is a great cooking secret. Besides "doctoring-up" spaghetti sauce or frozen pizza, give the suggestions below a try.

Start With	Add
Baked Beans	• Cooked bacon, sausage, ham, hot dogs or ground beef • Brown sugar, ketchup, barbecue sauce or molasses
Coleslaw	• Dried fruit pieces (raisins, apricots) • Canned fruits (pineapple tidbits, mandarin orange segments) • Extra fresh vegetables (celery, onion, broccoli, shredded carrots, bell peppers) • Cream-style horseradish • Sunflower seeds or dry roasted peanuts
Cream Soups (mushroom, chicken, celery)	• White wine or sherry and sliced mushrooms for a quick sauce for chicken • Sour cream and sliced mushrooms for a quick beef stroganoff sauce • Leftover meat and vegetables for an easy chowder
Pudding Mixes	• Use half-and-half or eggnog instead of milk • Substitute 2 to 4 tablespoons liqueur (Irish cream, Kahlua, creme de cacao) for part of the milk • Leftover rice for rice pudding—stir into hot pudding and serve warm.
Coffee	• Add extracts (vanilla, rum, coconut), spices (cinnamon, nutmeg, apple pie or pumpkin pie spice) or ground nuts (almonds, hazelnuts) to the coffee grounds to brew your own flavored coffee.

Harvest Bean Casserole

▼ 6 servings

Use either spicy or regular sausage—whichever suits your household—for this hearty casserole.

Prep: 12 min

Bake: 35 min

1 Serving: Calories 355
(Calories from Fat 80);
Fat 9g (Saturated 3g);
Cholesterol 55mg;
Sodium 1310mg;
Carbohydrate 50g
(Dietary Fiber 8g);
Protein 26g.

1 pound bulk turkey or pork breakfast sausage
1 can (28 ounces) baked beans
2 baking apples, thinly sliced
1 can (18 ounces) vacuum-packed sweet potatoes
3 medium green onions, sliced (1/3 cup)

1. Heat oven to 375°.

2. Cook sausage in 10-inch skillet over medium heat 8 to 10 minutes, stirring occasionally, until no longer pink; drain.

3. Place sausage in ungreased rectangular baking dish, 11 x 7 x 1½ inches. Stir in baked beans. Arrange apple slices over sausage mixture. Slice sweet potatoes over apples.

4. Cover and bake 30 to 35 minutes or until apples are tender. Sprinkle with onions.

▼ ▼ ▼ ▼ ▼ ▼ ▼ ▼ ▼ ▼ ▼ ▼ ▼ ▼ ▼ ▼ ▼ ▼

Wild Rice and Turkey Casserole

▼ 6 servings

Prep: 10 min

Bake: 65 min

1 Serving: Calories 175
(Calories from Fat 65);
Fat 7g (Saturated 2g);
Cholesterol 40mg;
Sodium 460mg;
Carbohydrate 12g
(Dietary Fiber 0g);
Protein 16g.

2 cups cut-up cooked turkey
2 1/4 cups boiling water
1/3 cup milk
1 small onion, chopped (1/4 cup)
1 can (10 3/4 ounces) condensed cream of mushroom soup
1 package (6 ounces) seasoned long grain and wild rice

1. Heat oven to 350°.

2. Mix all ingredients, including seasoning packet from rice mix, in ungreased 2-quart casserole.

3. Cover and bake 45 to 50 minutes or until rice is tender. Uncover and bake 10 to 15 minutes longer or until liquid is absorbed.

Harvest Bean Casserole ▶

Cornbread Beef Bake

▼ 6 servings

A cast-iron skillet works well for this casserole. However, if you don't have one, any ovenproof skillet works just fine.

Prep: 10 min

Bake: 40 min

1 Serving: Calories 395 (Calories from Fat 155); Fat 17g (Saturated 7g); Cholesterol 85mg; Sodium 530mg; Carbohydrate 43g (Dietary Fiber 6g); Protein 24g.

1 **pound lean ground beef**

1 **medium onion, chopped (1/2 cup)**

1 **can (14 1/2 ounces) Mexican-style stewed tomatoes, undrained**

1 **can (15 ounces) black beans, rinsed and drained**

1 **can (8 ounces) tomato sauce**

1/2 **cup frozen corn**

2 **teaspoons chili powder**

1 **can (11 1/2 ounces) refrigerated corn bread twists**

1. Heat oven to 350°.

2. Cook beef and onion in 10-inch ovenproof skillet over medium heat 8 to 10 minutes, stirring occasionally, until beef is brown; drain.

3. Stir in tomatoes, beans, tomato sauce, corn and chili powder; heat to boiling. Immediately top with corn bread twists left in round shape (do not unwind), pressing down gently. Bake uncovered 35 to 40 minutes or until corn bread is golden brown.

Cornbread Beef Bake ▶

Tortilla Casserole

▼ 6 servings

Prep: 15 min

Bake: 40 min

Stand: 10 min

1 Serving: Calories 465
(Calories from Fat 280);
Fat 31g (Saturated 16g);
Cholesterol 100mg;
Sodium 940mg;
Carbohydrate 21g
(Dietary Fiber 2g);
Protein 27g.

    1 pound ground beef
    1 medium onion, chopped (1/2 cup)
    1 jar (8 ounces) green or red salsa (1 cup)
1/2 cup sour cream
    1 can (10 3/4 ounces) condensed cream of chicken soup
    1 jar (2 ounces) sliced pimientos, drained
    6 corn tortillas (6 to 8 inches), cut into 1-inch strips
    2 cups shredded Cheddar cheese (8 ounces)

1. Heat oven to 350°.

2. Cook beef and onion in 10-inch skillet over medium heat 8 to 10 minutes, stirring occasionally, until beef is brown; drain.

3. Spread 1/2 cup of the salsa in bottom of ungreased square baking dish, 8 x 8 x 2 inches. Mix remaining salsa, the sour cream, soup and pimientos. Layer half of the tortilla strips, beef mixture, soup mixture and cheese on salsa; repeat.

4. Bake uncovered 30 to 40 minutes or until hot and bubbly. Let stand 10 minutes. Garnish with olives if desired.

Hamburger-Cabbage Casserole

▼ 6 servings

Prep: 10 min

Bake: 45 min

1 Serving: Calories 240
(Calories from Fat 110);
Fat 12g (Saturated 5g);
Cholesterol 45mg;
Sodium 570mg;
Carbohydrate 19g
(Dietary Fiber 2g);
Protein 16g.

    1 pound lean ground beef
    1 large onion, chopped (1 cup)
1/2 cup uncooked instant rice
1/2 teaspoon salt
1/2 teaspoon pepper
    1 can (10 3/4 ounces) condensed tomato soup
1/4 cup water
    4 cups coleslaw mix or shredded cabbage

1. Heat oven to 400°.

2. Cook beef and onion in 10-inch skillet over medium heat 8 to 10 minutes, stirring occasionally, until beef is brown; drain. Stir in remaining ingredients. Spoon into ungreased 2-quart casserole. Cover and bake 45 minutes or until hot and bubbly.

Betty Crocker's Top 10

Recipe Shortcuts for Casseroles and Oven Meals Dinners

1. ▶ Canned vegetables such as green beans, peas, corn, mixed vegetables

2. ▶ Canned soups such as Cheddar cheese, broccoli cheese, golden corn, and cream soups such as asparagus, celery, mushroom and onion

3. ▶ Canned or jarred gravies (chicken, beef, turkey, mushroom)

4. ▶ Frozen chopped onions—store-bought or from your freezer

5. ▶ Frozen vegetables

6. ▶ Frozen or pre-cooked lasagne sheets from the freezer case

7. ▶ Crunchy toppings such as seasoned bread crumbs, croutons or flavored potato chips

8. ▶ Frozen potato nuggets or potato wedges

9. ▶ Quicker cooking pasta such as orzo, elbow macaroni, small shells or vermicelli

10. ▶ Instant rice or potatoes

Cajun Pork Tenderloin with Vegetables

▼ 4 servings

If you'd like a milder flavor, just reduce the amount of Cajun spice.

Prep: 12 min

Roast: 35 min

Stand: 10 min

1 Serving: Calories 280 (Calories from Fat 90); Fat 10g (Saturated 3g); Cholesterol 65mg; Sodium 260mg; Carbohydrate 24g (Dietary Fiber 4g); Protein 27g.

2	teaspoons Cajun or Creole seasoning
1	pound pork tenderloin
2	medium sweet potatoes or yams (3/4 pound)
4	small zucchini (1 pound)
1 1/2	cups frozen small whole onions
2	tablespoons margarine, butter or spread, melted
1/2	teaspoon dried thyme leaves
1/4	teaspoon salt

1. Heat oven to 425°.

2. Rub Cajun seasoning into pork. Place in ungreased jelly roll pan, 15½ x 10½ x 1 inches. Insert meat thermometer horizontally into center of thickest part of pork.

3. Cut sweet potatoes and zucchini lengthwise into halves. Place sweet potatoes, zucchini and onions around pork. Drizzle margarine over vegetables. Sprinkle with thyme and salt.

4. Roast uncovered about 35 minutes or until thermometer reads 160°. Loosely cover pan with aluminum foil and let stand 10 minutes. Cut pork into thin slices. Serve with vegetables.

Cajun Pork Tenderloin with Vegetables ▶

Pizza Casserole

▼ 6 servings

Prep: 15 min

Bake: 35 min

1 Serving: Calories 365 (Calories from Fat 145); Fat 16g (Saturated 7g); Cholesterol 40mg; Sodium 970mg; Carbohydrate 39g (Dietary Fiber 1g); Protein 17g.

4 cups uncooked wagon wheel pasta (8 ounces)
1/2 pound bulk Italian sausage
1/4 cup sliced ripe olives
1 can (4 ounces) mushroom stems and pieces, drained
1 jar (28 ounces) spaghetti sauce
1 cup shredded mozzarella cheese (4 ounces)

1. Heat oven to 350°.

2. Cook and drain pasta as directed on package.

3. While pasta is cooking, cook sausage in 10-inch skillet over medium-high heat, stirring occasionally, until no longer pink; drain. Mix pasta, sausage and remaining ingredients except cheese in ungreased 2¹/₂-quart casserole.

4. Cover and bake about 30 minutes or until hot and bubbly. Sprinkle with cheese. Bake uncovered about 5 minutes or until cheese is melted.

Pineapple Brunch Bake

▼ 6 servings

Prep: 10 min

Bake: 29 min

1 Serving: Calories 285 (Calories from Fat 135); Fat 15g (Saturated 7g); Cholesterol 115mg; Sodium 1000mg; Carbohydrate 21g (Dietary Fiber 1g); Protein 17g.

1 1/2 cups chopped fully cooked ham
1 can (8 ounces) crushed pineapple in juice, drained
4 medium green onions, sliced (1/2 cup)
1 cup Bisquick® Original baking mix
1 cup milk
2 eggs
2 teaspoons mustard
1 cup shredded Colby-Monterey Jack cheese (4 ounces)

1. Heat oven to 400°. Grease pie plate, 9 x 1¹/₄ inches.

2. Sprinkle ham, pineapple and onions in pie plate.

3. Mix baking mix, milk, eggs and mustard until blended; pour over ham mixture.

4. Bake uncovered about 25 minutes or until knife inserted in center comes out clean. Sprinkle with cheese. Bake 3 to 4 minutes longer or until cheese is melted.

Pizza Casserole ▶

Chili Dog Wraps

▼ 5 servings

This Mexican-inspired casserole gives you another great way to serve the always popular hot dog.

Prep: 5 min

Bake: 25 min

1 Serving: Calories 550 (Calories from Fat 325); Fat 36g (Saturated 15g); Cholesterol 65mg; Sodium 2190mg; Carbohydrate 41g (Dietary Fiber 7g); Protein 22g.

10 corn or flour tortillas (6 to 8 inches in diameter)

10 hot dogs

 1 can (15 to 16 ounces) chili

 2 cups salsa

 1 cup shredded Cheddar or Monterey Jack cheese (4 ounces)

1. Heat oven to 350°. Grease rectangular baking dish, 13 x 9 x 2 inches.

2. Soften tortillas as directed on package. Place 1 hot dog and 3 tablespoons chili on each tortilla. Roll up tortillas; place seam side down in baking dish. Spoon salsa over tortillas.

3. Cover and bake 20 minutes. Sprinkle with cheese. Bake uncovered about 5 minutes longer or until cheese is melted.

Chili Dog Wraps ▶

Fish and Vegetable Packets

▼ 4 servings

Prep: 12 min

Bake: 20 min

1 Serving: Calories 130 (Calories from Fat 20); Fat 2g (Saturated 0g); Cholesterol 60mg; Sodium 400mg; Carbohydrate 7g (Dietary Fiber 2g); Protein 23g.

4 lean fish fillets (about 4 ounces each)

1 package (16 ounces) frozen broccoli, cauliflower and carrots, thawed

1 tablespoon chopped fresh or 1 teaspoon dried dill weed

1/2 teaspoon salt

1/4 teaspoon pepper

1/4 cup dry white wine or chicken broth

1. Heat oven to 450°.

2. Place each fish fillet on a 12-inch square of aluminum foil. Top each fish fillet with one-fourth of the vegetables. Sprinkle with dill weed, salt and pepper. Drizzle 1 tablespoon wine over each mound of vegetables.

3. Fold up sides of foil to make a tent; fold top edges over to seal. Fold in sides, making a packet; fold to seal. Place packets on ungreased cookie sheet.

4. Bake about 20 minutes or until vegetables are crisp-tender and fish flakes easily with fork.

Put the Freeze on Casseroles

Don't freeze your assets! When you're freezing casseroles, but need the dish for other uses, try this easy method. Line casserole and lasagna dishes with heavy-duty foil, allowing enough extra foil to completely seal food with a double fold. Freeze food right in the casserole or lasagna dish until completely frozen. Remove food and wrap again with foil or place in plastic freezer bag; label and date for future use. Casseroles and lasagna can either be thawed in the refrigerator or placed frozen in a cold oven. To cook, place in the same casserole or dish the mixture was frozen in—foil and all! If baking from the frozen state, allow an extra 15 to 30 minutes for cooking.

Fish and Vegetable Packets ▶

Flounder Florentine

▼ 4 servings

Prep: 8 min

Bake: 30 min

1 Serving: Calories 130
(Calories from Fat 20);
Fat 2g (Saturated 0g);
Cholesterol 55mg;
Sodium 300mg;
Carbohydrate 7g
(Dietary Fiber 2g);
Protein 23g.

> 2 packages (10 ounces each) frozen chopped spinach, thawed and squeezed to drain
> 1 pound flounder or other whitefish fillets, about 1/2-inch thick
> 1/4 teaspoon salt
> 1/2 cup roasted red bell peppers (from 7-ounce jar)
> 1/4 cup chopped fresh or 2 teaspoons dried basil leaves
> 1 tablespoon milk
> 1/8 teaspoon red pepper sauce

1. Heat oven to 400°.

2. Spread spinach evenly in ungreased rectangular pan, 11 x 7 x 2 inches. Arrange fish on spinach. Sprinkle with salt.

3. Place bell peppers, basil, milk and pepper sauce in blender or food processor. Cover and blend on high speed about 15 seconds or until smooth; pour over fish.

4. Cover and bake 25 to 30 minutes or until fish flakes easily with fork.

Tuna-Macaroni Casserole

▼ 6 servings

Prep: 15 min

Bake: 40 min

1 Serving: Calories 410
(Calories from Fat 180);
Fat 20g (Saturated 11g);
Cholesterol 50mg;
Sodium 770mg;
Carbohydrate 34g
(Dietary Fiber 1g);
Protein 25g.

> 1 package (7 ounces) elbow macaroni (2 cups)
> 2 cups grated Cheddar cheese (8 ounces)
> 1 medium onion, finely chopped (1/2 cup)
> 1 can (6 ounces) tuna, drained
> 1 can (10 3/4 ounces) condensed cream of mushroom or celery soup
> 1 soup can of milk

1. Heat oven to 350°. Grease 2-quart casserole.

2. Cook and drain macaroni as directed on package.

3. Mix macaroni and remaining ingredients in casserole. Bake uncovered 30 to 40 minutes or until hot and bubbly.

Flounder Florentine

Tuna-Broccoli Casserole

▼ 4 servings

Prep: 11 min

Bake: 40 min

1 Serving: Calories 480 (Calories from Fat 155); Fat 17g (Saturated 7g); Cholesterol 30mg; Sodium 880mg; Carbohydrate 59g (Dietary Fiber 4g); Protein 27g.

1 1/2 cups uncooked small pasta shells (6 ounces)
1 package (10 ounces) frozen broccoli cuts, thawed
1 can (6 ounces) tuna, drained
1 can (10 3/4 ounces) condensed Cheddar cheese soup
1 soup can of milk
1 cup crushed potato chips

1. Heat oven to 350°. Grease 2-quart casserole.

2. Mix all ingredients except potato chips in casserole. Sprinkle with potato chips. Bake uncovered 30 to 40 minutes or until hot and bubbly.

▼▼▼▼▼▼▼▼▼▼▼▼▼▼▼▼▼▼▼

Shrimp Supreme

▼ 4 servings

This colorful and creamy dish is sure to please all shrimp lovers. (Photograph on page 191.)

Prep: 8 min

Bake: 45 min

1 Serving: Calories 200 (Calories from Fat 90); Fat 10g (Saturated 6g); Cholesterol 145mg; Sodium 490mg; Carbohydrate 13g (Dietary Fiber 1g); Protein 16g.

1 package (5.3 ounces) mushroom and wild rice mix
1 package (3 ounces) cream cheese, softened
2 medium stalks celery, sliced (1 cup)
1 small red bell pepper, chopped (1/2 cup)
3 medium green onions, sliced (1/3 cup)
1 1/4 cups hot water
1 1/2 teaspoons lemon juice
3/4 pound uncooked peeled and deveined medium shrimp, thawed if frozen

1. Heat oven to 425°.

2. Mix rice mix, with seasoning packet and remaining ingredients except shrimp in ungreased 1½-quart casserole.

3. Cover and bake 30 minutes. Stir in shrimp. Cover and bake about 15 minutes longer or until shrimp are pink and firm.

Pastas and Pizzas

Tuscan Rigatoni and White Beans

▼ 6 servings

Tuscany is a region in Italy noted for its white bean dishes and hearty breads. So round out this Tuscan skillet meal with a robust loaf of bread.

Prep: 10 min

Cook: 16 min

1 Serving: Calories 400 (Calories from Fat 90); Fat 10g (Saturated 3g); Cholesterol 45mg; Sodium 970mg; Carbohydrate 55g (Dietary Fiber 5g); Protein 27g.

2 cups uncooked rigatoni pasta (6 ounces)

1 large onion, chopped (1 cup)

1 package (16 ounces) smoked turkey sausage, cut into 1/2-inch slices

1 can (15 to 16 ounces) cannellini beans, rinsed and drained

1/3 cup oil-packed sun-dried tomatoes, drained and chopped

1/3 cup chicken broth

1 tablespoon chopped fresh or 1 teaspoon dried rosemary leaves

1/3 cup shredded Parmesan cheese

1. Cook and drain pasta as directed on package.

2. While pasta is cooking, cook onion and sausage in 12-inch skillet over medium-high heat 2 to 3 minutes, stirring occasionally, until onion is tender.

3. Gently stir in pasta and remaining ingredients except cheese. Cook 3 to 5 minutes or until hot. Sprinkle each serving with cheese.

Preceding Page
Thai Chicken Pizza (page 238)

High Flavor Enhancers!

Big, bold flavors make food more interesting and add great taste—that's why we add ketchup, mustard, barbecue sauce, mayonnaise, hot sauce and black pepper to our foods. The advantage of these ingredients? They offer an explosive burst of flavor allowing you to use fewer ingredients—so the end result truly is that less is more! Pick some of your favorites from the list below to have on hand to put that extra dash or kick in your foods.

Wet Your Whistle

- Flavored vinegar: balsamic, raspberry and red wine
- Bottled marinades and gravy
- Olive oil and commercially prepared flavored oils
- Lemon/lime juice
- Mustards
- Prepared horseradish
- Oriental sauces/condiments: chili paste, fish sauce, hoisin, oyster, teriyaki, sweet-sour, etc.
- Salad dressing
- Salsa
- Pesto
- Condiments: ketchup, chili sauce, tartar sauce, chutney, etc.
- Vanilla

Buy It Dry

- Spices: anise, cumin, curry, five-spice powder, nutmeg, pepper and saffron
- Dried chilies, peppers and fruit
- Seasoning mixes: blackened, Thai, Cajun, Creole, pork and barbecue
- Seasoning packets: taco, gravy and sauces

Fresh and Flavorful

- Herbs: basil, chives, cilantro, dill and oregano
- Chilies, peppers and gingerroot
- Onions and garlic

Chicken-Pasta Salad

▼ 4 servings

    1 package (5 ounces) juniorettes (spiral macaroni)
    1 package (6 ounces) frozen Chinese pea pods, thawed
      and drained
    1/3 cup mayonnaise or salad dressing
    1/4 cup French dressing
    2 cups cut-up cooked chicken or turkey
    1 cup cherry tomatoes, cut in half

1. Cook macaroni as directed on package—except add pea
   pods about 2 minutes before macaroni is done; drain.
   Rinse macaroni and pea pods with cold water; drain.

2. While macaroni is cooking, mix mayonnaise and French
   dressing in large bowl. Add macaroni mixture, chicken
   and tomatoes; toss.

Prep: 5 min

Cook: 10 min

1 Serving: Calories 480
(Calories from Fat 235);
Fat 26g (Saturated 5g);
Cholesterol 80mg;
Sodium 380mg;
Carbohydrate 36g
(Dietary Fiber 2g);
Protein 27g.

▼ ▼

Smoked Turkey and Couscous

▼ 4 servings

    1 can (14 1/2 ounces) ready-to-serve chicken broth
    2 cups broccoli flowerets
    1 cup cut-up fully cooked smoked turkey
1 1/2 teaspoons chopped fresh or 1/2 teaspoon dried
      tarragon leaves
    1/2 cup uncooked couscous
    1/2 cup shredded Cheddar cheese (2 ounces)

1. Heat broth to boiling in 10-inch skillet. Stir in broccoli,
   turkey and tarragon. Cover and cook 3 to 4 minutes or
   until broccoli is crisp-tender.

2. Stir in couscous; remove from heat. Cover and let stand
   about 5 minutes or until liquid is absorbed.

3. Fluff couscous mixture with fork. Sprinkle with cheese.
   Cover and let stand 3 to 5 minutes or until cheese is
   melted.

Prep: 10 min

Stand: 10 min

Cook: 9 min

1 Serving: Calories 230
(Calories from Fat 70);
Fat 8g (Saturated 4g);
Cholesterol 45mg;
Sodium 460mg;
Carbohydrate 21g
(Dietary Fiber 2g);
Protein 20g.

Beef and Artichoke Fettuccine

▼ 6 servings

Prep: 10 min

Cook: 15 min

1 Serving: Calories 300
(Calories from Fat 110);
Fat 12g (Saturated 6g);
Cholesterol 80mg;
Sodium 260mg;
Carbohydrate 31g
(Dietary Fiber 3g);
Protein 20g.

8 ounces uncooked fettuccine

1 jar (6 ounces) marinated artichoke hearts, cut in half and marinade reserved

1 small onion, finely chopped (1/4 cup)

1 cup half-and-half

1/2 cup grated Parmesan cheese

2 cups cut-up cooked roast beef

1. Cook and drain pasta as directed on package.

2. While pasta is cooking, heat 1 tablespoon reserved marinade to boiling in 10-inch skillet over medium heat. Discard remaining marinade. Cook onion in marinade about 4 minutes or until crisp-tender, stirring occasionally.

3. Stir in half-and-half; heat until hot. Stir in cheese, artichoke hearts and beef; heat until hot. Stir in fettuccine and toss. Sprinkle with pepper if desired.

Beef and Artichoke Fettuccine ▶

Fiery Fettuccine

▼ 4 servings

Prep: 10 min

Cook: 15 min

1 Serving: Calories 555 (Calories from Fat 335); Fat 37g (Saturated 18g); Cholesterol 145mg; Sodium 850mg; Carbohydrate 43g (Dietary Fiber 2g); Protein 15g.

8 ounces uncooked fettuccine

1 cup whipping (heavy) cream

1 teaspoon Creole or Cajun seasoning

1 jar (7 ounces) roasted red bell peppers, drained

1/2 pound smoked sausage, cut into 1/4-inch slices

2 medium green onions, sliced (1/4 cup)

1. Cook and drain pasta as directed on package.

2. While pasta is cooking, place whipping cream, Creole seasoning and bell peppers in blender or food processor. Cover and blend on high speed until smooth.

3. Pour pepper mixture into 12-inch skillet. Cook over medium heat, stirring occasionally, until mixture thickens. Stir in sausage; heat through but do not boil.

4. Serve sausage mixture over fettuccine. Sprinkle with onions.

Quick Tip: Substitute 1 (7 ounce) container refrigerated Roasted Pepper Cream Sauce for the whipping cream, Creole seasoning and roasted red bell peppers.

Sausage and Peppers Pasta

▼ 4 servings

Prep: 15 min

Cook: 10 min

1 Serving: Calories 585 (Calories from Fat 290); Fat 32g (Saturated 12g); Cholesterol 90mg; Sodium 1140mg; Carbohydrate 44g (Dietary Fiber 2g); Protein 32g.

2 1/2 cups uncooked rigatoni (8 ounces)
    1 pound bulk Italian sausage
    2 medium bell peppers, cut into strips
    1 tablespoon chopped fresh parsley
 1/4 cup grated Parmesan cheese

1. Cook and drain pasta as directed on package.

2. While pasta is cooking, cook sausage and bell peppers in 10-inch skillet over medium heat 8 to 10 minutes, stirring frequently, until sausage is no longer pink; drain.

3. Toss with rigatoni and parsley. Sprinkle with cheese.

▼▼▼▼▼▼▼▼▼▼▼▼▼▼▼▼▼▼▼▼

Sweet-and-Sour Pasta Salad

▼ 6 servings

Here's a refreshing salad for summer entertaining—add sorbet or fresh watermelon slices for dessert.

Prep: 5 min

Cook: 10 min

1 Serving: Calories 255 (Calories from Fat 45); Fat 5g (Saturated 1g); Cholesterol 20mg; Sodium 1100mg; Carbohydrate 42g (Dietary Fiber 4g); Protein 14g.

    1 cup uncooked rosamarina (orzo) pasta (6 ounces)
    1 package (16 ounces) frozen stir-fry vegetables
    1 can (14 ounces) baby corn nuggets, drained
1 1/2 cups cubed fully cooked ham
 3/4 cup sweet-and-sour sauce

1. Cook pasta as directed on package, but do not drain.

2. Place frozen vegetables in colander. To drain pasta, pour over frozen vegetables in colander. Let stand until vegetables are thawed.

3. Place vegetables and pasta in large bowl. Add corn, ham and sweet-and-sour sauce; toss.

Sweet-and-Sour Pasta Salad ▶

Tuna-Vegetable Salad

▼ 6 servings

Want a cold salad, but don't want to wait for it to chill after you put it together? If so, rinse the tortellini and vegetables in cold water to thaw, and store the can of tuna and bottle of dressing in the refrigerator until ready to make the salad.

Prep: 5 min

1 Serving: Calories 185 (Calories from Fat 100); Fat 11g (Saturated 3g); Cholesterol 20mg; Sodium 430mg; Carbohydrate 6g (Dietary Fiber 1g); Protein 16g.

  1 **can (12 ounces) tuna, drained**

  1 **package (14 ounces) frozen pre-cooked salad tortellini, rinsed and drained**

  1 **package (16 ounces) frozen broccoli, cauliflower and carrots, thawed**

1/2 **cup creamy Parmesan or cucumber dressing**

Toss all ingredients.

▼ ▼

Tuna Spaghetti

▼ 4 servings

Prep: 10 min

Cook: 12 min

1 Serving: Calories 510 (Calories from Fat 235); Fat 26g (Saturated 8g); Cholesterol 30mg; Sodium 890mg; Carbohydrate 43g (Dietary Fiber 1g); Protein 27g.

  1 **package (7 ounces) spaghetti**

1/4 **cup (1/2 stick) margarine, butter or spread**

  2 **cloves garlic, finely chopped**

3/4 **cup half-and-half**

  1 **teaspoon dried basil leaves**

  1 **can (9 1/4 ounces) tuna, drained**

1/2 **cup sliced pimiento-stuffed olives**

1/4 **cup grated Parmesan cheese**

Cook and drain spaghetti as directed on package.

2. While spaghetti is cooking, melt margarine in 2-quart saucepan over medium-high heat. Cook garlic in margarine, stirring occasionally, until golden. Stir in half-and-half and basil; heat to boiling.

3. Stir in tuna, olives and cheese; cook until hot. Serve over spaghetti. Sprinkle with chopped fresh parsley if desired.

▽ ▽ ▽ ▽ ▽ ▽ ▽ ▽ ▽ ▽ ▽ ▽ ▽ ▽ ▽

Snappy Seafood Salad
▼ 4 servings

2	cups uncooked medium pasta shells (5 ounces)
2/3	cup mayonnaise or salad dressing
1	tablespoon chili sauce or cocktail sauce
1	small tomato, cut into 8 wedges
1/3	cup small pitted ripe olives
3	cups bite-size pieces lettuce
1	package (8 ounces) frozen imitation crabmeat chunks, thawed

Prep: 7 min

Cook: 11 min

1 Serving: Calories 470 (Calories from Fat 280); Fat 31g (Saturated 5g); Cholesterol 40mg; Sodium 850mg; Carbohydrate 36g (Dietary Fiber 2g); Protein 14g.

1. Cook and drain pasta as directed on package. Rinse with cold water; drain.

2. Mix mayonnaise and chili sauce in large bowl. Add pasta, tomato and olives; toss. Add lettuce and crabmeat; toss.

Quick Tip: Substitute Thousand Island dressing for the mayonnaise and chili sauce and use pre-bagged lettuce for the lettuce pieces.

Easy Saucy Secrets!

Creating tasty sauces for a main dishes or desserts by using a convenience product is super easy! Simple becomes sensational with a few personal touches as suggested below.

Savory Sauces

Start With	Stir In	Serve
Alfredo sauce (1 cup)	• Cooked bacon, chicken, seafood or meat (1/2 to 1 cup) • Cooked fresh or frozen vegetables (1/2 to 1 cup)	Over pasta, mashed or baked potatoes, rice or barley
Gravy (1 cup)	• Sour cream or yogurt (1/4 cup) • Cooked meats or poultry (1/2 to 1 cup) • Sliced mushrooms (1/4 to 1/2 cup)	Over noodles, rice, cooked potatoes, toast or biscuits
Yogurt or sour cream (1 cup)	• Picante sauce and red or green salsa (1/4 to 1/2 cup) • Chopped green onion or sliced ripe olives (2 to 4 tablespoons)	As a dip, in taco salads, burritos, tortilla roll-ups or to top cooked eggs
Barbecue sauce (1 cup)	• Orange marmalade or cranberry sauce (1/2 cup) • Bourbon (1 to 2 tablespoons) • Dijon mustard (1 to 2 tablespoons)	As a baste and sauce for grilled meats and poultry or as a sauce for cocktail hot dogs or meatballs
Pesto (1/2 cup)	• Mayonnaise (1/2 cup plus milk if desired to thin to desired consistency)	As a dressing for pasta or chicken salads
Sour cream (1 cup)	• Horseradish (1 to 2 tablespoons) • Dijon mustard (1 to 2 tablespoons) • Black pepper (1/8 to 1/4 teaspoon)	Use heated as a sauce for cooked beef and cold as a sandwich spread or dip.

Start With	Stir In	Serve
Seasoned tomato chunks or marinara sauce (1 cup)	• Whipping cream or Alfredo sauce (1/4 cup) • Cooked vegetables (as desired) • Cooked meats, sausage or poultry (1/2 to 1 cup)	Over cooked pasta

Easy Dessert Sauces

Start With	Stir In	Serve
Maple syrup (1 cup)	• Toasted nuts (1/4 cup) • Sour cream or plain yogurt (1/2 cup); whisk into syrup • Softened cream cheese (8 ounces); whisk into hot syrup	Over fruit, ice cream, yogurt or pound cake or unfrosted cake
Whole cranberry sauce (1 cup)	• Orange juice (1/2 cup) • Brandy (1 to 2 tablespoons) • Chopped pecans (1/4 cup)	Over ice cream, yogurt or pound cake or unfrosted cake
Chocolate fudge ice cream topping (1 cup)	• Peanut butter (1/4 cup) • Amaretto, Kahlúa, rum or brandy (2 to 4 tablespoons)	Over ice cream, yogurt or brownies

Minestrone Pasta

▼ 6 servings

Not only is this salad great served with grilled chicken, pork, beef or shrimp, it also makes a hearty meal.

Prep: 10 min

Cook: 11 min

1 Serving: Calories 550 (Calories from Fat 160); Fat 18g (Saturated 4g); Cholesterol 5mg; Sodium 810mg; Carbohydrate 86g (Dietary Fiber 10g); Protein 21g.

3 cups uncooked medium pasta shells (7 1/2 ounces)

2/3 cup Italian dressing

1/2 cup shredded Parmesan cheese

2 medium carrots, sliced (1 cup)

1 medium green bell pepper, chopped (1 cup)

1 can (15 to 16 ounces) kidney beans, rinsed and drained

1 can (15 to 16 ounces) garbanzo beans, rinsed and drained

1 can (14 1/2 ounces) Italian-style stewed or diced tomatoes, drained

Cook and drain pasta as directed on package. Toss pasta and remaining ingredients. Serve warm or cold.

Ravioli Marinara

▼ 6 servings

Prep: 5 min

Cook: 13 min

1 Serving: Calories 435 (Calories from Fat 115); Fat 13g (Saturated 5g); Cholesterol 35mg; Sodium 1420mg; Carbohydrate 67g (Dietary Fiber 8g); Protein 21g.

1 package (25 to 27 1/2 ounces) frozen beef- or cheese-filled ravioli

1 jar (28 ounces) chunky spaghetti sauce

1 package (16 ounces) frozen broccoli, green beans, pearl onions and red peppers

1 can (15 to 16 ounces) cannellini beans, rinsed and drained

1/4 cup grated Parmesan cheese

1. Cook and drain ravioli as directed on package.

2. While ravioli is cooking, mix spaghetti sauce, vegetables and beans in 4-quart saucepan. Heat to boiling; reduce heat to low. Simmer uncovered 6 to 8 minutes or until vegetables are tender.

3. Serve vegetable mixture over ravioli; sprinkle with cheese.

Minestrone Pasta ▶

Dill and Lemon Pepper Fettuccine

▼ 4 servings

Prep: 7 min

Cook: 11 min

1 Serving: Calories 315 (Calories from Fat 110); Fat 12g (Saturated 6g); Cholesterol 70mg; Sodium 490mg; Carbohydrate 46g (Dietary Fiber 5g); Protein 11g.

2 medium carrots
2 medium zucchini
8 ounces uncooked fettuccine
1 container (8 ounces) dill dip
3/4 teaspoon lemon pepper

1. Shave carrots and zucchini lengthwise into thin slices with vegetable peeler.

2. Cook fettuccine as directed on package—except add carrots and zucchini about 1 minute before fettuccine is done; drain.

3. Return fettuccine mixture to saucepan. Add dill dip and lemon pepper; toss. Serve immediately.

Salsa Pasta

▼ 4 servings

Prep: 7 min

Cook: 10 min

Stand: 5 min

1 Serving: Calories 365 (Calories from Fat 100); Fat 11g (Saturated 7g); Cholesterol 30mg; Sodium 760mg; Carbohydrate 56g (Dietary Fiber 6g); Protein 17g.

1 package (7 ounces) elbow macaroni (2 cups)
1 cup frozen whole kernel corn
1 jar (8 ounces) salsa (1 cup)
1 small green bell pepper, chopped (1/2 cup)
1 can (14 1/2 ounces) whole tomatoes, undrained
1 cup shredded Cheddar cheese (4 ounces)

1. Cook and drain macaroni as directed on package.

2. While macaroni is cooking, heat remaining ingredients except cheese to boiling in 2-quart saucepan over medium heat, breaking up tomatoes; reduce heat to low. Simmer uncovered 5 minutes.

3. Stir in macaroni. Sprinkle with cheese. Cover and let stand about 5 minutes or until cheese is melted. Serve with freshly ground pepper if desired.

Dill and Lemon Pepper Fettuccine ▶

Betty Crocker's Top 10

Recipe Shortcuts for Pastas and Pizzas

1. Fresh pasta from the deli counter or refrigerated case, such as meat-, cheese-, mushroom- or vegetable-filled tortellini or ravioli; angel hair, fettuccine and linguini

2. Quick-cooking dry pasta, such as ancini de pepe, angel hair, vermicelli, spaghetti, rings, small shells and elbow macaroni

3. Pre-cooked frozen pasta such as lasagna noodles and potato gnocchi

4. Frozen egg noodles—regular and fat-free

5. Ready-made pasta sauces from jars or cans or from the refrigerated case

6. Pre-made pizza crusts—thick or thin

7. English muffins and French bread to use as pizza crust

8. Purchased pizza sauce and jarred, sliced mushrooms and olives

9. Pre-shredded cheese

10. Jazz up frozen pizza by adding your favorite extras such as sliced olives, cooked meat, chopped onions, mushrooms, sun-dried tomatoes, peppers and extra cheese

Gorgonzola Linguine with Toasted Walnuts

▼ 4 servings

8 ounces uncooked linguine

1 tablespoon margarine, butter or spread

1 clove garlic, finely chopped

1 1/2 cups whipping (heavy) cream

1/4 cup dry white wine or chicken broth

1/4 teaspoon salt

1/2 cup crumbled Gorgonzola cheese (2 ounces)

1/4 cup chopped walnuts, toasted

1. Cook and drain linguine as directed on package.

2. While linguine is cooking, melt margarine in 2-quart saucepan over medium heat. Cook garlic in margarine, stirring occasionally, until golden.

3. Stir in whipping cream, wine and salt. Cook, stirring occasionally, until mixture begins to thicken slightly; reduce heat to medium-low.

4. Stir cheese into sauce. Cook, stirring occasionally, until cheese is melted. Toss linguine and sauce. Sprinkle with walnuts.

Prep: 10 min

Cook: 15 min

1 Serving: Calories 615 (Calories from Fat 370); Fat 41g (Saturated 22g); Cholesterol 110mg; Sodium 440mg; Carbohydrate 50g (Dietary Fiber 2g); Protein 14g.

Thai Chicken Pizza

▼ 6 servings

(Photograph on page 217)

Prep: 9 min

Bake: 20 min

1 Serving: Calories 580 (Calories from Fat 270); Fat 30g (Saturated 10g); Cholesterol 65mg; Sodium 1640mg; Carbohydrate 39g (Dietary Fiber 5g); Protein 43g.

6 flour tortillas (8 to 10 inches in diameter)

2/3 cup creamy peanut butter

1/4 cup soy sauce

2 tablespoons seasoned rice vinegar

2 teaspoons sugar

3 cups shredded mozzarella cheese (12 ounces)

2 cups chopped cooked chicken breast

1 package (16 ounces) frozen stir-fry vegetables, thawed

1. Heat oven to 400°.

2. Place tortillas on ungreased cookie sheet. Bake 5 minutes.

3. Mix peanut butter, soy sauce, vinegar and sugar; spread over tortillas. Top each with $1/4$ cup cheese. Spread chicken and vegetables evenly over tortillas. Sprinkle with remaining $1^1/2$ cups cheese.

4. Bake 10 to 15 minutes or until pizzas are hot and cheese is melted.

▼ ▼ ▼ ▼ ▼ ▼ ▼ ▼ ▼ ▼ ▼ ▼ ▼ ▼ ▼ ▼ ▼ ▼ ▼

Hawaiian Pizza

▼ 6 servings

Prep: 5 min

Bake: 10 min

1 Serving: Calories 500 (Calories from Fat 100); Fat 11g (Saturated 6g); Cholesterol 60mg; Sodium 890mg; Carbohydrate 75g (Dietary Fiber 4g); Protein 29g.

1 Italian bread shell or purchased pizza crust (12 to 14 inches in diameter)

1 can (8 ounces) tomato sauce

2 cups cubed cooked chicken

1 can (8 ounces) pineapple tidbits, well drained

1 cup shredded mozzarella cheese (4 ounces)

1. Heat oven to 400°.

2. Place bread shell on ungreased cookie sheet. Spread tomato sauce over bread shell. Top with chicken and pineapple. Sprinkle with cheese. Bake 8 to 10 minutes or until pizza is hot and cheese is melted.

Extra Quick Cooking Tricks

- When making a pasta dish that will be mixed with frozen vegetables, simply add the vegetables to the boiling pasta during the last several minutes of cooking for crisp-tender vegetables. Add vegetables earlier in the process for softer vegetables. Drain pasta and vegetables in a colander and continue with the recipe. Or if you don't want to cook your vegetables at all, place them in the bottom of the colander and when the pasta is cooked, just pour the hot water and pasta right over the vegetables—they will thaw instantly!

- Measuring honey or syrup? Spray measuring spoons and cups with cooking spray first—that sticky stuff will slide right out!

- Want meatloaf in a hurry? Instead of waiting for a whole loaf to bake, press the uncooked meatloaf mixture in muffin tins—you'll cut the baking time in half!

- How do you serve hard ice cream without using a hammer and chisel? Use an electric knife to cut slices of ice cream, or soften very hard ice cream in the refrigerator for 10 to 20 minutes before serving.

- To "frost" cupcakes in a hurry, dip cupcake tops into whipped topping or whipped cream, then sprinkle with nuts, miniature chocolate chips or candy sprinkles.

- Have you ever needed softened butter or margarine in a hurry, but didn't want to microwave it because it might get too soft or melt? Get out the cheese grater and grate the stick of butter or margarine against the large or small holes! Keep the paper or foil on and roll it up on the stick as you go to avoid greasy hands.

Pizza Mexicana

▼ 6 servings

Prep: 10 min

Bake: 10 min

1 Serving: Calories 375
(Calories from Fat 115);
Fat 13g (Saturated 7g);
Cholesterol 70mg;
Sodium 1180mg;
Carbohydrate 40g
(Dietary Fiber 2g);
Protein 27g.

6 pita breads (6 inches in diameter)
1 can (15 ounces) tomato sauce with tomato bits
2 cups shredded or chopped cooked chicken
1 can (4 ounces) chopped green chilies, drained
1 1/2 cups shredded taco-flavored cheese (6 ounces)

1. Heat oven to 350°.

2. Place pita breads on ungreased cookie sheet. Spread tomato sauce over pita breads. Top with chicken and chilies. Sprinkle with cheese. Bake 8 to 10 minutes or until pizzas are hot and cheese is melted.

▼▼▼▼▼▼▼▼▼▼▼▼

Pizza Monterey

▼ 6 servings

Prep: 14 min

Bake: 25 min

1 Serving: Calories 395
(Calories from Fat 215);
Fat 24g (Saturated 10g);
Cholesterol 55mg;
Sodium 980mg;
Carbohydrate 29g
(Dietary Fiber 3g);
Protein 19g.

1 can (10 ounces) refrigerated pizza crust dough
2 cups shredded Monterey Jack cheese (8 ounces)
1 package (16 ounces) frozen broccoli, cauliflower and carrots, thawed
1 cup cubed fully cooked ham
1/2 cup ranch dressing

1. Heat oven to 425°. Lightly grease 12-inch pizza pan or rectangular pan, 13 x 9 x 2 inches.

2. Unroll dough; press into pan. Bake about 10 minutes or until light golden brown.

3. Sprinkle 1 cup of the cheese over dough. Cut large pieces of vegetables into bite-size pieces if necessary. Spread vegetables and ham over dough. Drizzle with dressing. Sprinkle with remaining 1 cup cheese.

4. Bake 12 to 15 minutes or until crust is golden brown.

Pizza Mexicana ▶

Turkey Gyro Pizzas

▼ 4 servings

Prep: 10 min

Bake: 15 min

1 Serving: Calories 535
(Calories from Fat 215);
Fat 24g (Saturated 15g);
Cholesterol 120mg;
Sodium 990mg;
Carbohydrate 39g
(Dietary Fiber 2g);
Protein 43g.

4 pita breads (6 inches in diameter)
1/2 cup sour cream
1 1/2 teaspoons chopped fresh or 1/2 teaspoon dried mint leaves
1 1/2 cups shredded mozzarella cheese (6 ounces)
1/2 pound deli sliced turkey breast, cut into strips
1/2 cup chopped cucumber
1 small tomato, chopped (1/2 cup)
1 cup crumbled feta cheese (4 ounces)

1. Heat oven to 400°.

2. Place pita breads on ungreased cookie sheet. Mix sour cream and mint; spread evenly over pitas. Sprinkle each pita with ¼ cup mozzarella cheese. Top each pita with turkey, cucumber, tomato and feta cheese. Sprinkle remaining ½ cup mozzarella cheese over pitas.

3. Bake 10 to 15 minutes or until cheese is melted.

Deep-Dish Pepperoni Pizza Pie

▼ 6 servings

Prep: 10 min

Bake: 45 min

Stand: 5 min

1 Serving: Calories 505
(Calories from Fat 295);
Fat 33g (Saturated 15g);
Cholesterol 130mg;
Sodium 1460mg;
Carbohydrate 28g
(Dietary Fiber 1g);
Protein 25g.

1 package (15 ounces) refrigerated pie crusts
1 can (14 1/2 ounces) chunky pizza sauce
3 cups shredded mozzarella cheese (12 ounces)
6 ounces sliced pepperoni, chopped
1 can (4 ounces) mushroom stems and pieces, drained
2 eggs

1. Heat oven to 400°.

2. Place 1 pie crust in pie plate, 9 x 1¼ inches. Spread half of the pizza sauce over crust. Mix cheese, pepperoni, mushrooms and eggs; spread evenly over pizza sauce. Spread with remaining pizza sauce.

3. Top with second pie crust. Seal edges and flute. Cut 4 slits in top crust. Bake 35 to 45 minutes or until crust is golden brown. Let stand 5 minutes before cutting.

Turkey Gyro Pizzas ▶

Ranchero Beef Pizza

▼ 6 servings

Fully cooked and sliced barbecued beef is now available in the refrigerated meat section or deli of most grocery stores. If the slices of meat are large, cut them into small chunks before placing on top of the pizza.

1 Italian bread shell or purchased pizza crust
(12 to 14 inches in diameter)

3 cups shredded smoked or regular Cheddar cheese
(12 ounces)

1 pound cooked barbecued beef

4 slices red onion, separated into rings

1. Heat oven to 400°.

2. Place bread shell on ungreased cookie sheet. Sprinkle with 1 cup of the cheese. Top with beef and onion. Sprinkle with remaining 2 cups cheese. Bake 15 to 20 minutes or until hot.

Ranchero Beef Pizza ▶

Pizza Alfredo

▼ 6 servings

Prep: 10 min

Broil: 2 min

1 Serving: Calories 570
(Calories from Fat 360);
Fat 40g (Saturated 18g);
Cholesterol 100mg;
Sodium 1240mg;
Carbohydrate 28g
(Dietary Fiber 2g);
Protein 27g.

1 pound bulk Italian sausage
1 large onion, chopped (1 cup)
1 package (8 ounces) sliced mushrooms
1 container (10 ounces) refrigerated Alfredo sauce
1 twelve-inch loaf French bread, cut horizontally in half
1 cup shredded mozzarella cheese (4 ounces)

1. Set oven control to broil.

2. Cook sausage, onion and mushrooms in 10-inch skillet over medium-high heat until sausage is no longer pink; drain. Stir in Alfredo sauce.

3. Place bread halves, cut sides up, on ungreased cookie sheet. Spread with sausage mixture. Sprinkle with cheese. Broil with tops 5 inches from heat 1 to 2 minutes or until pizzas are hot and cheese begins to brown.

Tex-Mex Pizza

▼ 6 servings

Prep: 10 min

Bake: 10 min

1 Serving: Calories 555
(Calories from Fat 190);
Fat 21g (Saturated 11g);
Cholesterol 55mg;
Sodium 1200mg;
Carbohydrate 75g
(Dietary Fiber 6g);
Protein 22g.

1/4 pound bulk chorizo or pork sausage
1 Italian bread shell or purchased pizza crust (12 to 14 inches in diameter)
1 1/2 cups shredded Monterey Jack cheese (6 ounces)
1 jar (8 ounces) salsa (1 cup)
1 small bell pepper, chopped (1/2 cup)
1/2 cup canned black beans, rinsed and drained, or 1 can (2 1/4 ounces) sliced ripe olives, drained

1. Heat oven to 450°.

2. Cook sausage in 8-inch skillet over medium heat 8 to 10 minutes, stirring occasionally, until no longer pink; drain.

3. Place bread shell on ungreased cookie sheet. Sprinkle with 1 cup of the cheese. Top with salsa, sausage, bell pepper and beans. Sprinkle with remaining cheese. Bake 8 to 10 minutes or until pizza is hot and cheese is melted.

Pizza Alfredo ▶

Meatless Meathall Pizza

▼ 6 servings

This pizza tastes just like traditional Italian sausage pizza, you'd never know it was vegetarian!

Prep: 12 min

Bake: 20 min

1 Serving: Calories 300 (Calories from Fat 115); Fat 13g (Saturated 9g); Cholesterol 30mg; Sodium 810mg; Carbohydrate 25g (Dietary Fiber 2g); Protein 22g.

1 Italian bread shell or purchased pizza crust (12 to 14 inches in diameter)

2 frozen Italian-style vegetable burgers, thawed

3/4 cup pizza sauce

2 tablespoons sliced ripe olives

1 cup shredded mozzarella cheese (4 ounces)

1 cup shredded provolone cheese (4 ounces)

1. Heat oven to 425°.

2. Place bread shell on ungreased cookie sheet. Shape burgers into 1/2-inch balls. Spread pizza sauce over bread shell. Top with burger balls and olives. Sprinkle with cheeses. Bake 18 to 20 minutes or until cheese is melted and light golden brown.

Rice, Beans and Grains

Southern Stir-Fry

▼ 4 servings

Prep: 5 min

Cook: 8 min

1 Serving: Calories 180 (Calories from Fat 10); Fat 1g (Saturated 0g); Cholesterol 0mg; Sodium 380mg; Carbohydrate 41g (Dietary Fiber 8g); Protein 10g.

1	cup cold cooked white rice
1	cup frozen whole kernel corn
1 1/2	teaspoons chopped fresh or 1/2 teaspoon dried thyme leaves
1/2	teaspoon garlic salt
1/8	teaspoon ground red pepper (cayenne)
1	can (15 to 16 ounces) black-eyed peas, rinsed and drained
2	cups lightly packed spinach leaves

1. Spray 12-inch nonstick skillet with nonstick cooking spray; heat over medium-high heat.

2. Cook all ingredients except spinach in skillet, stirring occasionally, until hot. Stir in spinach. Cook until spinach begins to wilt.

Mexican Rice and Bean Bake

▼ 6 servings

Prep: 10 min

Bake: 35 min

Stand: 5 min

1 Serving: Calories 260 (Calories from Fat 90); Fat 10g (Saturated 5g); Cholesterol 90mg; Sodium 700mg; Carbohydrate 35g (Dietary Fiber 7g); Protein 14g.

2	cups cooked brown or white rice
2	eggs
1 1/2	cups picante sauce or salsa
1	cup shredded Cheddar cheese (4 ounces)
1	can (15 to 16 ounces) pinto beans, drained
1/4	teaspoon chili powder

1. Heat oven to 350°. Grease square baking dish, 8 x 8 x 2 inches.

2. Mix rice, eggs, 1/2 cup of the picante sauce and 1/2 cup of the cheese; press in bottom of baking dish.

3. Mix beans and remaining 1 cup picante sauce; spoon over rice mixture. Sprinkle with remaining 1/2 cup cheese and the chili powder.

4. Bake uncovered 30 to 35 minutes or until cheese is melted and bubbly. Let stand 5 minutes before serving.

◀ Preceding page
Mexican Polenta Pie (page 276)

Southern Stir-Fry ▶

Broccoli, Rice and Chili Beans

▼ 6 servings

Prep: 5 min

Cook: 10 min

Stand: 5 min

1 Serving: Calories 360 (Calories from Fat 115); Fat 13g (Saturated 7g); Cholesterol 30mg; Sodium 1260mg; Carbohydrate 50g (Dietary Fiber 8g); Protein 19g.

6 slices bacon, cut into 1-inch pieces
1 cup uncooked instant rice
2 cans (16 ounces each) hot chili beans, undrained
1 package (16 ounces) frozen broccoli cuts, thawed
1 cup shredded process cheese (8 ounces)

1. Cook bacon in 10-inch skillet over medium-high heat, stirring occasionally, until crisp; drain. Set aside.

2. Add rice, beans and broccoli to skillet. Heat to boiling; reduce heat to medium.

3. Cover and simmer 5 minutes; remove from heat. Sprinkle with bacon and cheese. Cover and let stand about 5 minutes or until liquid is absorbed and cheese is melted.

▼ ▼ ▼ ▼ ▼ ▼ ▼ ▼ ▼ ▼ ▼ ▼ ▼ ▼ ▼ ▼ ▼ ▼ ▼

Indian Peas with Vegetables

▼ 4 servings

This vegetarian dish has a mild curry flavor—if you're a curry fan, go ahead and add some more.

Prep: 5 min

Cook: 12 min

1 Serving: Calories 200 (Calories from Fat 35); Fat 4g (Saturated 1g); Cholesterol 0mg; Sodium 350mg; Carbohydrate 40g (Dietary Fiber 12g); Protein 13g.

1 tablespoon vegetable oil
1 teaspoon curry powder
2 jalapeño chilies, seeded and chopped
3 cups cauliflowerets (1 pound)
1/4 cup chicken broth
2 cups frozen green peas, thawed
1 can (15 ounces) black beans, rinsed and drained

1. Heat oil in 10-inch skillet over medium-high heat. Cook curry powder and chilies in oil 2 minutes, stirring occasionally.

2. Stir in cauliflowerets and broth. Cover and cook 3 to 4 minutes or until cauliflowerets are tender. Stir in peas and beans. Cook about 5 minutes, stirring occasionally, until hot.

Broccoli, Rice and Chili Beans ▶

Vegetable Rice Skillet

▼ 4 servings

Cooking the rice and vegetables in broth adds an extra flavor punch.

Prep: 5 min

Cook: 9 min

1 Serving: Calories 315 (Calories from Fat 115); Fat 13g (Saturated 5g); Cholesterol 20mg; Sodium 1540mg; Carbohydrate 40g (Dietary Fiber 4g); Protein 13g.

1 can (14 1/2 ounces) ready-to-serve vegetable broth

2 tablespoons margarine, butter or spread

1 package (16 ounces) frozen cauliflower, carrots and asparagus

1 package (6.2 ounces) long grain and wild rice fast-cooking mix

3/4 cup shredded Cheddar cheese (3 ounces)

1. Heat broth and margarine to boiling in 10-inch skillet. Stir in vegetables, rice and contents of seasoning packet. Heat to boiling; reduce heat to low.

2. Cover and simmer 5 to 6 minutes or until vegetables and rice are tender. Sprinkle with cheese.

Vegetable Rice Skillet ▶

Rice and Cheese Casserole

▼ 4 servings

Carrots and cheese make a great flavor combination in this satisfying casserole.

Prep: 10 min

Bake: 45 min

1 Serving: Calories 435 (Calories from Fat 215); Fat 24g (Saturated 13g); Cholesterol 160mg; Sodium 980mg; Carbohydrate 38g (Dietary Fiber 3g); Protein 20g.

1 cup uncooked instant rice

1 package (8 ounces) shredded process cheese (2 cups)

2 cups packaged shredded carrots

4 medium green onions, chopped (1/4 cup)

2 eggs

1/4 cup milk

1/3 cup dry bread crumbs

1 tablespoon margarine, butter or spread, melted

1. Heat oven to 350°. Grease square pan, 8 x 8 x 2 inches.

2. Prepare rice as directed on package.

3. Mix rice, cheese, carrots, onions, eggs and milk in pan. Sprinkle with bread crumbs. Drizzle with margarine. Bake uncovered 40 to 45 minutes or until knife inserted in center comes out clean.

Rice and Cheese Casserole ▶

Wild Rice–Pecan Patties

▼ 4 servings (8 patties)

These nutty patties are delicious served in sandwich buns and topped with cranberry sauce.

Prep: 12 min

Cook: 12 min

1 Serving: Calories 280
(Calories from Fat 125);
Fat 14g (Saturated 3g);
Cholesterol 85mg;
Sodium 360mg;
Carbohydrate 32g
(Dietary Fiber 2g);
Protein 8g.

2 cups cooked wild rice

1 cup soft bread crumbs

1/3 cup chopped pecans

1/2 teaspoon garlic salt

2 eggs

1 jar (2 1/2 ounces) mushroom stems and pieces, drained and finely chopped

1 jar (2 ounces) diced pimientos, drained

2 tablespoons vegetable oil

1. Mix all ingredients except oil.

2. Heat oil in 10-inch skillet over medium heat. Scoop wild rice mixture by ⅓ cupfuls into skillet; flatten to ½ inch. Cook about 3 minutes on each side or until light brown. Remove patties from skillet. Cover and keep warm while cooking remaining patties.

Wild Rice and Broccoli Timbales

▼ 4 servings

Fresh basil and spaghetti sauce add an Italian twist to this attractive dish.

Prep: 15 min

Cook: 10 min

1 Serving: Calories 230 (Calories from Fat 100); Fat 11g (Saturated 6g); Cholesterol 25mg; Sodium 670mg; Carbohydrate 29g (Dietary Fiber 4g); Protein 8g.

1 package (2 3/4 ounces) instant simmer-and-serve wild rice*

1 package (10 ounces) frozen chopped broccoli

1 1/3 cups water

1 tablespoon chopped fresh or 1 teaspoon dried basil leaves

1/4 teaspoon salt

1 package (3 ounces) cream cheese, softened

2 tablespoons grated Parmesan cheese

1 cup spaghetti or marinara sauce

1. Heat wild rice, broccoli, water, basil and salt to boiling in 2-quart saucepan, stirring occasionally to break up broccoli; reduce heat to low. Cover and simmer 6 to 7 minutes or until wild rice and broccoli are tender. Stir in cheeses until blended.

2. Meanwhile, heat spaghetti sauce in 1-quart saucepan over medium heat until hot; reduce heat to low, stirring occasionally.

3. Spray 10-ounce custard cup with nonstick cooking spray. To form timbales, press 3/4 cup wild rice mixture into cup; invert onto serving plate. Repeat with remaining mixture. Or, if desired, omit shaping mixture into timbales and spoon mixture onto serving plates.

4. Pour spaghetti sauce over timbales. Sprinkle with additional Parmesan cheese if desired.

*Two cups cooked instant wild rice can be substituted.

Wild Rice and Broccoli Timbales ▶

Red Beans and Rice

▼ 4 servings

The traditional Cajun red beans and rice is a favorite in New Orleans, the city whose nickname is "The Big Easy." The name is also perfect for this recipe, which is big on satisfaction and so easy to make!

Prep: 5 min

Cook: 14 min

1 Serving: Calories 295 (Calories from Fat 90); Fat 10g (Saturated 4g); Cholesterol 25mg; Sodium 1100mg; Carbohydrate 40g (Dietary Fiber 5g); Protein 16g.

1 package (4 1/2 ounces) Cajun-style rice and sauce mix
2 cups water
2 fully cooked spicy smoked sausage links (2 1/2 to 3 ounces), thinly sliced (from 16 ounce package)
1 can (15 to 16 ounces) kidney beans, rinsed and drained

1. Heat rice and sauce mix, water and sausage to boiling in 2-quart saucepan; reduce heat to low.

2. Cook uncovered about 10 minutes, stirring occasionally, until rice is tender. Stir in beans; heat 1 minute.

Red Beans and Rice ▶

Refried Bean Roll-Ups

▼ 4 servings

Prep: 15 min

Cook: 5 min

1 Serving: Calories 430 (Calories from Fat 110); Fat 12g (Saturated 4g); Cholesterol 15mg; Sodium 1190mg; Carbohydrate 71g (Dietary Fiber 9g); Protein 18g.

  1 can (16 ounces) refried beans

1/2 cup salsa

1/2 teaspoon chili powder

  8 flour tortillas (8 to 10 inches in diameter)

  1 cup shredded lettuce

1/2 cup shredded Monterey Jack cheese (2 ounces)

1. Mix beans, salsa and chili powder in 1-quart saucepan. Heat over medium heat about 5 minutes, stirring occasionally, until warm.

2. Spoon about 1/4 cup bean mixture onto center of each tortilla; spread slightly. Top with lettuce and cheese. Fold over sides and ends of tortillas. Serve with additional salsa if desired.

▼▼▼▼▼▼▼▼▼▼▼▼▼▼▼▼▼▼▼▼▼▼▼

Sweet Potatoes and Black Beans

▼ 4 servings

Prep: 10 min

Cook: 17 min

1 Serving: Calories 270 (Calories from Fat 10); Fat 1g (Saturated 0g); Cholesterol 0mg; Sodium 230mg; Carbohydrate 63g (Dietary Fiber 9g); Protein 11g.

  3 sweet potatoes, peeled and cut into 3/4-inch cubes (3 cups)

3/4 cup orange juice

  2 teaspoons cornstarch

  1 teaspoon pumpkin pie spice, apple pie spice or ground cinnamon

1/4 teaspoon ground cumin

  1 can (15 ounces) black beans, rinsed and drained

  1 cup cooked rice

1. Place sweet potatoes in 2-quart saucepan; add enough water just to cover sweet potatoes. Heat to boiling; reduce heat to low. Cover and simmer 10 to 12 minutes or until tender; drain and set aside.

2. Mix orange juice, cornstarch, pie spice and cumin in same saucepan. Heat to boiling. Boil about 1 minute, stirring constantly, until thickened.

3. Stir in sweet potatoes, beans and rice. Cook about 2 minutes or until hot.

Greek Pasta Salad

▼ 5 servings

1 1/4	cups uncooked rosamarina (orzo) pasta (8 ounces)
2	cups thinly sliced cucumber
1/2	cup chopped red onion
1/2	cup Italian dressing
1	medium tomato, chopped (3/4 cup)
1	can (15 to 16 ounces) garbanzo beans, rinsed and drained
1	can (4 ounces) sliced ripe olives, drained
1/2	cup crumbled feta cheese (2 ounces)

Prep: 15 min

Chill: 1 hr

1 Serving: Calories 425 (Calories from Fat 170); Fat 19g (Saturated 5g); Cholesterol 15mg; Sodium 670mg; Carbohydrate 56g (Dietary Fiber 5g); Protein 13g.

1. Cook and drain pasta according to package directions. Rinse with cold water; drain.

2. Mix all ingredients except cheese in glass or plastic bowl. Cover and refrigerate at least 1 hour to blend flavors but no longer than 24 hours. Top with cheese.

Mediterranean Couscous and Beans

▼ 4 servings

Prep: 5 min

Cook: 4 min

Stand: 5 min

1 Serving: Calories 540 (Calories from Fat 55); Fat 6g (Saturated 3g); Cholesterol 10mg; Sodium 620mg; Carbohydrate 108g (Dietary Fiber 9g); Protein 22g.

3 cups chicken broth

2 cups uncooked couscous

1/2 cup raisins or currants

1/4 teaspoon pepper

1/8 teaspoon ground red pepper (cayenne)

1 small tomato, chopped (1/2 cup)

1 can (15 to 16 ounces) garbanzo beans, rinsed and drained

1/3 cup crumbled feta cheese

1. Heat broth to boiling in 3-quart saucepan. Stir in remaining ingredients except cheese; remove from heat.

2. Cover and let stand about 5 minutes or until liquid is absorbed; stir gently. Sprinkle each serving with cheese.

Cook Now for Later

Leftover pasta or rice, whether planned or not, can be a real time-saver during the week when every minute counts to get an evening meal on the table.

Make extra pasta, rice or barley and refrigerate or freeze. (To prevent pasta from sticking, toss it with a small amount of oil.) Cooked pasta, rice or other grains can be covered and stored in the refrigerator for up to 5 days. To freeze, place desired amount in re-sealable plastic freezer bags or containers with lids, label and date. Freeze up to 6 months and thaw in refrigerator before using.

There are 3 ways to reheat pasta, rice and other grains—note that frozen pasta and grains must be thawed first.

1. Place in rapidly boiling water for up to 2 minutes. Drain and serve immediately.

2. Place in colander and pour boiling water over it until heated through. Drain and serve immediately.

3. Place in microwave-safe dish or container. Microwave tightly covered on high for 1 to 3 minutes or until heated through. Serve immediately.

Mediterranean Couscous and Beans ▶

Black Bean and Rice Burgers

▼ 4 servings

Black beans are packed with complex carbohydrates, fiber, vitamins, minerals and protein. They also have no cholesterol and are very low in fat and sodium. Beans have another plus—they are a tasty addition to almost any dish.

Prep: 10 min

Cook: 10 min

1 Serving: Calories 320 (Calories from Fat 55); Fat 6g (Saturated 3g); Cholesterol 10mg; Sodium 620mg; Carbohydrate 61g (Dietary Fiber 9g); Protein 14g.

- 1 can (15 to 16 ounces) black beans, rinsed and drained
- 1 cup cooked rice
- 1 small onion, finely chopped (1/4 cup)
- 2 tablespoons salsa
- 1/4 cup sour cream
- 1/4 cup salsa
- 4 hamburger buns, split
- Lettuce leaves

1. Mash beans. Mix beans, rice, onion and 2 tablespoons salsa.

2. Spray 10-inch skillet with nonstick cooking spray; heat over medium-high heat. Spoon bean mixture by $1/2$ cupfuls into skillet; flatten to $1/2$ inch. Cook 4 to 5 minutes on each side or until light brown. Remove patties from skillet. Cover and keep warm while cooking remaining patties.

3. Mix sour cream and $1/4$ cup salsa; spread on buns. Top with burgers and lettuce.

Betty Crocker's Top 10

Recipe Shortcuts for Rice, Beans and Grains

1. Rice—try white, brown, converted, instant, wild, jasmine or Arborio

2. Quick-cooking barley

3. Couscous—both plain and flavored mixes

4. Seasoned rice mixes, such as white and wild rice, herb and chicken-flavored

5. Dry packets of seasoning mixes, such as salad dressings, sauces and Mexican flavors

6. Packaged, seasoned grain mixes

7. Canned plain beans, such as kidney, garbanzo or black

8. Canned seasoned beans, such as chili beans

9. Canned baked beans you fix-up with extras, such as cooked bacon, molasses, brown sugar or diced ham

10. Packaged dehydrated beans to which you just add water, such as refried beans

Warm Bean and Spinach Salad

▼ 4 servings

This new salad idea bursts with flavor, color and texture. Try it when you want the lightness of a salad combined with the heartiness of a main dish.

Prep: 12 min

Cook: 3 min

1 Serving: Calories 365 (Calories from Fat 200); Fat 22g (Saturated 5g); Cholesterol 10mg; Sodium 680mg; Carbohydrate 34g (Dietary Fiber 8g); Protein 16g.

1	package (10 ounces) washed fresh spinach
1	can (15 to 16 ounces) cannellini beans, rinsed and drained
1	large bell pepper, coarsely chopped (1 1/2 cups)
2/3	cup Italian dressing
1/4	teaspoon garlic pepper
1/2	cup shredded mozzarella cheese (2 ounces)

1. Remove large stems from spinach; tear spinach into bite-size pieces. Place spinach in large bowl. Add beans; set aside.

2. Heat bell pepper and dressing to boiling in 1-quart saucepan; reduce heat to low. Cook uncovered 2 minutes, stirring occasionally. Stir in garlic pepper.

3. Pour bell pepper mixture over spinach and beans; toss. Sprinkle with cheese. Serve warm.

Warm Bean and Spinach Salad ▶

Three-Bean Barley Salad

▼ 4 servings

In this recipe, use quick-cooking barley to keep preparation time down.

Prep: 5 min

Chill: 1 hr

1 Serving: Calories 290
(Calories from Fat 170);
Fat 19g (Saturated 3g);
Cholesterol 0mg;
Sodium 410mg;
Carbohydrate 30g
(Dietary Fiber 6g);
Protein 6g.

> 1 can (15 ounces) three-bean salad, undrained
> 1 1/2 cups cooked barley
> 2 medium tomatoes, chopped (1 1/2 cups)
> 3 cups bite-size pieces salad greens
> 2 tablespoons sunflower nuts, toasted

1. Mix three-bean salad, barley and tomatoes. Cover and refrigerate about 1 hour or until chilled.

2. Spoon bean mixture onto salad greens. Sprinkle with nuts.

Quick Tip: Use quick-cooking barley versus regular barley and reduce the cooking time from 50 minutes to 12 minutes.

Polenta with Cheese

▼ 6 servings

Polenta comes from northern Italy. In America, it's often known as cornmeal mush.

Prep: 5 min

Cook: 15 min

1 Serving: Calories 200
(Calories from Fat 90);
Fat 10g (Saturated 6g);
Cholesterol 25mg;
Sodium 480mg;
Carbohydrate 19g
(Dietary Fiber 1g);
Protein 9g.

> 1 cup yellow cornmeal
> 1/2 cup water
> 3 cups boiling water
> 1 teaspoon salt
> 1 tablespoon margarine or butter
> 1 1/2 cups shredded Swiss or Gruyère cheese (6 ounces)

1. Mix cornmeal and 1/2 cup water in 2-quart saucepan. Stir in 3 cups boiling water and the salt. Cook, stirring constantly, until mixture thickens and boils; reduce heat to low.

2. Cover and simmer 10 minutes, stirring occasionally; remove from heat. Stir until smooth. Stir in margarine and 1 cup of the cheese. Sprinkle each serving with remaining cheese.

Three-Bean Barley Salad ▶

Grits and Black-Eyed Peas

▼ 4 servings

Look for instant grits in the cereal section of your supermarket.

Prep: 8 min

Bake: 40 min

1 Serving: Calories 315
(Calories from Fat 90);
Fat 10g (Saturated 6g);
Cholesterol 75mg;
Sodium 1340mg;
Carbohydrate 48g
(Dietary Fiber 10g);
Protein 18g.

4 packets (1 ounce each) instant grits (from 12-ounce package)

1 cup boiling water

1 jar (5 ounces) process cheese spread with bacon

1 egg, slightly beaten

1 can (15 to 16 ounces) black-eyed peas, rinsed and drained

1 can (14 1/2 ounces) diced tomatoes, drained

1. Heat oven to 350°. Grease square pan, 8 x 8 x 2 inches.

2. Empty grits into pan; stir in boiling water. Stir in cheese spread and egg; continue stirring until cheese is melted. Gently stir in black-eyed peas and tomatoes.

3. Bake uncovered 35 to 40 minutes or until firm.

▼ ▼ ▼ ▼ ▼ ▼ ▼ ▼ ▼ ▼ ▼ ▼ ▼ ▼ ▼ ▼ ▼ ▼ ▼

Barley-Vegetable Sauté

▼ 4 servings

Prep: 10 min

Cook: 8 min

1 Serving: Calories 365
(Calories from Fat 35);
Fat 4g (Saturated 1g);
Cholesterol 0mg;
Sodium 350mg;
Carbohydrate 83g
(Dietary Fiber 15g);
Protein 14g.

1 tablespoon margarine, butter or spread

1 large onion, chopped (1 cup)

1 clove garlic, finely chopped

4 cups cooked barley

2 tablespoons chopped fresh or 2 teaspoons dried thyme leaves

1/2 teaspoon salt

1 package (16 ounces) frozen whole kernel corn, thawed

1 package (10 ounces) frozen lima beans, thawed

1. Melt margarine in 10-inch skillet over medium-high heat. Cook onion and garlic in margarine about 2 minutes, stirring occasionally, until onion is crisp-tender.

2. Stir in remaining ingredients. Cook about 5 minutes, stirring occasionally, until hot.

Couscous-Stuffed Tomatoes

▼ 4 servings

These savory stuffed tomatoes are nice served with a crisp green salad and breadsticks.

2/3 cup uncooked couscous

4 medium tomatoes

1 small zucchini, coarsely shredded (1 cup)

2 tablespoons grated Parmesan cheese

1 tablespoon chopped fresh or 1 teaspoon dried basil leaves

1/4 teaspoon salt

1/4 teaspoon pepper

1. Heat oven to 350°. Grease square pan, 8 x 8 x 2 inches.

2. Cook couscous as directed on package. Meanwhile, cut ¹/₂-inch slice from top of each tomato; scoop out pulp and reserve for other use.

3. Stir remaining ingredients into couscous. Spoon mixture into tomatoes. Place tomatoes in pan. Bake uncovered about 35 minutes or until tomatoes are tender.

Prep: 15 min

Bake: 35 min

1 Serving: Calories 145 (Calories from Fat 10); Fat 1g (Saturated 1g); Cholesterol 2mg; Sodium 190mg; Carbohydrate 30g (Dietary Fiber 2g); Protein 6g.

Mexican Polenta Pie

(Photograph on page 249)

▼ 6 servings

Prep: 15 min

Bake: 40 min

Stand: 5 min

1 Serving: Calories 160
(Calories from Fat 55);
Fat 6g (Saturated 3g);
Cholesterol 50mg;
Sodium 410mg;
Carbohydrate 22g
(Dietary Fiber 3g);
Protein 8g.

3/4 cup cornmeal

2 cups water

1/4 teaspoon salt

1 egg, slightly beaten

1 can (15 to 16 ounces) chili beans, drained

3/4 cup shredded Monterey Jack cheese with jalapeño peppers (3 ounces)

1/3 cup crushed corn or taco chips

1. Heat oven to 375°. Grease pie plate, 9 x 1¼ inches.

2. Mix cornmeal, water and salt in medium 2-quart saucepan. Heat to boiling, stirring constantly; reduce heat to medium. Cook about 6 minutes, stirring frequently, until mixture is very thick. Remove from heat; quickly let stand 5 minutes, stir in egg.

3. Spread cornmeal mixture in pie plate. Bake uncovered 15 minutes. Spread beans over cornmeal mixture; sprinkle with cheese and corn chips.

4. Bake uncovered 20 minutes or until center is set. Let stand 5 minutes before serving.

Sandwiches, Soups and Chilies

Italian Vegetable Focaccia Sandwich

▼ 4 servings

Prep: 5 min

Bake: 30 min

1 Serving: Calories 540 (Calories from Fat 215); Fat 24g (Saturated 9g); Cholesterol 75mg; Sodium 1400mg; Carbohydrate 57g (Dietary Fiber 3g); Protein 27g.

1 cheese and herb focaccia bread (10 to 12 inches in diameter) cut horizontally in half

2 cups shredded mozzarella cheese (8 ounces)

2 cups deli marinated Italian vegetable salad, drained and coarsely chopped

1. Heat oven to 400°.

2. Place bottom half of bread on cookie sheet. Sprinkle with 1 cup of the cheese. Spread vegetables over cheese. Sprinkle with remaining cheese. Top with top of bread.

3. Bake 12 to 15 minutes or until golden brown. Cut into wedges.

Chicken BLT Sandwiches

▼ 4 sandwiches

Prep: 5 min

Cook: 20 min

1 Sandwich: Calories 325 (Calories from Fat 135); Fat 15g (Saturated 4g); Cholesterol 70mg; Sodium 520mg; Carbohydrate 19g (Dietary Fiber 2g); Protein 30g.

2 teaspoons vegetable oil

4 skinless boneless chicken breast halves (about 1 pound)

1/4 cup bacon-and-tomato or Thousand Island dressing

4 whole wheat sandwich buns, split

8 slices tomato

4 slices bacon, cooked

4 lettuce leaves

1. Heat oil in 10-inch skillet over medium-high heat. Cook chicken in oil 15 to 20 minutes, turning once, until juice of chicken is no longer pink when centers of thickest pieces are cut.

2. Spread dressing on cut sides of buns. Layer chicken, tomato, bacon and lettuce on bottoms of buns. Top with tops of buns.

Preceding Page
Italian Vegetable Focaccia Sandwich,
Tex-Mex Minestrone Soup (page 298)

Betty Crocker's Good and Easy Cookbook

Betty Crocker's Top 10

Recipe Shortcuts for Sandwiches, Soups and Chilies

1. Canned beef, chicken or Oriental broth—regular and reduced salt
2. Dry soup mixes with seasonings and packaged mixed beans for soup
3. Frozen soups from the grocery store
4. Fresh soup from the deli
5. Pre-sliced deli and packaged meats
6. Pre-sliced deli and packaged cheeses
7. Purchased jars of sandwich spread, such as mayonnaise/mustard, sweetened mayonnaise relish combinations and horseradish sauce
8. Purchased submarine or hoagie sandwiches
9. Pre-cooked and purchased sandwich fillings such as canned meats and seafood, meat spreads, barbecued meats, breaded chicken patties or grilled chicken breast fillets
10. Bagged lettuce mixtures to use in sandwiches

Ham and Cheese Tortilla Roll-Ups

▼ 5 servings

Looking for quick picnic ideas? Just pack the tortillas and the filling for this sandwich in your cooler. Bring along chips, fresh fruit, bottled water and some cookies to complete your meal.

Prep: 10 min

1 Serving: Calories 575 (Calories from Fat 270); Fat 30g (Saturated 12g); Cholesterol 60mg; Sodium 1020mg; Carbohydrate 58g (Dietary Fiber 3g); Protein 21g.

1 1/2 cups shredded Cheddar cheese (6 ounces)

1/4 cup mayonnaise or salad dressing

1/4 cup sour cream

1 can (11 ounces) whole kernel corn with red and green peppers, drained

10 flour tortillas (6 to 8 inches in diameter)

10 slices (1 ounce each) deli fully cooked ham

Cilantro sprigs, if desired

1. Mix cheese, mayonnaise, sour cream and corn.

2. Top each tortilla with 1 slice ham. Spread 2 tablespoons corn mixture over ham. Top with cilantro. Roll up. Serve immediately.

Ham and Cheese Tortilla Roll-Ups ▶

Quick Chicken Barbecue Sandwiches

▼ 6 servings

Prep: 5 min

Cook: 5 min

1 Serving: Calories 185 (Calories from Fat 35); Fat 4g (Saturated 1g); Cholesterol 15mg; Sodium 1000mg; Carbohydrate 28g (Dietary Fiber 1g); Protein 10g.

1   cup barbecue sauce
3   packages (2.5 ounces each) sliced smoked chicken, cut into 1-inch strips (3 cups)
6   hamburger buns, split

Mix barbecue sauce and chicken in 2-quart saucepan. Heat to boiling; reduce heat to low. Cover and simmer about 5 minutes or until hot. Fill buns with chicken mixture.

Timesaving Tricks

Chances are good that you're already "dovetailing"—doing several things at the same time. For example, when you put water on to boil, you go ahead and start another job, such as chopping onions, washing lettuce or setting the table. That's called dovetailing, and it's time efficient.

You'll also appreciate these dovetailing ideas:

- Turn the oven on to heat. While oven is heating, grease and flour baking sheets/pans and get recipe ingredients or baking mixes out.

- Adjust oven rack and turn the oven on to broil. Assemble recipes to be broiled while the broiler is heating.

- While dinner is in the oven, pour yourself a refreshing beverage and sit down to read the mail or newspaper! You could also put a load of wash in the machine or make the next day's lunches.

Quick Chicken Barbecue Sandwiches ▶

Hot Chicken Sub

▼ 6 servings

Want to shave 15 minutes off this sub's preparation time? Microwave the chicken breast patties—dinner's so fast it almost makes itself.

Prep: 10 min

Bake: 20 min

1 Serving: Calories 435 (Calories from Fat 200); Fat 22g (Saturated 4g); Cholesterol 25mg; Sodium 810mg; Carbohydrate 48g (Dietary Fiber 3g); Protein 14g.

6 frozen breaded chicken breast patties
1 loaf (1 pound) French bread, cut horizontally in half
1/2 cup creamy Italian dressing
Lettuce
1 large tomato, thinly sliced

1. Prepare chicken as directed on package.

2. Spread cut sides of bread with dressing. Layer lettuce, hot chicken patties and tomato on bottom half of bread. Top with top half of bread. Cut into 6 slices.

▼▼▼▼▼▼▼▼▼▼▼▼▼▼▼▼▼▼

Roast Beef Pocket Sandwiches

▼ 4 servings (2 pockets each)

Prep: 10 min

1 Serving: Calories 210 (Calories from Fat 65); Fat 7g (Saturated 3g); Cholesterol 35mg; Sodium 240mg; Carbohydrate 22g (Dietary Fiber 1g); Protein 16g.

1 cup plain yogurt
1 1/2 teaspoons chopped fresh or 1/2 teaspoon dried dill weed
1 teaspoon mustard
1 medium bell pepper, chopped (1 cup)
2 pita breads (6 inches in diameter), cut crosswise in half
1/3 pound thinly sliced roast beef
1 cup alfalfa sprouts

Mix yogurt, dill weed and mustard. Stir in bell pepper. Fill pita bread halves with yogurt mixture, beef and sprouts.

Quick Tip: Substitute 1 cup of dill dip from the deli or dairy case for the yogurt, fresh dill and mustard.

Hot Chicken Sub ▶

Ham and Apple Broiled Cheese Sandwiches

▼ 8 open-face sandwiches

Prep: 10 min

Broil: 4 min

1 Sandwich: Calories 210 (Calories from Fat 110); Fat 12g (Saturated 5g); Cholesterol 35mg; Sodium 490mg; Carbohydrate 16g (Dietary Fiber 1g); Protein 10g.

4	English muffins, split
2 1/2	tablespoons mayonnaise
2 1/2	tablespoons mustard
8	thin slices (1/2 ounce each) boiled or baked ham
1	medium apple, finely chopped (1 cup)
8	thin slices (1 ounce each) Cheddar or American cheese

1. Set oven control to broil. Place muffin halves on ungreased cookie sheet. Broil with tops 4 to 6 inches from heat until lightly toasted.

2. Spread mayonnaise and mustard on muffin halves. Top each with 1 slice ham, trimming overhanging edges. Spread each with 2 tablespoons apple. Top with cheese slice.

3. Broil with tops 4 to 6 inches from heat 1 to 2 minutes or until cheese is melted and light brown.

Rachel Sandwiches

▼ 6 sandwiches

Prep: 10 min

1 Serving: Calories 385 (Calories from Fat 205); Fat 23g (Saturated 7g); Cholesterol 45mg; Sodium 780mg; Carbohydrate 35g (Dietary Fiber 5g); Protein 14g.

4	ounces sliced Swiss cheese
1/4	pound sliced corned beef
3	cups creamy deli coleslaw
12	slices dark rye bread

Layer cheese, corned beef and coleslaw on 6 slices of bread. Top with remaining bread slices. Cut sandwiches in half.

Rachel Sandwiches ▶

Oriental-Style Chicken Noodle Soup

▼ 4 servings

Prep: 10 min

Cook: 8 min

1 Serving: Calories 225 (Calories from Fat 70); Fat 8g (Saturated 3g); Cholesterol 60mg; Sodium 570mg; Carbohydrate 16g (Dietary Fiber 1g); Protein 23g.

- 3 cups water
- 1 package (3 ounces) chicken-flavor ramen noodles
- 2 cups cut-up cooked chicken
- 2 medium stalks bok choy (with leaves), cut into 1/4-inch slices
- 1 medium carrot, sliced (1/2 cup)
- 1 teaspoon sesame oil, if desired

1. Heat water to boiling in 3-quart saucepan. Break block of noodles (reserve flavor packet). Stir noodles, chicken, bok choy and carrot into water. Heat to boiling; reduce heat to low. Simmer uncovered 3 minutes, stirring occasionally.

2. Stir in contents of flavor packet and sesame oil.

▼▼▼▼▼▼▼▼▼▼▼▼▼▼▼▼▼

Broiled Seafood Sandwiches

▼ 4 open-face sandwiches

Prep: 10 min

Broil: 2 min

1 Sandwich: Calories 405 (Calories from Fat 280); Fat 31g (Saturated 8g); Cholesterol 70mg; Sodium 490mg; Carbohydrate 15g (Dietary Fiber 2g); Protein 18g.

- 1 cup mixed bite-size pieces cooked crabmeat, lobster or shrimp*
- 1 cup shredded Swiss cheese (4 ounces)
- 1/2 cup mayonnaise or salad dressing
- 1 medium green onion, thinly sliced (2 tablespoons)
- 4 slices whole-grain bread, toasted

1. Set oven control to broil. Mix all ingredients except toast. Top toast slices with seafood mixture. Place sandwiches on ungreased cookie sheet.

2. Broil with tops 4 to 6 inches from heat about 2 minutes or until seafood mixture is hot and bubbly.

*1 cup bite-size pieces cooked fish (salmon, cod, halibut, tuna, swordfish) can be substituted for the crabmeat, lobster or shrimp.

Oriental-Style Chicken Noodle Soup ▶

Vegetable, Beef and Tortellini Soup

▼ 4 servings

Prep: 5 min

Cook: 10 min

1 Serving: Calories 190 (Calories from Fat 55); Fat 6g (Saturated 2g); Cholesterol 60mg; Sodium 1080mg; Carbohydrate 23g (Dietary Fiber 2g); Protein 13g.

4 cups water
1 package (1.4 ounces) vegetable soup and recipe mix
1 package (9 ounces) refrigerated beef-filled tortellini
1 package (10 ounces) frozen chopped spinach, thawed and squeezed to drain
Grated Parmesan cheese, if desired

1. Mix water and soup mix in 3-quart saucepan. Heat to boiling, stirring occasionally; reduce heat to low.

2. Stir in tortellini and spinach. Simmer uncovered about 5 minutes, stirring occasionally, until tortellini is tender. Sprinkle each serving with cheese.

Vegetable, Beef and Tortellini Soup ▶

Italian Vegetable Soup

▼ 8 servings

Prep: 10 min

Cook: 20 min

1 Serving: Calories 265
(Calories from Fat 145);
Fat 16g (Saturated 6g);
Cholesterol 45mg;
Sodium 900mg;
Carbohydrate 16g
(Dietary Fiber 3g);
Protein 17g.

	1	pound bulk Italian sausage

1 pound bulk Italian sausage

1 medium onion, sliced

1 1/2 cups water

2 tablespoons chopped fresh or 1 teaspoon dried basil leaves

2 medium zucchini or yellow summer squash, cut into 1/4-inch slices (4 cups)

1 can (16 ounces) whole tomatoes, undrained

1 can (15 to 16 ounces) garbanzo beans, drained

1 can (10 1/2 ounces) condensed beef broth

1. Cook sausage and onion in 3-quart saucepan over medium-high heat 8 to 10 minutes, stirring occasionally, until sausage is no longer pink; drain.

2. Stir in remaining ingredients, breaking up tomatoes. Heat to boiling; reduce heat to low. Cover and simmer about 5 minutes or until zucchini is tender.

3. Sprinkle each serving with grated Parmesan cheese if desired.

Italian Vegetable Soup ▶

Seafood Chowder in Bread Bowls

▼ 6 servings

These bread bowls add extra fun to eating soup! Set the table with serrated steak knives, as well as forks and spoons, to make eating the bowl as easy as spooning up this creamy chowder.

Prep: 8 min

Cook: 8 min

1 Serving: Calories 355 (Calories from Fat 70); Fat 8g (Saturated 3g); Cholesterol 55mg; Sodium 1130mg; Carbohydrate 57g (Dietary Fiber 5g); Protein 19g.

6 large hard rolls (about 3 1/2 inches in diameter)

2 cans (19 ounces each) ready-to-serve New England clam chowder

1 package (16 ounces) frozen potatoes, sweet peas and carrots

1 package (4 ounces) frozen cooked salad shrimp, thawed

1. Cut thin 2-inch round slice from tops of rolls. Remove bread from inside of each roll, leaving 1/2-inch shell on side and bottom. Reserve bread trimmings for another use.

2. Mix soup, vegetables and shrimp in 3-quart saucepan. Cook over medium-high heat, stirring occasionally, until vegetables are tender and soup is hot.

3. Fill soup bowls one-third full with soup. Place rolls on top of soup. Spoon additional soup into rolls, allowing some soup to overflow into bowls.

Seafood Chowder in Bread Bowls

Super Sandwich Selections

If the lunch bunch is betting bored of the same old leftovers or luncheon meats and peanut butter and jelly sandwiches on the usual bread, here are some new, quick and easy ideas. We've also included important food safety information for packing lunches.

Sandwich Idea

Tortilla Roll-Ups: Fill sandwiches as suggested below; roll up and wrap in plastic wrap.

- Spread tortillas with mayonnaise seasoned with taco seasoning mix; top with sliced turkey breast, lettuce, shredded cheese and sliced ripe olives.
- Spread tortillas with peanut butter; top with banana slices and raisins.
- Spread tortillas with plain or flavored cream cheese; top with chopped fresh vegetables.

Bread Ideas

Instead of sliced bread try your favorite sandwich fillings with:

- Mini-hoagie rolls
- Hot dog and hamburger buns
- Pita bread
- Soft bagels
- Focaccia bread

Snack Ideas

- Baby carrots
- Popcorn or pretzels
- Rice and popcorn cakes
- Dried fruit
- Cereal
- String cheese
- Cereal or breakfast bars
- Single-serve pudding or gelatin
- Yogurt

Super-Quick Lunches

- Purchased dry soups or noodles in a cup (just add boiling water or heat in the microwave)
- Pre-packaged lunches (meat, cheese, crackers) from the luncheon meat section of the grocery store
- Purchased meals in a cup that can be microwaved
- Purchased canned tuna lunch kits that include dressing and crackers

Smart Sandwich Strategies

The Night Before: To save time in the morning, assemble lunches the night before. If not already frozen, remember to place small size freezer packs in the freezer so they will be ready to go in the morning. Place juice boxes in the freezer—by lunchtime, juice will be thawed. Cookies and bars can be frozen as well. Don't freeze sandwiches, however, because when thawed they will be very soggy!

Cold Lunch Food Safety: Unless a refrigerator is available at work or school, perishable foods cannot stand at room temperature for more than two hours without the risk of bacterial growth and food poisoning. The safe way to carry lunches is to use freezer packs designed for coolers which are now available in small sizes perfect for insulated lunch bags and mini-coolers. Always keep these packs in the freezer so they will be ready-to-go. Wide-mouth thermos containers also work well for toting food. Pre-chill the thermos by filling it with *ice* water, replace cap and allow it to stand for 5 minutes; drain and fill with *completely chilled* food.

Hot Lunch Food Safety: To carry hot foods such as soup, chili, stew or casserole, use a wide-mouth thermos. Pre-heat the thermos by filling it with *very hot* water, replace cap and allow it to stand for 5 minutes; drain and fill with *very hot* food.

Lunch Bags: Items like insulated bags, mini-coolers, freezer packs, microwave containers with lids, plastic containers with lids, re-sealable plastic bags and foods in single-serving sizes make putting lunches together much easier.

Tex-Mex Minestrone Soup

▼ 5 servings

If you like your Mexican food hot, use hot salsa in this soup. (Photograph on page 277.)

Prep: 4 min

Cook: 12 min

1 Serving: Calories 215 (Calories from Fat 90); Fat 10g (Saturated 5g); Cholesterol 25mg; Sodium 940mg; Carbohydrate 26g (Dietary Fiber 8g); Protein 13g.

1 package (16 ounces) frozen garlic-seasoned pasta and vegetables

1 jar (16 ounces) thick-and-chunky salsa (2 cups)

1 can (15 ounces) black beans, rinsed and drained

1 can (2 1/4 ounces) sliced ripe olives, drained

2 cups water

1 teaspoon chili powder

1 cup shredded Cheddar cheese (4 ounces)

Sour cream, if desired

1. Mix all ingredients except cheese and sour cream in Dutch oven or 4-quart saucepan. Heat to boiling; reduce heat to low. Simmer uncovered 5 to 7 minutes, stirring occasionally, until vegetables are tender.

2. Top each serving with cheese and sour cream.

▼ ▼ ▼ ▼ ▼ ▼ ▼ ▼ ▼ ▼ ▼ ▼ ▼ ▼ ▼ ▼ ▼ ▼

Ham 'n Corn Chowder

▼ 4 servings

Prep: 10 min

Cook: 15 min

1 Serving: Calories 225 (Calories from Fat 65); Fat 7g (Saturated 3g); Cholesterol 25mg; Sodium 900mg; Carbohydrate 33g (Dietary Fiber 4g); Protein 11g.

1/2 cup chopped thinly sliced fully cooked ham

1 1/2 cups milk

1 package (16 ounces) frozen whole kernel corn

1 can (10 3/4 ounces) condensed cream of celery soup

2 medium green onions, sliced (1/4 cup)

Mix ham, milk, corn and soup in 3-quart saucepan. Heat to boiling, stirring occasionally; reduce heat to low. Simmer uncovered 10 minutes, stirring occasionally. Sprinkle with onions.

Ham 'n Corn Chowder ▶

California Beef Stew

▼ 4 servings

Prep: 5 min

Cook: 35 min

1 Serving: Calories 320
(Calories from Fat 135);
Fat 15g (Saturated 5g);
Cholesterol 60mg;
Sodium 780mg;
Carbohydrate 25g
(Dietary Fiber 7g);
Protein 28g.

> 1 pound beef stew meat
> 1 can (10 1/2 ounces) condensed beef consommé
> 1/2 cup dry red wine or water
> 1 package (16 ounces) frozen stew vegetables
> 1 can (6 ounces) pitted whole ripe olives, drained
> Chopped parsley, if desired

1. Mix beef, consommé and wine in Dutch oven. Heat to boiling, stirring occasionally; reduce heat to low. Cover and simmer 15 minutes.

2. Stir in vegetables. Cover and simmer about 15 minutes or until beef is tender. Stir in olives; heat through. Sprinkle each serving with parsley.

California Beef Stew ▶

Cincinnati-Style Chili

▼ 5 servings

Prep: 5 min

Cook: 20 min

1 Serving: Calories 465 (Calories from Fat 160); Fat 18g (Saturated 9g); Cholesterol 55mg; Sodium 930mg; Carbohydrate 56g (Dietary Fiber 8g); Protein 28g.

1/2	pound ground beef
1	large onion, chopped (1 cup)
1	can (16 ounces) whole tomatoes, undrained
1	can (15 to 16 ounces) kidney beans, undrained
1	can (8 ounces) tomato sauce
1	tablespoon chili powder
1	package (7 ounces) spaghetti
1 1/4	cups shredded Cheddar cheese (5 ounces)

1. Cook beef and about $3/4$ cup of the onions in 3-quart saucepan over medium heat 8 to 10 minutes, stirring occasionally, until beef is brown and onions are tender; drain.

2. Stir in tomatoes, beans, tomato sauce and chili powder; breaking up tomatoes. Cook uncovered over medium heat about 10 minutes, stirring occasionally, until desired consistency.

3. Meanwhile, cook and drain spaghetti as directed on package.

4. For each serving, spoon about $3/4$ cup beef mixture over 1 cup hot spaghetti. Sprinkle each serving with $1/4$ cup cheese and about 1 tablespoon remaining onion.

Quick Tip: Substitute 2 cans meat chili for the ground beef, onions, tomatoes, beans, tomato sauce and chili powder.

Cincinnati-Style Chili ▶

White Bean–Chicken Chili

▼ 6 servings

Love chili, but ready for a change of pace? Then try this flavorful white chili made with chicken.

Prep: 6 min

Cook: 13 min

1 Serving: Calories 245 (Calories from Fat 65); Fat 7g (Saturated 2g); Cholesterol 55mg; Sodium 400mg; Carbohydrate 22g (Dietary Fiber 5g); Protein 29g.

2 tablespoons margarine, butter or spread

1 large onion, coarsely chopped (1 cup)

2 cloves garlic, finely chopped

3 cups cubed cooked chicken breast

1/2 teaspoon ground cumin

2 cans (10 ounces each) diced tomatoes and green chilies

1 can (15 to 16 ounces) great northern beans, rinsed and drained

Sour cream, if desired

1. Melt margarine in Dutch oven over medium-high heat. Cook onion and garlic in margarine, stirring occasionally, until onion is tender.

2. Stir in remaining ingredients except sour cream. Heat to boiling; reduce heat to low. Simmer uncovered 2 to 3 minutes, stirring occasionally, until hot. Top each serving with sour cream.

Italian Chili

▼ 4 servings

Prep: 6 min

Cook: 15 min

1 Serving: Calories 710 (Calories from Fat 395); Fat 44g (Saturated 16g); Cholesterol 125mg; Sodium 2310mg; Carbohydrate 41g (Dietary Fiber 8g); Protein 46g.

1 1/4 pounds bulk Italian sausage
   1 large green bell pepper, coarsely chopped (1 1/2 cups)
   1 large onion, coarsely chopped (1 cup)
   2 cans (14 1/2 ounces each) Italian-style stewed tomatoes, undrained
   1 can (15 to 16 ounces) garbanzo beans, rinsed and drained
   1 can (8 ounces) tomato sauce
   1 cup shredded mozzarella cheese (4 ounces)

1. Cook sausage, bell pepper and onion in Dutch oven over medium-high heat 8 to 10 minutes, stirring occasionally, until sausage is no longer pink; drain.

2. Stir in tomatoes, beans and tomato sauce. Cook about 5 minutes, stirring occasionally, until hot. Sprinkle each serving with cheese.

▼ ▼ ▼ ▼ ▼ ▼ ▼ ▼ ▼ ▼ ▼ ▼ ▼ ▼ ▼ ▼ ▼ ▼ ▼

Picante Pork Chili

▼ 4 servings

Prep: 6 min

Cook: 15 min

1 Serving: Calories 280 (Calories from Fat 90); Fat 10g (Saturated 3g); Cholesterol 35mg; Sodium 850mg; Carbohydrate 37g (Dietary Fiber 10g); Protein 20g.

   1 medium onion, chopped (1/2 cup)
   1 medium green bell pepper, chopped (1 cup)
   1 clove garlic, finely chopped
1/2 pound ground pork
   1 cup salsa
   1 teaspoon chili powder
   1 can (15 to 16 ounces) pinto beans, rinsed and drained
   1 can (16 ounces) whole tomatoes, undrained

1. Cook onion, bell pepper, garlic and pork in 3-quart saucepan over medium heat, stirring frequently, until pork is no longer pink; drain if necessary.

2. Stir in remaining ingredients, breaking up tomatoes. Heat to boiling; reduce heat to low. Cover and simmer 10 minutes.

Salads and Vegetables

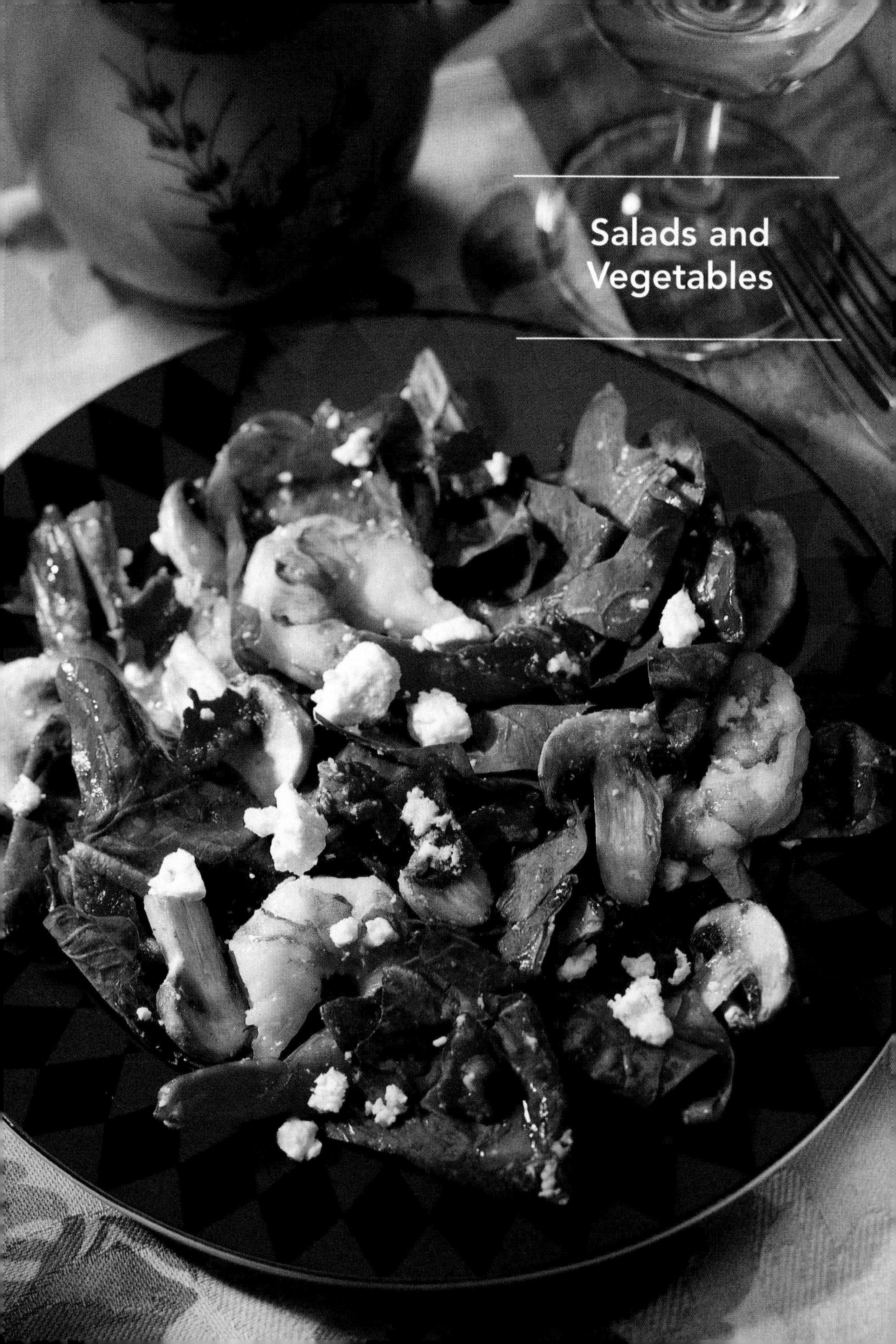

Chicken Salad Oriental

▼ 4 servings

Prep: 10 min

1 Serving: Calories 375 (Calories from Fat 205); Fat 23g (Saturated 4g); Cholesterol 55mg; Sodium 320mg; Carbohydrate 18g (Dietary Fiber 2g); Protein 26g.

1/4 cup vegetable oil

3 tablespoons sugar

2 tablespoons red wine or seasoned rice vinegar

1 tablespoon soy sauce

1/4 pound Chinese pea pods, strings removed (1 cup), cut diagonally in half

3 cups coleslaw mix

1 can (10 ounces) chunk light chicken, drained

1/2 cup sliced almonds, toasted

Mix oil, sugar, vinegar and soy sauce in large bowl. Add remaining ingredients; toss to coat. Serve immediately.

Spinach-Shrimp Salad with Hot Bacon Dressing

▼ 4 servings

Prep: 8 min

Cook: 10 min

1 Serving: Calories 200 (Calories from Fat 90); Fat 10g (Saturated 6g); Cholesterol 140mg; Sodium 590mg; Carbohydrate 8g (Dietary Fiber 1g); Protein 20g.

4 slices bacon, cut into 1-inch pieces

1/4 cup white vinegar

1 tablespoon sugar

1/4 teaspoon ground mustard (dry)

4 cups lightly packed bite-size pieces spinach leaves

1 cup sliced mushrooms (3 ounces)

1 cup crumbled feta cheese (4 ounces)

1/2 pound cooked, peeled and deveined medium shrimp

1. Cook bacon in 10-inch skillet over medium-high heat, stirring occasionally, until crisp. Stir in vinegar, sugar and mustard; continue stirring until sugar is dissolved.

2. Toss spinach, mushrooms, cheese and shrimp in large bowl. Drizzle hot bacon dressing over spinach mixture; toss to coat. Serve immediately.

◄ Preceding Page
Spinach-Shrimp Salad with
Hot Bacon Dressing

Chicken Salad Oriental ►

Couscous-Vegetable Salad

▼ 6 servings

Serve this flavorful salad with a loaf of French bread for a light dinner or with grilled chicken or steak for a heartier meal.

Prep: 11 min

Cook: 6 min

1 Serving: Calories 315 (Calories from Fat 180); Fat 20g (Saturated 4g); Cholesterol 5mg; Sodium 105mg; Carbohydrate 30g (Dietary Fiber 3g); Protein 7g.

1	cup uncooked couscous
1	tablespoon olive or vegetable oil
1	medium zucchini, cut into 1/4-inch slices (2 cups)
1	medium yellow summer squash, cut into 1/4-inch slices (1 1/2 cups)
1	large red bell pepper, cut into 1-inch pieces
1/2	medium red onion, cut into 8 wedges
1	container (7 ounces) refrigerated pesto with sun-dried tomatoes or regular pesto
2	tablespoons balsamic or cider vinegar

1. Prepare couscous as directed on package.

2. Meanwhile, heat oil in 10-inch nonstick skillet over medium-high heat. Cook zucchini, yellow squash, bell pepper and onion in oil about 5 minutes, stirring frequently, until crisp-tender.

3. Toss couscous, vegetable mixture, pesto and vinegar in large bowl. Serve warm or cool.

Couscous-Vegetable Salad ▶

Quick Caesar Salad

▼ 6 servings

Look for bags of pre-torn and washed salad greens that have romaine lettuce or a romaine lettuce blend—using them makes preparation time for this salad just about a minute!

Prep: 10 min

1 Serving: Calories 165 (Calories from Fat 115); Fat 13g (Saturated 3g); Cholesterol 5mg; Sodium 340mg; Carbohydrate 9g (Dietary Fiber 1g); Protein 4g.

1/2 cup Caesar dressing

1 large or 2 small bunches romaine, torn into bite-size pieces (10 cups)

1 cup Caesar or garlic-flavored croutons

1/3 cup freshly grated Parmesan cheese

Freshly ground pepper

Pour dressing into large salad bowl. Add romaine; toss until coated with dressing. Sprinkle with croutons, cheese and pepper; toss.

Quick Tip: Purchase a Caesar salad kit in the produce section of the store. It includes the lettuce, croutons, dressing and cheese.

Honey-Lime Fruit Salad

▼ 4 servings

Prep: 10 min

1 Serving: Calories 270
(Calories from Fat 70);
Fat 8g (Saturated 2g);
Cholesterol 0mg;
Sodium 10mg;
Carbohydrate 50g
(Dietary Fiber 4g);
Protein 4g.

1/2 cup honey
1/4 cup frozen limeade concentrate, thawed
  2 teaspoons poppy seeds, if desired
  4 cups cut-up fresh fruit
1/4 cup slivered almonds, toasted

Mix honey, limeade concentrate and poppy seeds in medium bowl. Carefully toss fruit with honey mixture. Sprinkle with almonds.

Quick Tip: Purchase cut-up fruit from the produce or deli area of the grocery store.

Sweet Potato Fries

▼ 4 servings

Instead of using the same old salt and pepper, try your favorite seasoning salt or herb blend on these low-fat fries.

Prep: 10 min

Bake: 30 min

1 Serving: Calories 170
(Calories from Fat 65);
Fat 7g (Saturated 1g);
Cholesterol 0mg;
Sodium 280mg;
Carbohydrate 28g
(Dietary Fiber 3g);
Protein 2g.

4 medium sweet potatoes (1 1/2 pounds)

2 tablespoons vegetable oil

1/2 teaspoon salt

1/4 teaspoon pepper

1. Heat oven to 450°. Grease jelly roll pan, 15$^1/_2$ x 10$^1/_2$ x 1 inch.

2. Cut potatoes into $^1/_2$-inch wedges. Toss potatoes and oil. Sprinkle with salt and pepper. Place potatoes in single layer in pan.

3. Bake uncovered 25 to 30 minutes, turning occasionally, until potatoes are golden brown and tender when pierced with fork.

How to Cut It for Quicker Cooking

Unfortunately, the phrase, "no matter how you cut it" doesn't apply to quick-cooking techniques. Imagine fresh, creamy, made-from-scratch mashed potatoes in 10 minutes, not 20 minutes! How food is cut up before it's cooked can affect its cooking time. Cutting potatoes, carrots, celery, onions, broccoli and other vegetables into small pieces will shorten cooking. Cutting meat into smaller pieces or flattening chicken breasts to about 1/4-inch thick will also speed up the cooking time.

Of course, if a particular size or shape is important to the finished dish, you may want to stay with your usual preparation method—and look for other time-saving ideas.

2-in-1 Dinners

Call it "power cooking," call it a smart move, just don't call it left-overs! Some cooks have mastered the craft of taking a little of this and a little of that from a previous meal and turning it into a terrific-tasting meal for another night. With a little extra planning, you can learn to cook once, but eat twice and still enjoy meals with pizzazz!

Most of us know the technique for using up leftovers—add a few things to refresh them, and there's your second meal. But consider this angle: Plan to make extra food the first time, so it can be used again in other ways. What are the advantages of planning meals this way? Just to name a few, you get variety, flexibility and less stress on the cook! To get you started on the right track, we've listed some ideas below to double your cooking power:

First Meal	Second Meal
Chili	Cincinnati-style Chili (served over spaghetti with shredded Cheddar cheese), chili dogs, spoon over cornbread
Meatballs	Meatball sandwiches on hoagie buns with cooked onions, bell pepper strips and spaghetti sauce; in stew, soup or stroganoff
Grilled Flank Steak	Fajitas, tacos, burritos or Caesar salad
Grilled Chicken Breasts	Hot or cold sandwiches, pasta and sauce, salads, burritos, tacos, enchiladas, fajitas, soups or chili
Roast Beef or Pork	Hash, stir-fry, soups, chili, stew, casseroles, hot or cold sandwiches, tacos, burritos, enchiladas, stroganoff or salads
Pasta	Any pasta or casserole recipe, use as a side-dish instead of rice or potatoes, lo mein, stir-fry, spaghetti or pasta pie

Garlic-Parmesan Potatoes

▼ 8 servings

This is fancy enough for entertaining, yet so easy! You'll want to serve it to company, and it's also a great time-saving idea for holiday meals.

Prep: 5 min

Bake: 30 min

1 Serving: Calories 185 (Calories from Fat 100); Fat 11g (Saturated 5g); Cholesterol 25mg; Sodium 230mg; Carbohydrate 19g (Dietary Fiber 1g); Protein 4g.

1 package (1.25 pounds) refrigerated mashed potatoes (2 2/3 cups)

1 cup sour cream

1/3 cup grated Parmesan cheese

2 large cloves garlic, finely chopped

20 frozen potato wedges with skins (from 24-ounce package)

2 tablespoons grated Parmesan cheese

Chopped fresh chives, if desired

1. Heat oven to 400°. Spray quiche dish, 9 x 1½ inches, with nonstick cooking spray.

2. Mix mashed potatoes, sour cream, ⅓ cup cheese and the garlic in quiche dish; spread evenly. Arrange potato wedges in spoke fashion with 2 wedges in center on mashed potato mixture. Sprinkle with 2 tablespoons cheese.

3. Bake 25 to 30 minutes or until hot. Sprinkle with chives. Cut into wedges.

Garlic-Parmesan Potatoes ▶

Roasted Seasoned Vegetables

▼ 4 servings

Here's a delicious new way to fit vegetables into your family meals. They'll ask you to make this again and again!

Prep: 6 min

Bake: 35 min

1 Serving: Calories 355 (Calories from Fat 80); Fat 9g (Saturated 2g); Cholesterol 0mg; Sodium 1900mg; Carbohydrate 70g (Dietary Fiber 7g); Protein 6g.

  2 tablespoons vegetable oil

 12 baby-cut carrots

  8 small red potatoes, cut into fourths

  1 medium zucchini, cut into 1-inch slices

  1 medium onion, cut into 8 wedges

  1 pouch original seasoning mix for oven-browned fresh potatoes (from 3-ounce package)

1. Heat oven to 425°.

2. Pour oil into rectangular pan, 13 x 9 x 2 inches, spreading oil to coat bottom of pan.

3. Place carrots, potatoes, zucchini and onion in shaker bag from package. Add seasoning mix; shake just until vegetables are coated. Empty vegetables into pan. Bake uncovered 25 to 35 minutes or until carrots are tender.

Roasted Seasoned Vegetables ▶

Grilling Vegetables

Grilling is a favorite cooking method for vegetables, imparting a distinctive and delicious flavor.

1. Grill vegetables 4 to 5 inches over medium heat.

2. Brush occasionally with melted margarine or butter, olive or vegetable oil, or your favorite bottled or homemade salad dressing to prevent them from drying out.

3. Use the chart below as an easy guide for *approximate* grilling times; types of grills and weather conditions vary and will affect the time.

Timetable for Grilling Vegetables

Time	Vegetable
10 minutes	Carrots, small whole, partially cooked* Cherry tomatoes, whole Mushrooms, whole Onions, cut into 1/2-inch slices Potatoes, cut into 1-inch wedges, partially cooked*
15 minutes	Bell peppers, cut into 1-inch strips Eggplant, cut into 1/4-inch slices Green beans, whole Pattypan squash, whole Zucchini, cut into 3/4-inch pieces
20 minutes	Asparagus spears, whole Broccoli spears, cut lengthwise in half Cauliflowerets, cut lengthwise in half Corn on the cob, husked and wrapped in aluminum foil

*Before grilling, cook in boiling water 5 to 10 minutes or just until crisp-tender.

▼ ▼ ▼ ▼ ▼ ▼ ▼ ▼ ▼ ▼ ▼ ▼ ▼ ▼

Caesar Vegetable Medley

▼ 6 servings

Tired of the same old peas and carrots? For extraordinary veggies, try this flavorful side dish.

2 tablespoons olive or vegetable oil

2 packages (16 ounces each) frozen cauliflower, carrots and snow pea pods

1 envelope (1.2 ounces) Caesar salad dressing mix

1. Heat oil in 10-inch nonstick skillet over medium-high heat.

2. Add vegetables and dressing mix to oil. Cover and cook 5 to 7 minutes, stirring frequently until vegetables are crisp-tender.

Prep: 2 min

Cook: 7 min

1 Serving: Calories 115 (Calories from Fat 45); Fat 5g (Saturated 1g); Cholesterol 0mg; Sodium 450mg; Carbohydrate 13g (Dietary Fiber 0g); Protein 4g.

Betty Crocker's Top 10

Recipe Shortcuts for Salads and Vegetables

▶ **1.** Packaged lettuce mixtures with or without dressing and croutons

▶ **2.** Packaged coleslaw or broccoli slaw mixes and bottled coleslaw dressing

▶ **3.** Shelf-stable and refrigerated salad dressing; dry salad dressing mixes

▶ **4.** Fresh vegetable mixes or individual cut-up vegetables from the produce section—look for stir-fry mixtures, broccoli, carrots, cauliflower, rutabaga and turnips

▶ **5.** Frozen vegetable mixtures with or without sauces

▶ **6.** Dry mixes or seasoned liquids to season oven-roasted potatoes or vegetables

▶ **7.** Spice or herb blends to sprinkle on vegetables

▶ **8.** Purchased salad topping sprinkles from the spice aisle and packaged croutons

▶ **9.** Butter-flavored sprinkles

▶ **10.** Salad and fixings from the grocery store or restaurant salad bar

Pesto Vegetables

▼ 5 servings

Prep: 5 min

Cook: 10 min

1 Serving: Calories 135 (Calories from Fat 100); Fat 11g (Saturated 3g); Cholesterol 5mg; Sodium 125mg; Carbohydrate 7g (Dietary Fiber 2g); Protein 4g.

1 **package (16 ounces) frozen broccoli, cauliflower and carrots**

1/3 **cup pesto**

2 **tablespoons grated Parmesan cheese**

Cook and drain vegetables as directed on package. Toss vegetables and pesto. Sprinkle with cheese.

Pesto Vegetables ▶

Sesame Pea Pods

▼ 6 servings

Prep: 10 min

Cook: 5 min

1 Serving: Calories 40
(Calories from Fat 25);
Fat 3g (Saturated 0g);
Cholesterol 0mg;
Sodium 2mg;
Carbohydrate 3g
(Dietary Fiber 1g);
Protein 1g.

  1 tablespoon sesame oil

1/2 pound Chinese pea pods, strings removed (2 cups)

  1 tablespoon sesame seeds

  1 medium red or yellow bell pepper, cut into thin strips

1. Heat oil in 10-inch skillet over medium-high heat. Add pea pods and sesame seeds. Cook about 2 minutes, stirring, until pea pods are crisp-tender.

2. Stir in bell pepper. Cook about 2 minutes, stirring, until bell pepper is crisp-tender.

Sesame Pea Pods ▶

Ginger Glazed Carrots

▼ 6 servings

Prep: 12 min

Cook: 10 min

1 Serving: Calories 75
(Calories from Fat 35);
Fat 4g (Saturated 3g);
Cholesterol 10mg;
Sodium 50mg;
Carbohydrate 11g
(Dietary Fiber 2g);
Protein 1g.

6 medium carrots, thinly sliced (3 cups)
2 tablespoons packed brown sugar
2 tablespoons margarine or butter
1/2 teaspoon ground ginger

1. Heat 1 inch water to boiling in 3-quart saucepan; add carrots. Heat to boiling; reduce heat to medium. Cover and simmer about 5 minutes or until crisp-tender; drain and set aside.

2. Cook brown sugar, margarine and ginger in same saucepan over medium heat, stirring constantly, until bubbly. Stir in carrots. Cook 2 to 4 minutes over low heat, stirring occasionally, until carrots are glazed and hot.

Ginger Glazed Carrots ▶

Zesty Salsa Corn

▼ 6 servings

Prep: 5 min

Cook: 5 min

1 Serving: Calories 85
(Calories from Fat 10);
Fat 1g (Saturated 0g);
Cholesterol 00mg;
Sodium 130mg;
Carbohydrate 19g
(Dietary Fiber 3g);
Protein 3g.

> 1 package (16 ounces) frozen corn
>
> 1/2 cup salsa
>
> 1/4 cup sliced ripe olives

Cook corn according to package directions. Stir in salsa and olives; cook until hot.

Quick Eggs and Breads

Sausage and Egg Breakfast Pizza

▼ 4 servings

If you'd like a little variety, add a few vegetables such as chopped tomato, green bell pepper or mushrooms before topping with the final cheese layer.

Prep: 6 min

Cook: 6 min

Bake: 12 min

1 Serving: Calories 485 (Calories from Fat 350); Fat 39g (Saturated 18g); Cholesterol 410mg; Sodium 1090mg; Carbohydrate 2g (Dietary Fiber 0g); Protein 31g.

1 package (8 ounces) brown-and-serve pork sausage links, cut into 1/2-inch pieces

6 eggs, beaten

4 Italian bread shells (6 inches in diameter)

1 1/2 cups shredded Cheddar cheese (6 ounces)

1. Heat oven to 400°. Spray 10-inch nonstick skillet with non-stick cooking spray; heat over medium heat. Cook sausage in skillet 3 minutes or until brown. Remove from heat; set aside.

2. Pour eggs into skillet. As mixture begins to set at bottom and side, gently lift cooked portions with spatula so that thin, uncooked portion can flow to bottom. Do not stir. Cook 4 to 5 minutes or until eggs are thickened throughout but still moist.

3. Place bread shells on ungreased cookie sheets. Sprinkle with half of the cheese. Top each with eggs and sausage. Sprinkle with remaining cheese. Bake 10 to 12 minutes or until cheese is melted.

◀ Preceding Page
Vegetable Frittata (page 343)

Sausage and Egg Breakfast Pizza ▶

Betty Crocker's Top 10

Recipe Shortcuts for Quick Eggs and Bread

1. Liquid egg products, refrigerated or frozen

2. Cartons of seasoned quiche filling from the freezer case

3. Scramble eggs by stirring in your favorite omelet fillings— it's quicker than an omelet

4. Extra eggs—make them for dinner instead of breakfast

5. Frozen egg, pancake or waffle breakfast meal combinations

6. Frozen doughnuts, rolls and coffee cakes—just thaw and serve

7. Canned dough products such as biscuits, breadsticks, dinner and sweet rolls

8. Packaged bread and muffin mixes

9. Frozen bread dough and rolls

10. Prepare your own breakfast sandwiches using scrambled or fried eggs and serve between bagels, corn muffins, English muffins or biscuits

Tex-Mex Scrambled Eggs

▼ 4 servings

  2 teaspoons vegetable oil

  3 corn tortillas (5 to 6 inches in diameter), cut into thin strips

  1 small onion, chopped (1/4 cup)

  8 eggs, beaten

  1 cup salsa

1/4 cup sour cream

  2 medium green onions, chopped (2 tablespoons)

Prep: 10 min

Cook: 11 min

1 Serving: Calories 255 (Calories from Fat 145); Fat 16g (Saturated 5g); Cholesterol 435mg; Sodium 570mg; Carbohydrate 16g (Dietary Fiber 3g); Protein 15g.

1. Heat oil in 10-inch nonstick skillet over medium-high heat. Cook tortilla strips and 1/4 cup onion in oil about 5 minutes, stirring frequently, until tortilla strips are crisp.

2. Pour eggs over tortilla mixture; reduce heat to medium. As mixture begins to set at bottom and side, gently lift cooked portions with spatula so that thin, uncooked portion can flow to bottom. Do not stir. Cook 4 to 5 minutes or until eggs are thickened throughout but still moist.

3. Top each serving with salsa, sour cream and green onions.

Home-Style Scrambled Eggs

▼ 4 servings

Do your scrambled eggs end up looking more like rice or peas than the fluffy, moist, thick eggs from a restaurant? The trick is to avoid stirring them as much as possible while they cook.

Prep: 10 min

Cook: 11 min

1 Serving: Calories 250 (Calories from Fat 170); Fat 19g (Saturated 5g); Cholesterol 320mg; Sodium 630mg; Carbohydrate 11g (Dietary Fiber 1g); Protein 10g.

6 eggs
3/4 teaspoon salt
3 tablespoons water
1/4 cup (1/2 stick) margarine, butter or spread
1 cup refrigerated diced potatoes with onions or frozen hash brown potatoes
1 small zucchini, chopped (1 cup)
1 medium tomato, seeded and chopped (3/4 cup)

1. Beat eggs, salt and water.

2. Melt margarine in 10-inch skillet over medium heat. Cook potatoes, zucchini and tomato in margarine, stirring occasionally, until hot.

3. Pour egg mixture over vegetable mixture. As mixture begins to set at bottom and side, gently lift cooked portions with spatula so that thin, uncooked portion can flow to bottom. Do not stir. Cook 3 to 5 minutes or until eggs are thickened throughout but still moist.

Home-Style Scrambled Eggs ▶

Southwestern Egg Bake

▼ 6 servings

Make-ahead recipes like this one turn brunch into a relaxed meal. Prepare the stuffing mixture and refrigerate up to a day in advance. Add eggs and bake 20 minutes before serving time.

Prep: 8 min

Bake: 28 min

1 Serving: Calories 520 (Calories from Fat 295); Fat 33g (Saturated 13g); Cholesterol 320mg; Sodium 1020mg; Carbohydrate 41g (Dietary Fiber 3g); Protein 18g.

2 cups corn bread stuffing crumbs
1 can (15 1/4 ounces) whole kernel corn, drained
1 can (4 ounces) chopped green chilies
1/2 cup sour cream
7 eggs
1 cup shredded Monterey Jack cheese (4 ounces)
Salsa, if desired

1. Heat oven to 400°. Spray rectangular baking dish, 13 x 9 x 2 inches, with nonstick cooking spray.

2. Mix stuffing, corn, chilies, sour cream and 1 egg in large bowl. Spread evenly in baking dish.

3. Make 6 indentations in stuffing mixture with back of spoon. Break 1 egg into each indentation. Pierce yolk of each egg with fork.

4. Bake uncovered 20 to 25 minutes or until egg whites and yolks are firm, not runny. Sprinkle cheese over stuffing mixture. Bake 2 to 3 minutes or until cheese is melted. Serve with salsa.

Southwestern Egg Bake ▶

Crustless Spinach Quiche

▼ 6 servings

This flavorful egg dish will be a hit at your next brunch or lunch—it also makes entertaining a snap!

Prep: 5 min

Bake: 33 min

1 Serving: Calories 350 (Calories from Fat 245); Fat 27g (Saturated 12g); Cholesterol 220mg; Sodium 610mg; Carbohydrate 9g (Dietary Fiber 1g); Protein 19g.

2 cups shredded mozzarella cheese (8 ounces)

1/2 cup whipping (heavy) cream

1/3 cup pesto

1 package (10 ounces) frozen chopped spinach, thawed and squeezed to drain

5 eggs

1 cup chunky spaghetti sauce

1. Heat oven to 375°. Spray quiche dish, 9 x 1½ inches, with nonstick cooking spray.

2. Mix 1½ cups of the cheese, the whipping cream, pesto, spinach and eggs until well blended; pour into quiche dish.

3. Bake 25 to 30 minutes or until knife inserted in center comes out clean. Sprinkle with remaining ½ cup cheese. Bake 2 to 3 minutes or until cheese is melted.

4. Meanwhile, heat spaghetti sauce in small saucepan until hot; keep warm. To serve, cut into wedges. Serve with spaghetti sauce.

Quick Microwave Tips

The following tips provide quick, practical helps for preparing food. Foods are grouped alphabetically—be sure to use *microwavable utensils only*. For more tips, refer to the charts in the front and back inside covers.

Timetable

Food, Utensil and Tips		Amount	
Dried Fruit (softening) 2-cup measure; cover tightly	High (100%)	1 cup raisins or apricot halves sprinkled with 1 teaspoon water	45 seconds to 1 minute, let stand a few minutes
Fruit, refrigerated (warming) Place on floor of microwave	High (100%)	1 medium	15 seconds
Honey (crystallized) Jar or plastic container with lid removed; uncovered	High (100%)	8-ounce jar or plastic container	30 seconds to 2 minutes, stirring every 30 seconds
Ice Cream (softening) Original container; remove any foil	Low (10%)	1/2 gallon	1 1/2 minutes, rotating 1/2 turn after 1 minute
Syrup (heating) Measuring cup or pitcher; uncovered. Stir before serving.	High (100%)	1/2 cup	45 to 60 seconds
Vegetables or Fruits, frozen (thawing) Remove outer wrap from box; pierce box or bag with fork. Place on paper towel. Turn over after half the time; drain.	Medium-low (30%)	9- to 12-ounce package 16-ounce bag	6 to 10 minutes 8 to 12 minutes
Water (boiling) Glass measuring cup	High (100%)	1 cup	2 to 3 minutes

Vegetable Frittata

▼ 6 servings

(Photograph on page 331)

2 tablespoons margarine, butter or spread
2 medium bell peppers, chopped (1 cup)
1 medium onion, chopped (1/2 cup)
8 eggs
1/2 teaspoon salt
1/8 teaspoon pepper
1/2 cup shredded Swiss cheese (2 ounces)

1. Melt margarine in ovenproof 10-inch nonstick skillet over medium heat.

2. Cook bell peppers and onion in margarine, stirring occasionally, until onion is tender.

3. Beat eggs, salt and pepper in medium bowl. Stir in $1/2$ cup cheese. Pour egg mixture over pepper mixture. Cover and cook over medium-low heat 8 to 10 minutes or until eggs are set and light brown on bottom.

4. Set oven control to broil. Broil frittata with top 4 to 6 inches from heat about 2 minutes or until golden brown. Cut into wedges.

Prep: 10 min

Cook: 14 min

Broil: 2 min

1 Serving: Calories 175 (Calories from Fat 115); Fat 13g (Saturated 5g); Cholesterol 290mg; Sodium 350mg; Carbohydrate 4g (Dietary Fiber 1g); Protein 11g.

Bacon and Swiss Waffles

▼ Five 8-inch waffles

Serve these hearty waffles with cheese sauce or syrup.

Prep: 5 min

Bake: 8 min

1 8-Inch Waffle:
Calories 650
(Calories from Fat 315);
Fat 35g (Saturated 15g);
Cholesterol 200mg;
Sodium 1600mg;
Carbohydrate 56g
(Dietary Fiber 1g);
Protein 29g.

    2 cups Bisquick® Original baking mix
1 1/2 cups milk
    2 eggs
    1 cup shredded Swiss cheese (4 ounces)
  1/4 cup Bac-Os®

1. Beat baking mix, milk and eggs in large bowl with wire whisk or hand beater until smooth. Stir in cheese and bacon.

2. Pour onto hot waffle iron (grease if necessary). Bake until steaming slows and waffle is golden brown. Remove carefully.

Oven French Toast

▼ 8 servings

Prep: 10 min

Refrigerate: 8 hr

Bake: 18 min

1 Serving: Calories 270
(Calories from Fat 110);
Fat 12g (Saturated 3g);
Cholesterol 135mg;
Sodium 420mg;
Carbohydrate 34g
(Dietary Fiber 1g);
Protein 8g.

  1/3 cup margarine, butter or spread, melted
  2/3 cup orange juice
    3 tablespoons honey
    5 eggs
   16 slices French bread, each 1-inch thick
       Powdered sugar, if desired
       Maple-flavored syrup, if desired

1. Divide margarine between jelly roll pan, $15^1/_2$ x $10^1/_2$ x 1 inch, and rectangular pan, 13 x 9 x 2 inches.

2. Beat orange juice, honey and eggs until foamy. Dip bread into egg mixture; place in pans. Drizzle any remaining egg mixture over bread. Cover and refrigerate 8 hours but no longer than 24 hours.

3. Heat oven to 450°. Bake uncovered 16 to 18 minutes, turning once, until golden brown. Serve with powdered sugar and maple syrup.

Bacon and Swiss Waffles ▶

Honey Pancakes

▼ About 12 pancakes

Prep: 8 min

Cook: 10 min

1 Pancake: Calories 245
(Calories from Fat 100);
Fat 11g (Saturated 3g);
Cholesterol 20mg;
Sodium 390mg;
Carbohydrate 34g
(Dietary Fiber 0g);
Protein 2g.

2 cups Bisquick® Original baking mix
1 cup milk
2 tablespoons honey
1 egg
Honey-Cinnamon Syrup (below)

1. Beat baking mix, milk, honey and egg with wire whisk or hand beater until well blended.

2. Pour batter by scant ¼ cupfuls onto hot griddle (grease if necessary). Cook until pancakes are dry around edges. Turn; cook until golden. Serve with Honey-Cinnamon Syrup.

Honey-Cinnamon Syrup

3/4 cup honey
1/2 cup margarine, butter or spread
1/2 teaspoon ground cinnamon

Heat all ingredients, stirring occasionally, until hot.

Ham-Dijon Muffins

▼ 12 muffins

Try different flavors of mustard in these robust muffins, such as honey mustard or hot mustard—whatever suits your mood and meal at which they will be served.

Prep: 10 min

Bake: 20 min

1 Muffin: Calories 155 (Calories from Fat 70); Fat 8g (Saturated 2g); Cholesterol 25mg; Sodium 330mg; Carbohydrate 17g (Dietary Fiber 1g); Protein 5g.

1	egg
2	cups Bisquick® Original baking mix
2/3	cup milk
2	tablespoons vegetable oil
2	tablespoons country-style Dijon mustard
1/4	pound fully cooked ham, chopped (3/4 cup)

1. Heat oven to 400°. Grease bottoms only of 12 medium muffin cups, $2^{1}/_{2}$ x $1^{1}/_{4}$ inches, or line with paper baking cups.

2. Beat egg slightly in medium bowl. Stir in baking mix, milk, oil and mustard just until moistened. Fold in ham. Divide batter evenly among muffin cups.

3. Bake 18 to 20 minutes or until light golden brown. Immediately remove from pan. Refrigerate any remaining muffins.

Quick French Onion Biscuits

▼ 6 biscuits

These drop biscuits take only minutes from start to finish! Refrigerated dips are available in several flavors, so feel free to substitute one of your favorite flavors for the onion-flavored dip and create your own flavored bread to complement your meal.

Prep: 4 min

Bake: 12 min

1 Biscuit: Calories 230 (Calories from Fat 110); Fat 12g (Saturated 5g); Cholesterol 15mg; Sodium 840mg; Carbohydrate 26g (Dietary Fiber 0g); Protein 4g.

2	cups Bisquick® Original baking mix
1/4	cup milk
1	container (8 ounces) French onion dip

1. Heat oven to 450°.

2. Mix all ingredients until soft dough forms. Drop dough into 6 mounds onto ungreased cookie sheet. Bake 10 to 12 minutes or until light golden brown. Serve warm.

Ham-Dijon Muffins ▶

Banana-Gingerbread Muffins

▼ 16 muffins

For a quick snack or dessert, frost muffins with canned vanilla frosting.

Prep: 5 min

Bake: 20 min

1 Muffin: Calories 160 (Calories from Fat 25); Fat 3g (Saturated 1g); Cholesterol 25mg; Sodium 140mg; Carbohydrate 7g (Dietary Fiber 0g); Protein 26g.

2 medium ripe bananas, mashed (1 cup)

3/4 cup quick-cooking oats

3/4 cup water

2 eggs

1 package (14.5 ounces) gingerbread cake and cookie mix

1. Heat oven to 375°. Grease bottoms only of 16 medium muffin cups, 2¹/₂ x 1¹/₄ inches, or line with paper baking cups.

2. Mix all ingredients until well blended. Divide batter evenly among muffin cups.

3. Bake 15 to 20 minutes or until toothpick inserted in center comes out clean. Immediately remove from pan.

Banana-Gingerbread Muffins

Caramel Apple Breakfast Rolls

▼ 8 rolls

Regular applesauce can be used in place of the cinnamon-flavored, if you like; just stir ¹/₄ teaspoon ground cinnamon into the applesauce.

Prep: 7 min

Bake: 20 min

1 Roll: Calories 200 (Calories from Fat 55); Fat 6g (Saturated 3g); Cholesterol 15mg; Sodium 240mg; Carbohydrate 35g (Dietary Fiber 1g); Protein 3g.

1/2 cup packed dark or light brown sugar

1/2 cup whipping (heavy) cream

1/4 cup chopped pecans

  1 can (11 ounces) refrigerated soft breadsticks

1/3 cup cinnamon-flavored applesauce

1. Heat oven to 350°.

2. Mix brown sugar and whipping cream in ungreased round pan, 8 x 1¹/₂ inches, sprinkle with pecans.

3. Unroll breadstick dough, but do not separate into breadsticks. Spread applesauce over dough. Roll up dough from short end; separate at perforations. Place coiled dough in pan.

4. Bake 15 to 20 minutes or until golden brown. Cool 1 minute. Invert pan onto heatproof tray or serving plate. Let stand 1 minute so caramel will drizzle over rolls.

Caramel Apple Breakfast Rolls ▶

Glazed Cinnamon-Raisin Scones

▼ 8 scones

We've eliminated the traditional kneading step for scones, making these quick, easy and even more tender.

Prep: 10 min

Bake: 12 min

1 Scone: Calories 225 (Calories from Fat 70); Fat 8g (Saturated 4g); Cholesterol 40mg; Sodium 440mg; Carbohydrate 36g (Dietary Fiber 1g); Protein 3g.

Glaze (below)
2 cups Bisquick® Original baking mix
1/3 cup raisins or currants
1/3 cup whipping (heavy) cream or milk
3 tablespoons sugar
1 teaspoon ground cinnamon
1 egg

1. Heat oven to 425°. Grease cookie sheet.

2. Prepare Glaze; set aside.

3. Mix remaining ingredients until soft dough forms. Spread dough into 8-inch circle on cookie sheet. Cut into 8 wedges, but do not separate.

4. Bake 10 to 12 minutes or until golden brown. Drizzle Glaze over warm scones. Carefully separate wedges. Serve warm.

Glaze

1/2 cup powdered sugar
1 tablespoon whipping (heavy) cream

Mix ingredients.

Glazed Cinnamon-Raisin Scones ▶

Make It and Freeze It

Do you usually do two or more things at once? Most busy people do. Use this same time management skill for getting ingredients prepared ahead of time. It's easy to do—the only difficult part is remembering to do it! For example, if you're already chopping onions, chop an extra and freeze for future use. Below you will find additional ideas to help you get ahead of the game.

Produce

- Chop onions, bell peppers, celery and carrots. Place desired amount in resealable plastic freezer bags or containers with lids, label and date. Freeze up to 1 month. To use, add directly to food being cooked without thawing. Or to sauté, thaw slightly just to break pieces apart. Use in soups, stews, chilies, stir-fries and casseroles.

Bread

- Make bread crumbs (seasoned with your favorite herbs and spices or unseasoned) or croutons out of extra or stale bread. Place desired amount in resealable plastic freezer bags or containers with lids, label and date. Freeze up to 6 months.

Meat

- Make extra uncooked hamburger or turkey patties. Place waxed paper between each patty, wrap tightly, label and date. Freeze up to 4 months. To use patties, thaw before cooking.

- Cook ground beef and drain. Place desired amount in resealable plastic freezer bags or containers with lids, label and date. Freeze up to 3 months. Use in soups, stews, chilies, stir-fries and casseroles.

- Make extra meatballs; uncooked or cooked. Arrange meatballs in single layer on baking pan or cookie sheet; freeze. Remove meatballs from baking pan. Place desired amount in resealable plastic freezer bags or containers with lids, label and date. Freeze up to 6 months. Use cooked meatballs directly from freezer in cooked recipes. If using uncooked meatballs, make sure that you cook them until meatballs are no longer pink in center and juice is clear.

Great Grilling

Raspberry-Glazed Chicken Breasts

▼ 6 servings

For a different, equally delicious taste, substitute apricot jam for the raspberry jam and balsamic vinegar for the red wine vinegar.

Prep: 5 min

Marinate: 1 hr

Grill: 20 min

Cook: 2 min

1 Serving: Calories 220 (Calories from Fat 25); Fat 3g (Saturated 1g); Cholesterol 60mg; Sodium 70mg; Carbohydrate 23g (Dietary Fiber 0g); Protein 25g.

  6 **skinless boneless chicken breast halves (about 1 1/2 pounds)**
2/3 **cup raspberry jam**
1/4 **cup red wine vinegar**
  2 **tablespoons chopped fresh cilantro**
1/2 **teaspoon pepper**

1. Place chicken in shallow glass dish. Mix remaining ingredients; pour over chicken. Cover and refrigerate 1 hour, turning chicken once.

2. Heat coals or gas grill.

3. Remove chicken from marinade; reserve marinade. Cover and grill chicken 4 to 6 inches from medium heat 15 to 20 minutes, brushing with marinade and turning occasionally, until juice of chicken is no longer pink when centers of thickest pieces are cut.

4. Heat remaining marinade to boiling; boil 1 minute, stirring occasionally. Serve with chicken.

To Broil: Set oven control to broil. Place chicken on rack in broiler pan. Broil with tops 4 to 6 inches from heat 7 minutes; turn. Brush with marinade. Broil about 7 minutes longer or until juice of chicken is no longer pink when centers of thickest pieces are cut.

Preceding Page
Grilled Shrimp Kabobs (page 390)

Raspberry-Glazed Chicken Breasts ▶

▼ ▼ ▼ ▼ ▼ ▼ ▼ ▼ ▼

Grilled Teriyaki Chicken

▼ 4 servings

Prep: 5 min

Marinate: 2 hr

Grill: 20 min

1 Serving: Calories 230
(Calories from Fat 25);
Fat 3g (Saturated 1g);
Cholesterol 60mg;
Sodium 750mg;
Carbohydrate 27g
(Dietary Fiber 2g);
Protein 26g.

4 skinless boneless chicken breast halves (about
   1 pound)

1/2 cup teriyaki baste and marinade

1 medium bell pepper, cut into strips

1 can (8 ounces) sliced pineapple in juice, drained

1. Place chicken in shallow glass dish. Pour teriyaki marinade over chicken. Turn chicken to coat with marinade. Cover and refrigerate 2 hours.

2. Heat coals or gas grill.

3. Remove chicken from marinade; reserve marinade. Cover and grill chicken, bell pepper strips and pineapple slices 4 to 6 inches from medium heat 15 to 20 minutes, brushing with marinade and turning occasionally, until juice of chicken is no longer pink when centers of thickest pieces are cut. Discard any remaining marinade.

4. Serve chicken with bell pepper and pineapple.

To Broil: Set oven control to broil. Place chicken, bell pepper strips and pineapple slices on rack in broiler pan. Broil with tops of chicken 4 to 6 inches from heat 15 to 20 minutes, brushing with marinade and turning occasionally, until juice of chicken is no longer pink when centers of thickest pieces are cut.

Grilled Teriyaki Chicken ▶

Try a Meal Exchange!

Why not give yourself a break one night a week or once a month by taking turns cooking a meal for friends or family. This is how it works:

The Casual Get-Together:

- Set aside one evening each week or month for "Family Night Out" and rotate the host family responsibilities between participants.

- The host family is responsible for cooking the meal and cleaning up.

- Keep the foods simple, such as those listed below:

  - Crackers and cheese, pretzels, dips, salsa and chips

  - Tossed salads, coleslaw or fresh vegetables

  - Casseroles, stir-fries, meatloaf, spaghetti, pizza, grilled burgers, steak or chicken

  - Ice cream, yogurt, cookies, brownies or bars

- Put out "munchies" to start, which allows the visiting family to relax while the host family is preparing the meal. Plan to serve the meal 15 to 30 minutes after everyone arrives.

- Plan to end the evening early since it's a weeknight, and everyone is busy and tired!

The Dinner Drop-Off:

- Instead of having your friends or family in your home, simply arrange to drop off the meal! A home-cooked meal sure beats take-out or fast-food as a quick dinner option!

Grilled Citrus Chicken

▼ 6 servings

6 skinless boneless chicken breast halves (about 1 1/2 pounds)

1/2 cup frozen orange juice concentrate, thawed

1/4 cup vegetable oil

1/4 cup lemon juice

2 tablespoons grated orange peel

1/2 teaspoon salt

1 clove garlic, finely chopped

Prep: 5 min

Marinate: 2 hr

Grill: 20 min

Cook: 2 min

1 Serving: Calories 250 (Calories from Fat 110); Fat 12g (Saturated 3g); Cholesterol 60mg; Sodium 240mg; Carbohydrate 10g (Dietary Fiber 0g); Protein 25g.

1. Place chicken in shallow glass dish. Mix remaining ingredients; pour over chicken. Turn chicken to coat with marinade. Cover and refrigerate 2 to 3 hours, turning chicken occasionally.

2. Heat coals or gas grill.

3. Remove chicken from marinade; reserve marinade. Cover and grill chicken 4 to 6 inches from medium heat 15 to 20 minutes, brushing with marinade and turning occasionally, until juice of chicken is no longer pink when centers of thickest pieces are cut.

4. Heat remaining marinade to boiling; boil 1 minute, stirring occasionally. Serve with chicken.

To Broil: Set oven control to broil. Place chicken on rack in broiler pan. Broil with tops 4 to 6 inches from heat 15 to 20 minutes, brushing with marinade and turning occasionally, until juice of chicken is no longer pink when centers of thickest pieces are cut.

Quick Tip: Substitute 1 cup bottled citrus-flavored marinade for the orange juice, oil, lemon juice, orange peel and salt.

Sassy Grilled Chicken

▼ 6 servings

Prep: 5 min

Grill: 20 min

1 Serving: Calories 260 (Calories from Fat 145); Fat 16g (Saturated 5g); Cholesterol 90mg; Sodium 190mg; Carbohydrate 1g (Dietary Fiber 0g); Protein 28g.

1/2 cup ranch dressing

2 tablespoons French or Catalina dressing

6 skinless boneless chicken breast halves (about 1 1/2 pounds)

1. Heat coals or gas grill.

2. Mix dressings; set aside.

3. Cover and grill chicken 4 to 6 inches from medium heat 15 to 20 minutes, brushing frequently with dressing mixture and turning once, until juice of chicken is no longer pink when centers of thickest pieces are cut. Discard any remaining dressing mixture.

To Broil: Set oven control to broil. Place chicken on rack in broiler pan. Broil with tops 4 to 6 inches from heat 15 to 20 minutes, brushing frequently with dressing mixture and turning once, until juice of chicken is no longer pink when centers of thickest pieces are cut.

▼ ▼ ▼ ▼ ▼ ▼ ▼ ▼ ▼ ▼ ▼ ▼ ▼ ▼ ▼ ▼ ▼ ▼ ▼

Grilled Garlic Drumsticks

▼ 4 servings

Prep: 5 min

Grill: 40 min

1 Serving: Calories 180 (Calories from Fat 125); Fat 14g (Saturated 3g); Cholesterol 45mg; Sodium 180mg; Carbohydrate 0g (Dietary Fiber 0g); Protein 14g.

2 tablespoons olive or vegetable oil

1/4 teaspoon salt

1/8 teaspoon ground red pepper (cayenne)

1 clove garlic, finely chopped

4 chicken drumsticks (about 1 1/2 pounds)

Chopped fresh cilantro, if desired

1. Heat coals or gas grill.

2. Mix oil, salt, red pepper and garlic; brush on chicken.

3. Cover and grill chicken 4 to 6 inches from medium heat 30 to 40 minutes, turning 2 or 3 times, until juice is no longer pink when centers of thickest pieces are cut. Sprinkle with cilantro.

To Broil: Set oven control to broil. Place chicken on rack in broiler pan. Broil with tops 4 to 6 inches from heat 30 to 40 minutes, turning 2 or 3 times, until juice is no longer pink when centers of thickest pieces are cut.

Peanutty Chicken Kabobs

▼ 4 servings

1/3 cup crunchy peanut butter

1/3 cup boiling water

   1 tablespoon grated gingerroot or 1 teaspoon ground ginger

   1 tablespoon lemon juice

1/8 teaspoon crushed red pepper

   1 pound skinless boneless chicken breast halves or thighs, cut into 1 1/2-inch pieces

   Chopped peanuts, if desired

Prep: 15 min

Grill: 25 min

1 Serving: Calories 260 (Calories from Fat 125); Fat 14g (Saturated 3g); Cholesterol 60mg; Sodium 160mg; Carbohydrate 5g (Dietary Fiber 1g); Protein 29g.

1. Heat coals or gas grill.

2. Mix all ingredients except chicken and peanuts; reserve 1/4 cup.

3. Thread chicken on four 11-inch metal skewers, leaving space between each piece. Brush chicken with half of the reserved peanut butter mixture.

4. Cover and grill kabobs 4 to 6 inches from medium heat 15 to 25 minutes, turning and brushing occasionally with remaining peanut butter mixture, until chicken is golden brown on outside and no longer pink in center.

To Broil: Set oven control to broil. Place kabobs on rack in broiler pan. Broil with tops 4 to 6 inches from heat 5 minutes; turn. Broil 4 to 5 minutes longer or until chicken is no longer pink in center.

Betty Crocker's Top 10

Recipe Shortcuts for Great Grilling

1. Partially cook meat and poultry in the microwave oven (see page 376).

2. Use a gas grill for instant heat.

3. Use an indoor grill for convenience, inclement weather or if you cannot have an outdoor grill.

4. Form ground meat patties only 1/4- to 1/2-inch thick for quicker cooking.

5. Thinner cuts of meat or poultry cook faster.

6. Try marinated chicken or turkey pieces from the meat case, many are individually packaged.

7. Skinless, boneless chicken breasts cook faster than bone-in pieces.

8. Kabobs with meat, poultry and vegetables make a quick meal— many grocery meat counters sell ready-made kabobs, both plain and marinated.

9. Fish baskets make turning fish easy without it falling apart—they can double as a vegetable basket too.

10. Grill potatoes or vegetables in foil packets along with the meat, poultry or fish.

Dilly Turkey Slices

▼ 4 servings

Look for dill dip in the refrigerated section of your supermarket.

- **1 pound uncooked turkey breast slices, about 1/4-inch thick**
- **1/2 cup purchased dill dip**
- **2 tablespoons vegetable oil**
- **1/4 teaspoon pepper**

1. Place turkey in shallow dish. Mix remaining ingredients; pour over turkey. Cover and refrigerate 1 hour, turning turkey occasionally.

2. Heat coals or gas grill.

3. Remove turkey from marinade; reserve marinade. Cover and grill turkey 4 to 6 inches from medium heat 8 to 12 minutes, brushing with marinade and turning once, until turkey is no longer pink in center. Discard remaining marinade. Serve with additional dill dip if desired.

To Broil: Set oven control to broil. Place turkey on rack in broiler pan. Broil with tops 4 to 6 inches from heat 3 to 4 minutes, brushing with marinade and turning once, until turkey is no longer pink in center.

Prep: 10 min

Marinate: 1 hr

Grill: 12 min

1 Serving: Calories 230 (Calories from Fat 110); Fat 12g (Saturated 5g); Cholesterol 75mg; Sodium 270mg; Carbohydrate 2g (Dietary Fiber 0g); Protein 28g.

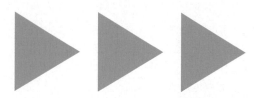

Grilled Parmesan Turkey Burgers

▼ 4 servings

Because of their lower fat content, turkey patties may stick to the grill unless the grill is oiled first. For safety reasons, always oil a grill rack before coals are lit or gas is turned on.

  1 pound ground turkey
1/3 cup grated Parmesan cheese
  1 tablespoon chopped fresh chives
1/4 teaspoon pepper
1/8 teaspoon salt
     Red onion rings, if desired
  4 hamburger buns, split and toasted

1. Lightly oil grill rack. Heat coals or gas grill.

2. Mix all ingredients except buns. Shape mixture into 4 patties, each about 1/2-inch thick.

3. Cover and grill patties 4 to 6 inches from medium heat 12 to 15 minutes, turning once, until no longer pink in center. Serve on buns with grilled or raw onion rings.

To Broil: Set oven control to broil. Place patties on rack in broiler pan. Broil with tops 4 to 6 inches from heat 12 to 15 minutes, turning once, until no longer pink in center.

Grilled Parmesan Turkey Burgers ▶

Tomato-and-Pesto-Stuffed Sirloin

▼ 6 servings

You can use the stuffing technique here for other delicious fillings such as basil pesto, flavored cheese spread or roasted garlic.

Prep: 10 min

Grill: 24 min

1 Serving: Calories 155 (Calories from Fat 70); Fat 8g (Saturated 2g); Cholesterol 55mg; Sodium 150mg; Carbohydrate 1g (Dietary Fiber 0g); Protein 20g.

4   beef tenderloin steaks (1 1/4-inches thick and about 3 inches in diameter)

1/3   cup refrigerated pesto with sun-dried tomatoes (from 7-ounce container)

1/8   teaspoon pepper

1. Heat coals or gas grill.

2. Make a horizontal cut into side of each steak, cutting to—but not through—opposite side and leaving about ¹/₂ inch uncut at each side, to form pocket. Spoon pesto evenly into pocket. Secure opening with toothpicks. Sprinkle pepper over both sides of beef.

3. Cover and grill beef 4 to 6 inches from medium heat 5 to 10 minutes for medium doneness, turning once, or until desired doneness.

To Broil: Set oven control to broil. Place beef on rack in broiler pan. Broil with top 4 to 6 inches from heat 5 to 10 minutes for medium doneness, turning once, or until desired doneness.

Tomato-and-Pesto-Stuffed Sirloin ▶

Peppered Steak with Brandy Cream Sauce

▼ 6 servings

Prep: 10 min

Grill: 16 min

Cook: 10 min

1 Serving: Calories 275 (Calories from Fat 145); Fat 16g (Saturated 7g); Cholesterol 95mg; Sodium 160mg; Carbohydrate 2g (Dietary Fiber 0g); Protein 31g.

3 teaspoons cracked black pepper

6 beef tenderloin steaks, about 3/4-inch thick (about 1 1/2 pounds)

1 tablespoon margarine, butter or spread

1/4 cup finely chopped shallots or green onions

1/4 cup brandy or beef broth

1/2 cup beef broth

1/2 cup sour cream

1. Heat coals or gas grill.

2. Press pepper onto both sides of beef. Grill beef uncovered 4 to 6 inches from medium heat 14 to 16 minutes for medium doneness, turning once, or until desired doneness.

3. Meanwhile, melt margarine in 1-quart saucepan over medium heat. Cook shallots in margarine, stirring occasionally, until tender.

4. Stir in brandy and broth. Cook over medium-high heat about 5 minutes or until mixture is slightly reduced. Stir in sour cream. Serve with beef.

To Broil: Set oven control to broil. Place beef on rack in broiler pan. Broil with tops 4 to 6 inches from heat 14 to 16 minutes for medium doneness, turning once, or until desired doneness.

Peppered Steak with Brandy Cream Sauce ▶

Turkey Burger Tactics

Ground turkey has a very mild flavor on its own, but by adding one of the ingredients below, you instantly create juicy burgers with lots of flavor!

1. To one pound of lean ground turkey or turkey breast, stir in 1/3 cup or 1 package of one of the items from the list below.

2. Shape into 1/4- to 1/2-inch patties and cook as desired, turning once, until turkey is no longer pink in center and juices run clear.

3. Serve on buns with your favorite toppings.

Use 1/3 cup of one of the following:

- Salsa
- Chili sauce
- Barbecue sauce
- Spaghetti sauce
- Pizza sauce
- Teriyaki sauce
- Sweet-and-sour sauce
- Salad dressing
- Chutney
- Pesto
- Alfredo sauce

Use 1 package (1 to 1 1/2 ounces) of one of the following:

- Dry salad dressing mix
- Taco seasoning mix
- Gravy mix
- Sloppy joe mix
- Spaghetti sauce mix

Supreme Burgers

▼ 8 burgers

> 2 pounds ground beef
> 1 envelope (about 1 1/2 ounces) onion soup mix
> 1 cup sour cream
> 1/2 cup dry bread crumbs
> 1/8 teaspoon pepper

1. Heat coals or gas grill.

2. Mix all ingredients. Shape mixture into 8 patties, about 3/4-inch thick.

3. Grill patties uncovered 4 to 6 inches from medium heat 10 to 15 minutes, turning once, until beef is no longer pink in center and juice is clear.

To Broil: Set oven control to broil. Place patties on rack in broiler pan. Broil with tops 4 to 6 inches from heat 10 to 15 minutes, turning once, until beef is no longer pink in center and juice is clear.

Prep: 10 min

Grill: 15 min

1 Burger: Calories 325 (Calories from Fat 200); Fat 22g (Saturated 10g); Cholesterol 85mg; Sodium 560mg; Carbohydrate 9g (Dietary Fiber 0g); Protein 23g.

Crunchy Teriyaki Burgers

▼ 6 burgers

> 1 1/2 pounds ground beef
> 1/2 cup finely chopped water chestnuts
> 1/2 cup teriyaki sauce

1. Mix beef and water chestnuts. Shape mixture into 6 patties, about 3/4-inch thick.

2. Place patties in shallow glass or plastic dish. Pour teriyaki sauce over patties. Cover and refrigerate at least 3 hours but no longer than 24 hours, turning once.

3. Heat coals or gas grill.

4. Remove patties from marinade; reserve marinade. Grill patties uncovered 4 to 6 inches from medium heat 10 to 15 minutes, brushing frequently with marinade and turning once, until beef is no longer pink in center and juice is clear. Discard any remaining marinade.

To Broil: Follow broiling instructions above.

Prep: 10 min

Marinate: 3 hr

Grill: 15 min

1 Burger: Calories 250 (Calories from Fat 145); Fat 16g (Saturated 7g); Cholesterol 65mg; Sodium 740mg; Carbohydrate 5g (Dietary Fiber 0g); Protein 21g.

Microwave-to-Grill—
A Head Start when Grilling

You can cut grilling time in half! How? By teaming the micro-wave oven with your barbecue grill. Foods such as broiler-fryer chicken pieces, turkey breasts and ribs are especially suited for microwave-to-grill cooking. Grilling time is often cut in half, food is more moist and there are fewer flare-ups because much of the fat cooks away from the foods during microwaving.

Microwave-to-Grill Directions:

1. Place the food with thickest parts to outside edges, in rectangular or square microwavable dish. Cover with plastic wrap, folding back one corner to vent.

2. Microwave on high about 4 minutes per pound, rotating dish after half the cooking time, until edges begin to cook; drain.

3. Immediately place food on the heated grill and grill until done.

Grilled Honey-Mustard Pork Chops

▼ 4 servings

The sweet honey glaze on these chops browns easily, so watch the chops carefully and make sure the coals are not too hot.

- **1/4 cup honey**
- **2 tablespoons Dijon mustard**
- **1 tablespoon orange juice**
- **1 teaspoon cider vinegar**
- **4 pork butterfly loin chops, 1 inch thick (about 1 pound)**

1. Heat coals or gas grill.

2. Mix all ingredients except pork. Cover and grill pork 4 to 6 inches from medium heat 14 to 16 minutes, brushing occasionally with honey mixture and turning once, until slightly pink in center.

To Broil: Set oven control to broil. Place pork on rack in broiler pan. Broil with tops 4 to 6 inches from heat 14 to 16 minutes, brushing occasionally with honey mixture and turning once, until slightly pink in center.

Prep: 7 min

Grill: 16 min

1 Serving: Calories 215 (Calories from Fat 65); Fat 7g (Saturated 3g); Cholesterol 55mg; Sodium 130mg; Carbohydrate 18g (Dietary Fiber 0g); Protein 20g.

Zesty Pork Chops

For a complete grilled meal, cut zucchini lengthwise in half, brush with oil, season with salt and pepper and cook with the pork chops. Add buttered French bread during the last 3 to 5 minutes, and you have your whole dinner!

Prep: 5 min

Grill: 15 min

1 Serving: Calories 265 (Calories from Fat 70); Fat 8g (Saturated 3g); Cholesterol 65mg; Sodium 60mg; Carbohydrate 25g (Dietary Fiber 0g); Protein 23g.

2/3 cup packed brown sugar

1/4 cup prepared horseradish

1 tablespoon lemon juice

6 fully cooked smoked pork chops, about 1/2-inch thick (about 1 1/4 pounds)

1. Heat coals or gas grill.

2. Heat brown sugar, horseradish and lemon juice to boiling in 1-quart saucepan, stirring constantly. Brush on pork.

3. Cover and grill pork 4 to 6 inches from medium-high heat about 15 minutes, turning once, until hot. Serve remaining sauce with pork.

To Broil: Set oven control to broil. Place pork on rack in broiler pan. Broil with tops 4 to 6 inches from heat 3 minutes; turn. Broil 3 to 5 minutes longer or until hot.

Easy Grilled Ribs

▼ 4 servings

Any seasoning blend can be used as a dry rub for ribs—use your favorite.

Prep: 10 min

Grill: 1 1/2 hr

1 Serving: Calories 645
(Calories from Fat 450);
Fat 50g (Saturated 19g);
Cholesterol 200mg;
Sodium 150mg;
Carbohydrate 1g
(Dietary Fiber 0g);
Protein 48g.

　3　**pounds pork baby backribs**
　2　**tablespoons pork seasoning blend**
　　　Barbecue sauce, if desired

1. Heat coals or gas grill.

2. Cut pork into serving pieces. Rub seasoning into both sides of pork.

3. Cover and grill pork 5 to 6 inches from low heat $1^{1}/_{4}$ to $1^{1}/_{2}$ hours, turning occasionally, until tender. Serve with barbecue sauce.

To Bake: Heat oven to 325°. Place pork, meaty sides up, on rack in shallow roasting pan. Bake uncovered $1^{1}/_{4}$ to $1^{1}/_{2}$ hours, turning twice, until tender.

Reuben Brats

▼ 4 servings

Prep: 5 min

Cook: 16 min

Grill: 10 min

1 Serving: Calories 560
(Calories from Fat 370);
Fat 41g (Saturated 15g);
Cholesterol 95mg;
Sodium 1860mg;
Carbohydrate 30g
(Dietary Fiber 6g);
Protein 24g.

1	can or bottle (12 ounces) beer or 2 cups water
4	uncooked fresh bratwurst links (about 1 pound)
2	tablespoons Thousand Island dressing
4	rye or whole wheat bratwurst buns, split
1/2	cup shredded Swiss cheese (2 ounces)
1	cup sauerkraut, drained

1. Heat coals or gas grill.

2. Heat beer to boiling in 2-quart saucepan. Add bratwurst; reduce heat to low. Cover and simmer 15 minutes; drain.

3. Cover and grill bratwurst 4 to 6 inches from medium heat 5 to 10 minutes, turning once, until brown.

4. Spread dressing on cut sides of buns. Top with cheese, bratwurst and sauerkraut (sauerkraut can be heated if desired).

To Broil: Set oven control to broil. Place bratwurst on rack in broiler pan. Broil with tops 4 to 6 inches from heat 5 to 10 minutes, turning once, until brown.

Reuben Brats ▶

Pizza Dogs

▼ 8 servings

Prep: 10 min

Grill: 15 min

1 Serving: Calories 310 (Calories from Fat 160); Fat 18g (Saturated 7g); Cholesterol 30mg; Sodium 890mg; Carbohydrate 25g (Dietary Fiber 1g); Protein 13g.

8 beef or turkey hot dogs

1/2 cup pizza sauce

8 hot dog buns, split

1 cup shredded mozzarella cheese (4 ounces)

4 medium green onions, sliced (1/2 cup)

1. Heat coals or gas grill.

2. Grill hot dogs uncovered 4 to 6 inches from medium heat about 15 minutes, turning frequently, until hot.

3. Meanwhile, heat pizza sauce until hot; keep warm. Serve hot dogs on buns. Top with cheese, pizza sauce and onions.

To Broil: Set oven control to broil. Place hot dogs on rack in broiler pan. Broil with tops 4 to 6 inches from heat about 15 minutes, turning frequently, until hot.

Grilled Italian Sausage Kabobs

▼ 6 servings

Prep: 15 min

Cook: 11 min

Grill: 25 min

1 Serving: Calories 400 (Calories from Fat 280); Fat 31g (Saturated 11g); Cholesterol 90mg; Sodium 1250mg; Carbohydrate 7g (Dietary Fiber 1g); Protein 24g.

1 1/2 pounds Italian sausage links
   2 medium zucchini, cut into 1-inch pieces
   2 medium bell peppers, cut into 1 1/2-inch pieces
   6 large pimiento-stuffed olives
1/2 cup pizza sauce

1. Heat coals or gas grill.

2. Cook sausage in 10-inch skillet over medium heat about 10 minutes, turning occasionally, until partially cooked; drain. Cool about 5 minutes. Cut into 1½-inch pieces.

3. Thread sausage, zucchini and bell pepper pieces alternately on each of six 15-inch metal skewers, leaving space between each piece. Place olive on end of each skewer.

4. Cover and grill kabobs 4 to 6 inches from medium heat 20 to 25 minutes, turning and brushing 2 or 3 times with pizza sauce, until sausage is no longer pink in center and vegetables are crisp-tender.

5. Heat remaining pizza sauce to boiling; boil 1 minute, stirring frequently. Serve with kabobs.

To Broil: Set oven control to broil. Place kabobs on rack in broiler pan. Broil with tops 4 to 6 inches from heat 20 to 25 minutes, turning and brushing 2 or 3 times with pizza sauce, until sausage is no longer pink in center and vegetables are crisp-tender.

Grilled Italian Sausage Kabobs ▶

Easy Grilled Fish Fillets

▼ 4 servings

Prep: 5 min

Grill: 14 min

1 Serving: Calories 145
(Calories from Fat 65);
Fat 7g (Saturated 2g);
Cholesterol 60mg;
Sodium 690mg;
Carbohydrate 0g
(Dietary Fiber 0g);
Protein 21g.

1 pound fish fillets or steaks, 1/2 to 3/4 inch thick
  Salt and pepper to taste
2 tablespoons margarine or butter, melted

1. Heat coals or gas grill.

2. Cut fish into 4 serving pieces. Sprinkle both sides of fish with salt and pepper. Brush both sides with margarine.

3. Cover and grill fish 4 to 6 inches from medium heat 15 to 25 minutes, turning once, until fish flakes easily with fork.

To Broil: Set oven control to broil. Place fish on rack in broiler pan. Broil with tops 4 to 6 inches from heat 10 to 14 minutes, turning once, until fish flakes easily with fork.

Easy Grilled Fish Fillets ▶

Grilled Shrimp Kabobs

▼ 6 servings

(*Photograph on page 357*)

Prep: 15 min

Marinate: 4 hr

Grill: 10 min

1 Serving: Calories 225 (Calories from Fat 145); Fat 16g (Saturated 3g); Cholesterol 110mg; Sodium 400mg; Carbohydrate 9g (Dietary Fiber 2g); Protein 13g.

1 pound uncooked peeled and deveined medium shrimp, thawed if frozen

12 cherry tomatoes

2 medium yellow summer squash, cut into 1/2-inch slices

2 medium zucchini, cut into 1/2-inch slices

6 large pitted ripe olives

3/4 cup Italian dressing

1. Place all ingredients except dressing in rectangular baking dish, 13 x 9 x 2 inches. Pour dressing over mixture. Cover and refrigerate 4 hours.

2. Heat coals or gas grill.

3. Remove shrimp and vegetables from marinade; reserve marinade. Thread shrimp, tomatoes, squash and zucchini alternately on each of six 15-inch metal skewers, leaving space between each piece. Place olive on end of each skewer.

4. Cover and grill kabobs 4 to 6 inches from medium heat 5 to 10 minutes, turning and brushing 2 or 3 times with marinade, until shrimp are pink and firm. Discard any remaining marinade.

To Broil: Set oven control to broil. Place kabobs on rack in broiler pan. Broil with tops 4 to 6 inches from heat 5 to 10 minutes, turning and brushing 2 or 3 times with marinade, until shrimp are pink and firm.

Betty Crocker's Good and Easy Cookbook

Delicious Desserts

Double Hot Fudge Pudding Cake

▼ 6 servings

As this dessert bakes, it magically forms a layer of fudgy brownie with a delicious hot fudge pudding underneath.

Prep: 6 min

Bake: 40 min

1 Serving: Calories 330 (Calories from Fat 100); Fat 11g (Saturated 3g); Cholesterol 35mg; Sodium 210mg; Carbohydrate 55g (Dietary Fiber 2g); Protein 5g.

1 package (10.25 ounces) fudge brownie mix

3 tablespoons vegetable oil

3 tablespoons water

1 egg

1 package (4-serving size) chocolate fudge pudding and pie filling (not instant)

2 cups very hot water

Ice cream, if desired

1. Heat oven to 400°.

2. Mix brownie mix (dry), oil, 3 tablespoons water and the egg in 1½-quart casserole; stir with spoon about 50 strokes.

3. Mix pudding and pie filling (dry) and 2 cups very hot water; carefully pour over brownie batter.

4. Bake uncovered 35 to 40 minutes or until pudding bubbles around edges of casserole. Serve warm with ice cream.

Preceding Page
Quick Cherry Cobbler (page 393)

Quick Cherry Cobbler

 6 servings

Heating the filling in the oven while the oven is heating saves time as ovens generally take 10 minutes to preheat. If cobbler fillings aren't heated first, the dough may still have raw spots after baking. (Photograph on page 391.)

1 can (21 ounces) cherry or peach pie filling*
1/2 teaspoon almond extract, if desired
1 cup Bisquick® Original baking mix
1 tablespoon sugar
1/4 cup milk
1 tablespoon margarine, butter or spread, softened
Sugar, if desired

Prep: 10 min

Bake: 30 min

1 Serving: Calories 285 (Calories from Fat 45); Fat 5g (Saturated 1g); Cholesterol 0mg; Sodium 310mg; Carbohydrate 60g (Dietary Fiber 2g); Protein 2g.

1. Mix pie filling and almond extract in ungreased square pan, 8 x 8 x 2 inches. Place in cold oven. Heat oven to 400°; let heat 10 minutes. Remove pan from oven.

2. While pie filling is heating, mix baking mix, sugar, milk and margarine with fork until soft dough forms. Drop dough by 6 spoonfuls onto warm cherry mixture. Sprinkle with sugar.

3. Bake 18 to 20 minutes or until topping is light brown.

*If using peach pie filling, substitute vanilla for the almond extract.

Triple Chocolate Rocky Road Bars

▼ 16 bars

Prep: 10 min

Bake: 25 min

1 Bar: Calories 235 (Calories from Fat 90); Fat 10g (Saturated 5g); Cholesterol 15mg; Sodium 110mg; Carbohydrate 33g (Dietary Fiber 0g); Protein 3g.

  1 package (17.5 ounces) double chocolate chunk cookie mix
1/4 cup vegetable oil
  2 tablespoons water
  1 egg
1/2 tub (16-ounce size) chocolate ready-to-spread frosting (1 cup)
1/3 cup miniature marshmallows
  1 tablespoon chopped peanuts, if desired

1. Heat oven to 350°.

2. Mix cookie mix (dry), oil, water and egg with spoon until dough forms. Press in ungreased square pan, 8x8x2 inches.

3. Bake 20 to 25 minutes or just until set. Cool completely.

4. Mix frosting and marshmallows; spread over bars. Sprinkle with peanuts. Cut into about 2-inch squares.

Triple Chocolate Rocky Road Bars ►

Betty Crocker's Top 10

Recipe Shortcuts for Delicious Desserts

▶ **1.** Ready-made desserts from a grocery store, bakery or restaurant

▶ **2.** Frozen pies, cakes, cheesecakes and cobblers

▶ **3.** Ice cream, sorbets and frozen yogurt served with purchased toppings

▶ **4.** Fresh fruit

▶ **5.** Single-serve packages of pudding or gelatin

▶ **6.** Ready-made cookies, brownies or bars

▶ **7.** Cookies made from refrigerated or frozen cookie doughs

▶ **8.** Flavored coffee, espresso, cappucino mixes or hot chocolate served with whipped cream and sprinkles and purchased biscotti

▶ **9.** A trip to your favorite soft-serve ice cream restaurant or drive-through

▶ **10.** S'mores made in the microwave oven

Candy-Topped Chocolate Chip Bars

▼ 16 bars

To dress up these tempting bars a bit more, add your favorite sprinkles or finely chopped nuts over the chocolate "frosting."

1 package (17.5 ounces) chocolate chip cookie mix
1/2 cup (1 stick) margarine or butter, softened
1 egg
1 bar (4 ounces) milk chocolate candy, broken into pieces

1. Heat oven to 350°.

2. Mix cookie mix (dry), margarine and egg with spoon until thoroughly blended (mixture will be crumbly until dough forms). Press in ungreased square pan, 8 x 8 x 2 inches.

3. Bake 25 to 28 minutes or until light golden brown.

4. Immediately place chocolate pieces on baked layer. Let stand about 5 minutes or until softened; spread evenly. Cool 30 minutes. Cut into about 2-inch squares while warm. Cool completely.

Prep: 7 min

Bake: 28 min

1 Bar: Calories 230 (Calories from Fat 110); Fat 12g (Saturated 5g); Cholesterol 15mg; Sodium 140mg; Carbohydrate 28g (Dietary Fiber 0g); Protein 2g.

▼▼▼▼▼▼▼▼▼▼▼▼▼▼▼▼▼▼▼▼▼▼

Caramel Baked Pears

▼ 3 servings

1 can (29 ounces) pear halves in juice, drained (6 halves)
1/4 cup caramel ice-cream topping
Ground cinnamon

1. Heat oven to 350°.

2. Drain pear halves, cut sides down, on paper towels.

3. Place pear halves, cut sides down, in pie plate, 9 x 1¼ inches. Drizzle with ice-cream topping. Bake 8 to 12 minutes or until warm. Spoon ice-cream topping in pan over pears. Sprinkle with cinnamon.

Prep: 5 min

Bake: 12 min

1 Serving: Calories 175 (Calories from Fat 0); Fat 0g (Saturated 0g); Cholesterol 0mg; Sodium 105mg; Carbohydrate 47g (Dietary Fiber 4g); Protein 1g.

▼ ▼ ▼ ▼ ▼ ▼ ▼ ▼ ▼

Quick Praline Bars

▼ About 2 dozen

Prep: 12 min

Cook: 4 min

Bake: 10 min

1 Square: Calories 90
(Calories from Fat 50);
Fat 6g (Saturated 2g);
Cholesterol 0mg;
Sodium 90mg;
Carbohydrate 10g
(Dietary Fiber 0g);
Protein 0g.

24 graham cracker squares
1/2 cup packed brown sugar
1/2 cup (1 stick) margarine or butter
1/2 teaspoon vanilla
1/2 cup chopped pecans

1. Heat oven to 350°.

2. Arrange graham crackers in single layer in ungreased jelly roll pan, 15½ x 10½ x 1 inch.

3. Heat brown sugar and margarine to boiling in 2-quart saucepan. Boil 1 minute, stirring constantly; remove from heat. Stir in vanilla.

4. Pour sugar mixture over crackers; spread evenly. Sprinkle with pecans. Bake 8 to 10 minutes or until bubbly; cool slightly.

Quick Praline Bars ▶

Quick Rice and Raisin Pudding

▼ 4 servings

Prep: 5 min

Cook: 2 min

Stand: 5 min

1 Serving: Calories 195 (Calories from Fat 10); Fat 1g (Saturated 1g); Cholesterol 5mg; Sodium 170mg; Carbohydrate 43g (Dietary Fiber 0g); Protein 4g.

1 cup uncooked instant rice

1 cup milk or water

1/4 cup raisins

3 tablespoons sugar

1/4 teaspoon salt

1/4 teaspoon ground cinnamon or nutmeg

Mix all ingredients in 2-quart saucepan. Heat to boiling, stirring constantly; remove from heat. Cover and let stand 5 minutes.

▼▼▼▼▼▼▼▼▼▼▼▼▼▼▼▼▼▼▼

Chocolate-Laced Kiwifruit with Orange Sauce

▼ 4 servings

Prep: 10 min

Cook: 5 min

1 Serving: Calories 125 (Calories from Fat 35); Fat 4g (Saturated 2g); Cholesterol 2mg; Sodium 25mg; Carbohydrate 21g (Dietary Fiber 2g); Protein 3g.

1/2 cup plain or vanilla yogurt

1 tablespoon frozen orange juice concentrate, partially thawed

4 large kiwifruit, peeled and cut into 1/4-inch slices

2 tablespoons semisweet chocolate chips

1 teaspoon shortening

1. Mix yogurt and juice concentrate. Spoon 2 tablespoons yogurt mixture onto each of 4 dessert plates. Arrange 1 sliced kiwifruit on yogurt mixture on each plate.

2. Heat chocolate chips and shortening over low heat, stirring constantly, until chocolate is melted. Drizzle chocolate over kiwifruit.

Quick Tip: Substitute chocolate-flavored syrup for the chocolate chips and shortening.

Chocolate-Laced Kiwifruit with Orange Sauce ▶

Caramel-Pineapple Sundaes

▼ 4 servings

These rich-flavored sundaes taste like pineapple upside-down cake—with no baking!

Prep: 10 min

Cook: 3 min

1 Serving: Calories 460 (Calories from Fat 90); Fat 10g (Saturated 5g); Cholesterol 130mg; Sodium 230mg; Carbohydrate 86g (Dietary Fiber 1g); Protein 7g.

- 1 can (8 ounces) crushed pineapple in juice, very well drained
- 1/2 cup caramel ice-cream topping
- 4 individual sponge cake cups
- 1 pint vanilla ice cream (2 cups)

1. Heat pineapple and ice-cream topping in 1-quart saucepan over medium heat, stirring occasionally, until warm.

2. Place sponge cake cups on individual serving plates. Place one scoop ice cream on each sponge cake cup. Spoon about 1/4 cup pineapple sauce over each sundae.

Pound Cake with Maple-Nut Topping

▼ 4 servings

Prep: 7 min

1 Serving: Calories 430 (Calories from Fat 250); Fat 28g (Saturated 13g); Cholesterol 90mg; Sodium 150mg; Carbohydrate 40g (Dietary Fiber 1g); Protein 5g.

- 1/2 package (8-ounce size) cream cheese, softened
- 1/4 cup maple-flavored syrup
- 1/4 cup coarsely chopped pecans
- 4 slices pound cake, 1-inch thick

1. Mix cream cheese, maple syrup and pecans.

2. Spoon topping onto cake.

Angel Food– Coconut Cream Cake

▼ 12 servings

1 purchased round angel food cake (8 or 9 inches in diameter)
1 can (21 ounces) coconut pie filling
1 container (8 ounces) frozen whipped topping, thawed
2 tablespoons coconut, lightly toasted

1. Split cake horizontally to make 4 layers. (To split, mark side of cake with toothpicks and cut with long, thin serrated knife.)

2. Place bottom layer on serving plate; spread with 1/3 cup of the pie filling. Repeat with 2 more layers. Replace top cake layer.

3. Frost top and sides of cake with whipped topping. Sprinkle top with coconut. Store in refrigerator.

Prep: 15 min

1 Serving: Calories 260 (Calories from Fat 90); Fat 10g (Saturated 7g); Cholesterol 50mg; Sodium 170mg; Carbohydrate 38g (Dietary Fiber 0g); Protein 4g.

Tiramisu Toffee Dessert

▼ 12 servings

Now you can make this popular restaurant dessert for your guests in almost no time at all!

Prep: 15 min

Chill: 1 hr

1 Serving: Calories 455 (Calories from Fat 250); Fat 28g (Saturated 17g); Cholesterol 100mg; Sodium 120mg; Carbohydrate 47g (Dietary Fiber 0g); Protein 4g.

1 package (10.75 ounces) frozen pound cake, thawed and cut into 9 slices

3/4 cup strong coffee

1 cup sugar

1/2 cup chocolate-flavored syrup

1 package (8 ounces) cream cheese, softened

2 cups whipping (heavy) cream

2 bars (1.4 ounces each) chocolate-covered toffee candy, chopped

1. Arrange cake slices on bottom of rectangular baking dish, 11 x 7 x 1½ inches, cutting cake slices if necessary to cover bottom of dish. Drizzle coffee over cake.

2. Beat sugar, chocolate syrup and cream cheese in large bowl with electric mixer on medium speed until smooth. Add whipping cream. Beat on medium speed until light and fluffy. Spread over cake. Sprinkle with candy.

3. Cover and refrigerate at least 1 hour, but no longer than 24 hours to set dessert and blend flavors.

Tiramisu Toffee Dessert ▶

Lemon–Blueberry Flan Cake

▼ 8 servings

Flan sponge cake is available in the produce section of most grocery stores and is sold next to the individual shortcake cups.

Prep: 5 min

1 Serving: Calories 255 (Calories from Fat 100); Fat 11g (Saturated 7g); Cholesterol 70mg; Sodium 160mg; Carbohydrate 36g (Dietary Fiber 1g); Protein 4g.

1 container (8 ounces) soft cream cheese

3 containers (4 ounces each) snack-size lemon pudding

1 package (7.05 ounces) flan sponge cake

3 cups fresh blueberries

1. Mix cream cheese and pudding until smooth.

2. Place sponge cake on serving plate. Spread pudding mixture in center of cake. Top with blueberries. Serve immediately, or refrigerate until serving time. Cover and refrigerate any remaining cake.

▼▼▼▼▼▼▼▼▼▼▼▼▼▼▼▼▼▼▼▼▼

Easy Key Lime Pie

▼ 8 servings

Prep: 5 min

Chill: 1 hr

1 Serving: Calories 375 (Calories from Fat 170); Fat 19g (Saturated 12g); Cholesterol 20mg; Sodium 170mg; Carbohydrate 46g (Dietary Fiber 0g); Protein 5g.

1 can (14 ounces) sweetened condensed milk

1/2 cup Key lime or regular lime juice

1 container (8 ounces) frozen whipped topping, thawed

1 package (6 ounces) ready-to-use chocolate-flavored or graham cracker pie crust

Grated lime peel, if desired

1. Beat milk and lime juice in large bowl with electric mixer on medium speed until smooth and thickened. Fold in whipped topping.

2. Spoon lime mixture into pie crust. Cover and refrigerate about 1 hour or until set. Cover and refrigerate any remaining pie. Garnish with grated lime peel.

Easy Key Lime Pie ▶

Banana Cream Trifle

▼ 6 servings

You'll find yourself making this dessert over and over—it's so easy and so good.

Prep: 15 min

1 Serving: Calories 470 (Calories from Fat 145); Fat 16g (Saturated 12g); Cholesterol 25mg; Sodium 480mg; Carbohydrate 76g (Dietary Fiber 2g); Protein 7g.

1 package (4-serving size) vanilla instant pudding and pie filling

2 cups cold milk

1 package (16 ounces) frozen banana breakfast quick bread loaf, thawed and cut into 1-inch cubes (about 6 cups)

3 ripe medium bananas, sliced

1 container (8 ounces) frozen whipped topping, thawed

1. Prepare pudding and pie filling in large bowl as directed on package for pudding, using 2 cups milk.

2. Layer half of the bread cubes, pudding, banana slices and whipped topping in 2-quart serving bowl. Repeat with remaining ingredients.

3. Cover and refrigerate until serving time but no longer than 24 hours. Cover and refrigerate any remaining dessert.

Quick Tip: Substitute 4 ready-to-eat, single-serve size vanilla pudding containers for the box of pudding and pie filling and milk.

Banana Cream Trifle ▶

Raspberry-Chocolate Cream

▼ 4 servings

Prep: 5 min

1 Serving: Calories 200 (Calories from Fat 115); Fat 13g (Saturated 11g); Cholesterol 0mg; Sodium 45mg; Carbohydrate 22g (Dietary Fiber 2g); Protein 1g.

1 pint raspberries
1 container (8 ounces) frozen whipped topping, thawed
1/2 cup chocolate-flavored syrup

Layer ¹/₂ of whipped topping, 1 tablespoon syrup and ¹/₈ of raspberries in each of 4 dessert dishes. Repeat with remaining ingredients.

Quick Lemon-Cheese Dessert

▼ 6 servings

Prep: 4 min

Chill: 1 hr

1 Serving: Calories 440 (Calories from Fat 250); Fat 28g (Saturated 14g); Cholesterol 50mg; Sodium 520mg; Carbohydrate 41g (Dietary Fiber 0g); Protein 6g.

1 package (8 ounces) cream cheese, softened
1 1/2 cups milk
1 package (4-serving size) lemon instant pudding and pie filling
1 to 2 tablespoons grated lemon peel
1 package (6 ounces) ready-to-use graham cracker pie crust

1. Beat cream cheese and ¹/₂ cup of the milk in small bowl with electric mixer on medium speed until blended. Add remaining milk, the pudding and pie filling (dry) and lemon peel. Beat on low speed 1 to 2 minutes or just until blended (do not underbeat).

2. Pour cream cheese mixture into pie crust. Cover and refrigerate at least 1 hour but no longer than 24 hours. Cover and refrigerate any remaining dessert.

Raspberry-Chocolate Cream ▶

▼ ▼ ▼ ▼ ▼ ▼ ▼ ▼ ▼

Creamy Caramel-Peach Parfaits

▼ 6 servings

When peaches are in season, try this tempting recipe with chopped fresh peaches.

Prep: 6 min

1 Serving: Calories 370 (Calories from Fat 110); Fat 12g (Saturated 10g); Cholesterol 0mg; Sodium 170mg; Carbohydrate 66g (Dietary Fiber 2g); Protein 2g.

2/3 **cup caramel ice-cream topping**
1 **container (8 ounces) frozen whipped topping, thawed**
1 **can (29 ounces) sliced peaches, drained and cut into pieces**
5 **soft molasses cookies, broken up**

1. Fold ice-cream topping into whipped topping in small bowl.

2. Layer cookies, whipped topping mixture and peaches in 6 parfait or other tall glasses. Sprinkle with cookie crumbs, if desired. Serve immediately, or refrigerate until serving time.

Creamy Caramel-Peach Parfaits ▶

Frozen Chocolate Mousse

▼ 8 servings

Crushed shortbread or coconut cookies or crumbled macaroons are delicious sprinkled on this airy mousse.

Prep: 8 min

Freeze: 4 hr

1 Serving: Calories 240 (Calories from Fat 170); Fat 19g (Saturated 12g); Cholesterol 65mg; Sodium 40mg; Carbohydrate 16g (Dietary Fiber 0g); Protein 1g.

   2 **cups whipping (heavy) cream**
1/4 **cup almond-, chocolate- or coffee-flavored liqueur**
   1 **can (5.5 ounces) chocolate-flavored syrup (1/2 cup)**

1. Beat whipping cream in large bowl with electric mixer on high speed until stiff. Fold in liqueur and chocolate syrup.

2. Pour whipped cream mixture into ungreased square pan, 9 x 9 x 2 inches.

3. Cover and freeze at least 4 hours but no longer than 48 hours. Cut into squares. Serve immediately. Cover and freeze any remaining dessert.

Sugar Cookie Tarts

▼ 4 servings

Be as inventive as you please with these tarts! Let kids pick their own fruit combinations and assemble the cookie tarts just their way.

Prep: 10 min

1 Serving: Calories 250 (Calories from Fat 145; Fat 16g (Saturated 8g); Cholesterol 25mg; Sodium 170mg; Carbohydrate 25g (Dietary Fiber 1g); Protein 3g.

1/2 **cup soft cream cheese with strawberries or pineapple**
   4 **round sugar cookies (4 inches in diameter)**
      Desired toppings (sliced fresh fruit, miniature chocolate chips, chopped pecans, toasted sliced almonds or jam)

Spread about 2 teaspoons cream cheese over each cookie. Arrange desired toppings above on cream cheese. Store in refrigerator.

Sugar Cookie Tarts ▶

Cookie Dunkers

▼ 4 servings

Think of this fun idea as a no-cook, no-hassle cookie fondue. Try any of your favorite cookies, such as chocolate chip, peanut butter or sugar. If you like, offer various candy sprinkles or chopped nuts, too.

Prep: 5 min

1 Serving: Calories 390 (Calories from Fat 110); Fat 12g (Saturated 6g); Cholesterol 5mg; Sodium 260mg; Carbohydrate 67g (Dietary Fiber 1g); Protein 4g.

1/2 cup chocolate fudge ice-cream topping, heat if desired

1/2 cup butterscotch or caramel ice-cream topping, heat if desired

1/2 cup frozen (thawed) whipped topping

12 cookies, any flavor (about 2 1/2 inches in diameter)

1. Place the ice-cream toppings and the whipped topping in separate small shallow bowls.

2. Dip cookies into ice-cream topping, then into whipped topping.

Foiling Messy Clean-ups

Some things just seem to have a thousand uses, and aluminum foil is one of those versatile items. Lining dishes or pans with foil makes clean-up quick and easy. When preparing foods with exposed bones (such as ribs) use heavy-duty foil, which won't rip or tear as easily. When the food is ready, just lift out the foil, crumple it up and toss it out—or rinse and recycle it. You can also purchase disposable aluminum pans—perfect for holiday turkeys and hams—and toss or recycle when finished. Here are more foil-friendly ideas:

- **Broiler Pans, Baking Dishes, Baking Sheets and Casseroles:** Line broiler pan with foil and spray rack with nonstick cooking spray.

- **Bars and Candy:** Line baking dish with foil, extending foil 1 to 2 inches over ends of dish. Cool completely and lift bars or candy out of pan. Another bonus of this method is bars and candy that can be cut evenly and easily!

Cookie Dunkers ▶

Malted Milk Ball Ice-Cream Dessert

▼ 12 servings

Ice-cream sandwiches form the base of this unbelievably easy and fun candy-flavored dessert.

Prep: 8 min

Freeze: 3 hr

1 Serving: Calories 480 (Calories from Fat 205); Fat 23g (Saturated 14g); Cholesterol 25mg; Sodium 230mg; Carbohydrate 66g (Dietary Fiber 2g); Protein 4g.

3 1/3 cups malted milk balls (10 1/2 ounces)

1 container (12 ounces) frozen whipped topping, thawed

12 frozen rectangular ice-cream sandwiches

1 cup hot fudge sauce, warmed if desired

1. Place malted milk balls in re-sealable plastic bag. Tap with rolling pin or meat mallet until coarsely crushed. Reserve ¹/₃ cup.

2. Mix 3 cups crushed malted milk balls and whipped topping.

3. Arrange ice-cream sandwiches on bottom of rectangular pan, 13 x 9 x 2 inches, cutting sandwiches if necessary to cover bottom of pan. Spread whipped topping mixture over ice-cream sandwiches. Sprinkle with reserved crushed malted milk balls. Cover and freeze about 2 to 3 hours or until firm.

4. Cut into squares. Top with fudge sauce. Cover and freeze any remaining dessert.

Malted Milk Ball Ice-Cream Dessert ▶

Menus

▼ **Parmesan-Dijon Chicken 84**
Spinach and Potatoes Alfredo 58
Pre-packaged lettuce with salad dressing
and croutons

▼ **Salsa Chicken Sandwiches 59**
Potato-Corn Salad 70
Pre-cut fresh vegetables

▼ **Easy Stroganoff Meatballs 102**
Frozen egg noodles
Frozen vegetables

▼ **Teriyaki Chicken Stir-Fry 124**
Instant rice
Frozen egg rolls

▼ **Tortellini with Fresh Vegetables 134**
Quick Caesar Salad 312
French bread

▼ **Pizza Casserole 208**
Pre-packaged lettuce
Garlic bread

▼ **Ranchero Beef Pizza 244**
Pre-cut fresh vegetables
Chips

▼ **Gorgonzola Linguine with Toasted Walnuts** 237
Pre-packaged lettuce with salad dressing
and croutons
Tiramisu Toffee Dessert 404

▼ **Mediterranean Couscous and Beans** 266
Fresh fruit
Pita bread

▼ **Chicken Salad Oriental** 308
Crusty dinner rolls

▼ **Warm Bean and Spinach Salad** 270
Breadsticks

▼ **Honey Pancakes** 346
Fresh fruit
Brown-and-serve sausage

▼ **Easy Grilled Fish Fillets** 388
Pesto Vegetables 324
Packaged seasoned rice or noodle mix

▼ **Tex-Mex Minestrone Soup** 298
Cornbread

Helpful Nutrition and Cooking Information

NUTRITION GUIDELINES:

Daily Values are set by the Food and Drug Administration and are based on the needs of most healthy adults. Percent Daily Values are based on an average diet of 2,000 calories per day. Your daily values may be higher or lower depending on your calorie needs.

Recommended intake for a daily diet of 2,000 calories:

Total Fat	Less than 65 g
Saturated Fat	Less than 20g
Cholesterol	Less than 300mg
Sodium	Less than 2,400mg
Total Carbohydrate	300g
Dietary Fiber	25g

CRITERIA USED FOR CALCULATING NUTRITION INFORMATION:

- The first ingredient is used wherever a choice is given (such as 1/3 cup sour cream or plain yogurt).

- The first ingredient amount is used wherever a range is given (such as 2 to 3 teaspoons milk).

- The first serving number is used wherever a range is given (such as 4 to 6 servings).

- "If desired" ingredients are not included, whether mentioned in the ingredient list or in the recipe directions as a suggestion (such as sprinkle with brown sugar if desired).

- Only the amount of a marinade or frying oil that is absorbed during preparation is calculated.

Cooking Terms Glossary:

Beat: Make smooth with a vigorous stirring motion using a spoon, wire whisk, egg beater or electric mixer.

Boil: Heat liquid until bubbles keep rising and breaking on the surface.

Chop: Cut food into small, uneven pieces; a sharp knife, food chopper or food processor may be used.

Core: Cut out the stem end and remove the seeds.

Cut in: Mix fat into a flour mixture with a pastry blender with a rolling motion or cutting with a fork or two knives until particles are size specified.

Dice: Cut into cubes smaller than 1/2 inch.

Drain: Pour off liquid or let it run off through the holes in a strainer or colander, as when draining cooked pasta or ground beef. Or, remove pieces of food from a fat or liquid and set them on paper towels to soak up excess moisture.

Flute: Flatten pastry evenly on rim of pie plate and press firmly around rim with tines of fork.

Grate: Rub against small holes of grater to cut into tiny pieces.

Grease: Spread the bottoms and side of a disk or pan with solid vegetable shortening using a pastry brush or paper towel.

Knead: Curve your fingers and fold dough toward you, then push it away with the heels of your hands, using a quick rocking motion.

Mix: Combine to distribute ingredients evenly using a spoon, fork, blender or an electric mixer.

Peel: Cut off the skin with a knife or peel with fingers.

Pipe: Press out frosting from a decorating bag using steady pressure to form a design or write a message. To finish a design, stop the pressure and lift the pint up and away.

Roll or **Pat:** Flatten and spread with a floured rolling pin or hands.

Ingredients Used in Recipe Testing and Nutrition Calculations:

- Large eggs, canned ready-to-use chicken broth, 2% milk, 80%-lean ground beef and vegetable-oil spread with less than 65% fat. These are used as they are the most commonly purchased ingredients within those categories.

- Regular long-grain white rice wherever cooked rice is listed, unless indicated.

- Nonfat, low-fat or low-sodium products are not used, unless indicated.

- Solid vegetable shortening (not margarine, butter and nonstick cooking sprays, as they can cause sticking problems) is used to grease pans, unless indicated.

Equipment Used in Recipe Testing:

- Cookware and bakeware *without* nonstick coatings are used, unless indicated.

- Wherever a baking *pan* is specified in a recipe, a *metal* pan is used; wherever a baking *dish* or pie *plate* is specified, ovenproof *glass* or *ceramic* ovenware is used.

- A portable electric hand mixer is used for mixing *only when mixer speeds are specified* in the recipe directions.

Metric Conversion Guide

VOLUME

U.S. Units	Canadian Metric	Australian Metric
1/4 teaspoon	1 mL	1 ml
1/2 teaspoon	2 mL	2 ml
1 teaspoon	5 mL	5 ml
1 tablespoon	15 mL	20 ml
1/4 cup	50 mL	60 ml
1/3 cup	75 mL	80 ml
1/2 cup	125 mL	125 ml
2/3 cup	150 mL	170 ml
3/4 cup	175 mL	190 ml
1 cup	250 mL	250 ml
1 quart	1 liter	1 liter
1 1/2 quarts	1.5 liters	1.5 liters
2 quarts	2 liters	2 liters
2 1/2 quarts	2.5 liters	2.5 liters
3 quarts	3 liters	3 liters
4 quarts	4 liters	4 liters

MEASUREMENTS

Inches	Centimeters
1	2.5
2	5.0
3	7.5
4	10.0
5	12.5
6	15.0
7	17.5
8	20.5
9	23.0
10	25.5
11	28.0
12	30.5
13	33.0
14	35.5
15	38.0

WEIGHT

U.S. Units	Canadian Metric	Australian Metric
1 ounce	30 grams	30 grams
2 ounces	55 grams	60 grams
3 ounces	85 grams	90 grams
4 ounces (1/4 pound)	115 grams	125 grams
8 ounces (1/2 pound)	225 grams	225 grams
16 ounces (1 pound)	455 grams	500 grams
1 pound	455 grams	1/2 kilogram

TEMPERATURES

Fahrenheit	Celsius
32°	0°
212°	100°
250°	120°
275°	140°
300°	150°
325°	160°
350°	180°
375°	190°
400°	200°
425°	220°
450°	230°
475°	240°
500°	260°

Note: The recipes in this cookbook have not been developed or tested using metric measures. When converting recipes to metric, some variations in quality may be noted.

Betty Crocker's Good and Easy Cookbook

Index

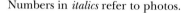

Numbers in *italics* refer to photos.